Pocahontas

AND THE

Powhatan Dilemma

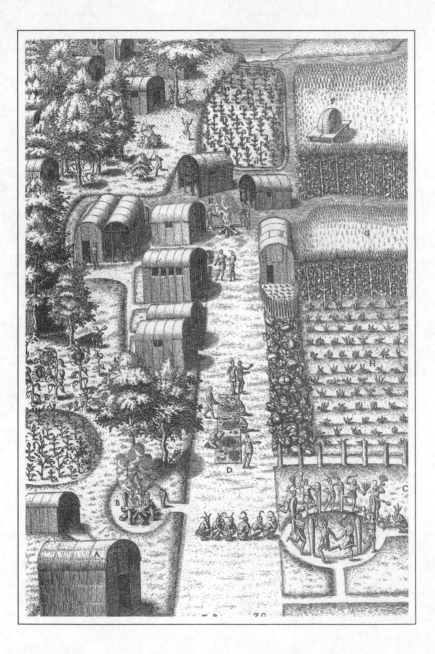

Pocahontas

AND THE

Powhatan Dilemma

Camilla Townsend

AN AMERICAN PORTRAIT

HILL AND WANG

A division of Farrar, Straus and Giroux
New York

Hill and Wang
A division of Farrar, Straus and Giroux
18 West 18th Street, New York 10011

Printed in the United States of America
Published in 2004 by Hill and Wang
First paperback edition, 2005

The Library of Congress has cataloged the hardcover edition as follows:
Townsend, Camilla, 1965–
    Pocahontas and the Powhatan dilemma / by Camilla Townsend.— 1st ed.
    p.   cm.
    Includes index.
    ISBN-13: 978-0-8090-9530-8
    ISBN-10: 0-8090-9530-0 (hc: alk. paper)
    1. Pocahontas, d. 1617.   2. Powhatan women—Biography.   3. Powhatan
Indians—History.   4. Powhatan Indians—Government relations.
5. Rolfe, John, 1585–1622.   I. Title.

E99.P85P5797 2004
975.561692—dc22

                                                            2003027915

Paperback ISBN-13: 978-0-8090-7738-0
Paperback ISBN-10: 0-8090-7738-8

Designed by Cassandra J. Pappas
Map designed by Jeffrey L. Ward

www.fsgbooks.com

Frontispiece: "Town of Secoran," Theodor de Bry, 1590

To my mother and father

Contents

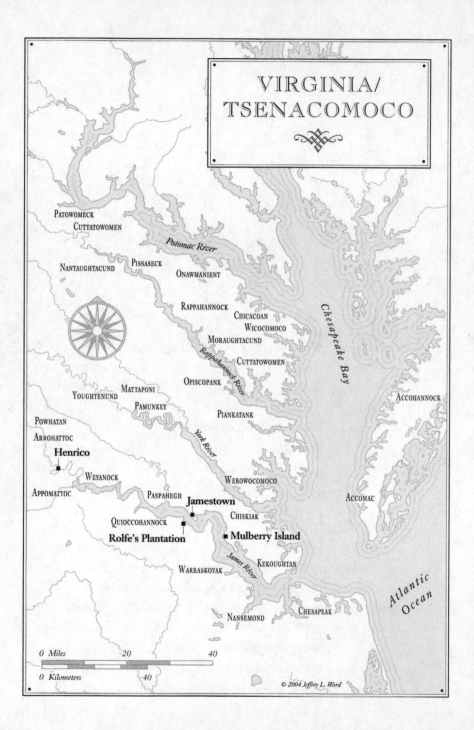

VIRGINIA/ TSENACOMOCO

PATOWOMECK
CUTTATOWOMEN

Potomac River

NANTAUGHTACUND   PISSASECK
                 ONAWMANIENT

                    RAPPAHANNOCK
                          CHICACOAN
                          WICOCOMOCO
                    MORAUGHTACUND
                          CUTTATOWOMEN
Rappahannock River

              OPISCOPANK
YOUGHTENUND MATTAPONI
             PAMUNKEY   PIANKATANK

POWHATAN
ARROHATTOC   *York River*

Henrico

     WEYANOCK
APPOMATTOC   WEROWOCOMOCO
        PASPAHEGH   **Jamestown**
                              CHISKIAK
   QUIOCCOHANNOCK
Rolfe's Plantation   ■ **Mulberry Island**

                   James River KEKOUGHTAN
        WARRASKOYAK

              NANSEMOND   CHESAPEAK

Chesapeake Bay

ACCOHANNOCK

ACCOMAC

Atlantic Ocean

0 Miles   20   40

0 Kilometers   40

© 2004 Jeffrey L. Ward

Preface

As it turned out, England was gray. Everything about it was gray—the stonework, the weathered wood, the filthy water slapping the docks. Pocahontas had long wondered what this country would be like. In Virginia she had seen beautiful books bound in red leather, her British husband's embroidered doublets, weapons with bejeweled handles—all from England. But now from the deck of the ship she saw that the town of Plymouth was simply gray. Whether she had time or energy to be disappointed, we will never know. Other thoughts must have been uppermost in her mind as she faced the enormity of what was before her. For now she knew: she knew the answers to the many questions, asked and unasked, that her father, high chief of all the Powhatans, had sent her here with. She knew for certain that her father and her people must ultimately lose.

Pocahontas, we must remember, was a real person. She was not always a myth. Long before she became an icon, she was a child who walked and played beneath the towering trees of the Virginia woods, and then an adult woman who learned to love—and to hate—English men. Myths can lend meaning to our days, and they can inspire wonderful movies. They are also deadly to our understanding. They diminish the influence of facts, and a historical figure's ability to make us think; they diminish our ability to see with fresh eyes. What has the myth of Pocahontas kept hidden? And if the real woman could speak, what might she tell us about our country's inception?

When the colonists of the Virginia Company struggled ashore in 1607 to found the settlement they called Jamestown, they hoped that theirs would be the first British colony in the Americas to endure; previous efforts in Canada and at Roanoke had ended in disaster. Jamestown did survive—but at great cost. The settlers died by the hundreds, adhering to a set of assumptions as to their place and purpose. For the first few years they resisted becoming subsistence farmers and instead demanded that the Indians grow corn for them. And so they starved.

The local Algonkian-speaking tribes were organized into a single paramount chieftainship under Powhatan, and one of his daughters, the outgoing Pocahontas, was a great favorite at the Jamestown fort. The colonists hoped that through her they might prevail upon Powhatan to make his people tributaries of the English. And in hindsight a version of that hope became accepted as fact. Captain John Smith later claimed that a smitten Pocahontas had thrown herself in front of him to save his life when, at their very first meeting, Powhatan meant to kill him; the story was retold and reprinted with alacrity and survives to this day.

In reality, the English kidnapped Pocahontas in the midst of a war against her people, and kept her prisoner for many months while they waited for her father to agree to tribute payments of corn. Pocahontas ended the conflict when she converted to Christianity and married a colonist named John Rolfe. She and several of her family members then chose to travel to Europe, not as prisoners but as free agents intent on gathering information that might clarify the Algonkians' future course.

The mythical Pocahontas who loved John Smith, the English, the Christian faith, and London more than she loved her own father or people or faith or village deeply appealed to the settlers of Jamestown and the court of King James. That Pocahontas also inspired the romantic poets and patriotic myth-makers of the nineteenth century, as well as many twentieth-century producers of toys, films, and books. With one accord, all these storytellers subverted her life to satisfy their own need to believe that the Indians loved and admired them (or their cultural forebears) without resentments, without guile. She deserves better. A woman as brave as Pocahontas—who endured a kidnapping, explored an alien faith, dared to marry a foreigner, and faced the voyage across the sea for the sake of her people—deserves a great deal more. She was as brave as all her people—not a simple joyful worshipper of English men or power, but a real and complicated woman with her own plans, goals, and ideas. She is worthy of our respect, not condescension.

When we allow her own story to unfold, we see not only that she herself was more than we thought, but that the moment of this country's inception was different from what we have been led to believe. We Americans prefer to think our early colonists were unlike the English who went to Ireland or the Spanish who went to Mexico, that our forebears wanted to found towns and work the land themselves rather than demand that others work for them. But Pocahontas knew otherwise: the English wanted to be lords of the manor, and they wanted the Indians to be something akin to serfs. It took the English years, in fact, to relinquish that hope, and they finally did so only because the Indians' refusal to comply was so adamant. When we consider the real events of Pocahontas's life, we learn more not only about another human being but about our own past, and ourselves.

Pocahontas

AND THE

Powhatan Dilemma

ONE

Amonute's People

Casa cunnakack, peya quagh acquintin uttasantasough?
(In how many daies will there come hither any more English ships?)
—Powhatan query, recorded 1608–1609,
quoted in John Smith, *A Map of Virginia* (1612)

The canoe bearing the news skimmed rapidly over the water. It was a spring day in 1607, and the rivers and streams of Tsenacomoco were swollen with rain and melted snow that came cascading down to the tidewater from the western mountains. The boat's messengers were bound for the main settlement of Powhatan, their paramount chief, and they used the riverine network that connected his dominions to move with their customary speed. There may have been an added urgency to the well-timed dips of their paddles, though, for they carried important news. The strangers on the three great ships that had entered the bay near the place where the Chesapeakes lived were not leaving. On the contrary, they seemed to be seeking a water supply and a camping ground—in short, a place to stay.[1]

The messengers drew near Powhatan's village of Werowocomoco, or "King's House." It was on the north shore of the Pamunkey (the York River, in today's world). Strangers unfamiliar with the area might have passed by without seeing anything other than a lovely bay, for the village was nestled back in the trees, but to these men the spot was well known, with a long history of power. It was a remarkable bay, like no other on the river: three creeks made their way in almost perfect symmetry down to the enfolded semicircle of water. To the left of the central creek, it was perfectly flat. But to the right, a knob of land rose up twenty-five feet, a fitting platform for a king.[2]

The men had to leave their canoe in a cove formed by the creek wrapping around the side of the village. Toward the rear a spring gushed, and beyond that lay the people's fishing weirs. Here the village land sloped gradually down to the water. But if, as often happened, several of the men sprang lightly off their craft right at the riverfront rather than entering the secluded cove, they had to follow a path up the twenty-foot bluff before they could see the village spreading out on either side, reaching into the ancient woods. It covered at least fifty acres, spreading over a much larger territory than like numbers of people usually chose to claim. Normally it was impractical to live like this. Powhatan, however, was a chief of chiefs. He had a point to make to visitors. And he had prisoners of war to do some of the requisite work. If the messengers turned around, they could see the whole bay spread before them and, beyond it, the wide grayness of the slow-moving Pamunkey. Herons stood patiently near the shore; ospreys swooped low, seeking unsuspecting fish.[3]

That evening the sky over the water glowed as it always did as the sun prepared to slip down behind the river. The summer light filtered into the woods, illuminating bits of stone or wood or leaf with low beams shot with gold. Powhatan may have received the messengers in state, as was his wont, reclining on a low platform at one end of his eighty-foot longhouse, the wall mats pinned back to let the breeze carry away some of the smoke from the hearth, his wives and children listening. Or he may have spoken alone and outdoors to those who brought the tidings, leaving his family to learn what there was to learn through village gossip. Werowocomoco, with its constant activity, was a poor place to keep a secret.

Sometime soon the chief's nine-year-old daughter, Pocahontas, would have heard the whole story.[4] News of this magnitude invariably entered the rumor mill: great boats had come again, this time perhaps to stay. Even a nine-year-old child who had never seen a ship would have understood what was anchored in the bay—boats larger than any canoe, able to catch the wind with huge blankets more finely woven than any net, perhaps something like the ones wealthy chiefs acquired through long-distance trade. These boats were widely known, their arrival even anticipated, for at least one appeared off the coast every few seasons. Mostly they just passed by. Some were driven by storms into the mouths of the four rivers of Powhatan's kingdom and sought shelter for a few days before departing.

Twice before, though, in Powhatan's long memory, such strangers had come with the intent to stay. Both times it had boded ill. Over forty years ago, when he was young, a kinsman—the son of the chiefly family of a neighboring tribe—was kidnapped when he dared to board one of the great boats. The strangers returned with him ten years later, after he had traveled over the sea and back again. By then he was a full-grown man who spoke their tongue; he had acquired one of their names, "Luis." He told everyone that the strangers came from a land of thousands and should be killed, or many more would come. His tribe took his advice and killed them all, sparing only a child. More came anyway. Vengeful, powerful, and ignorant, they attacked with deadly force, but wreaked their retribution on the wrong tribe.

Then about twenty years ago, when Powhatan was already a chief and had begun to conquer many of the tribes he now ruled, more strangers arrived, this time to the south of his lands, where the Roanoke and Croatan lived. These coat-wearers, as his people began to call them, were from a different tribe—"English" they called themselves, insisting they were not "Spanish."[5] It was said that they, too, took at least one chief's son hostage. And they, too, came and went, came and went. Once a group of them traveled northward and stayed for a few months with the Chesapeake tribe on the coast, just across the river from Powhatan's lands, before returning to their settlement at Roanoke. There they starved and declined until the few remaining fled the little colony and were probably sold as slaves among inland tribes.

Only four years ago, in 1603, there had been another incident that everyone still remembered, probably even those as young as Pocahontas. More English had come, this time to the place where the Rappahannock lived, right in the middle of Tsenacomoco. No one was foolish enough to board the boat, but the coat-wearers still managed to seize some men, killing others who tried to stop them. Powhatan and the *werowance*—the chief—of the Rappahannock wondered if these coat-wearers, too, would return.

Now in April 1607 they asked themselves if those who had come this time were the same men. The relatives of the kidnapped Rappahannocks, remembering the story of the return of "Luis," would have heard the news of the ship with greater and more heart-stopping interest than did Pocahontas. They lacked information, had only some of the puzzle pieces. They could not know that the earlier ship had indeed come on a reconnaissance mission for the present expedition, but that its crew was composed of different men. Nor could they know that their kinsmen had already died: in 1603 some "Virginia Indians" had been made to demonstrate their handling of canoes on the Thames, and their subsequent deaths had gone unremarked in a city where thousands were perishing of the plague.[6]

Indeed, there was much that the Indians could not then know about the Europeans' interest in them, and about how the short-lived

Spanish mission, the failed colony at Roanoke, and the recent English arrivals were all part of a much larger geopolitical contest. Confusing the Indians' minimal knowledge of Europe, however, with no knowledge at all—or worse, with essential innocence—would be to misread the historical record and do them a disservice. Powhatan clearly knew there was more to the story; he undoubtedly would have given much to have had more information earlier on.

Later Pocahontas and others interacting with the newcomers would learn the whole history. There had, as they knew, been dozens of European ships plying the continent's eastern seaboard in the preceding century. Perhaps Giovanni da Verrazano in 1524 was the first of them to pass the four rivers of Tsenacomoco (now the James, the York, the Rappahannock, and the Potomac), but the Spanish settling farther south had been the most frequent passersby as they worked to perfect their cartography of the New World. They recognized that the economic potential of this territory paled in comparison to that of the warm and resource-rich lands of Mexico, Peru, and the Caribbean, but they believed some sort of northern settlement could still be useful. Colonists might discover a sea route to the Pacific, capture Indian slaves, and trade for valuable furs. And a settlement would provide a deterrent to French ambitions, as well as a port for beleaguered Spanish ships tossed by storms and chased by the much-feared English pirates.

The Spanish had their own version of the story of the kidnapped Luis, which, combined with what the Indians knew, yields a much fuller picture. In 1561 a fleet on an exploratory expedition seized a young lord who was probably of the Chiskiak people and almost certainly a cousin of Powhatan, if not a nearer relation. Some of the Spanish claimed he had come with them of his own free will, to learn their language and their religion, but it is impossible that he could have understood all that was about to happen; other chroniclers said his family did not know he had been taken. He was taken to Spain, then sent to Mexico to be educated by Dominicans. There, living among the conquered Aztecs, the man who said he was called "Paquiquineo" at home was baptized and given the princely name Don Luis de Velasco, after the viceroy of New Spain. A few years later, one of the Spaniards who had been involved in organizing the expedition that took him became adelantado of Florida. Determined to settle the coast, and needing to communicate with the natives, Pedro Menéndez de Avilés asked the Spanish king if the valuable boy could be given into his care. Thus Don Luis was sent to Havana, and in 1566 he set sail with thirty soldiers and two Dominican friars to find his homeland.

Don Luis failed to recognize anything familiar. Or so he said. Perhaps his fellow travelers didn't press him. Many of those on board were eager to return to Spain, whither they sailed when a storm gave them a good excuse to say they had lost their bearings. In 1567, discouraged but still hopeful, the eager adelantado of Florida himself went to Spain and got himself named governor of Cuba. In 1570, Don Luis sailed back to Havana, along with a group of Jesuits seeking a foothold in the Americas whom either he or Menéndez had succeeded in interesting in the project of settling the coast. The missionaries sailed north without any soldiers. It was a most unusual decision, but Cuba and Florida had none to spare just then, and the Jesuits wanted to be free of the reins of government. Besides, Don Luis promised that all would be well. This time he had no trouble finding his homeland: halfway up the James River, he and his black-robed friends were welcomed joyfully by his kin.[7]

Luis helped the fathers find a place to build their mission. He said he had mistakenly led them up the wrong river: they would travel north over a narrow neck of land to the next river up and settle where his brother now ruled, quite near his own home village. He stayed with the Jesuits for a few nights, as their equipment was unpacked from the boat, and explained something of the region to them. One of the men prepared a letter to send back on their ship, which was to return to Havana to collect further supplies: "Don Luis has turned out as well as was hoped, he is most obedient to the wishes of Father."[8] Luis had explained that it would be impolitic and unnecessary to abduct and send back another Indian boy as the Spaniards had planned: "In no way does it seem best to me to send you any Indian boy, as the pilot [of the ship] will explain." Don Luis waited until the ship left with its letter. Then—after ten years—he went home.

The fathers waited at their mission settlement for Luis to return to them, but he did not come back. They languished, without food or converts. They sent pleading messages to his village. There was no response. Finally, after the winter, three of them decided to visit him: they cast public reclamations in his face, shaming to any Algonkian, and no doubt reminded him of the coming wrath of his Spanish sponsors if he did not mend his ways. Luis promised he would return to the mission.

He did so, leading the war party that came to kill the strangers and remove all trace of their presence from the land. The three who had visited him were already dead, having met their fate on their way back to the settlement. Only a young boy named Alonso was spared and adopted, over Don Luis's objections. Luis said the boy should die so as not to tell tales, but he was overruled by those who did not know the power of their new enemies.

The next year the supply ship came but could not find the mission. The crew seized two Indians. One jumped overboard; the other was brought back to Havana. There he was questioned in chains— perhaps he was tortured, following European custom—but he would or could communicate only that Alonso alone was left alive. A year later the governor himself led a punitive mission to find Luis. On the James River, in the general area of the first landing, one of the expedition's ships came upon a group of Indians who showed no fear and boarded the boat when the Spanish invited them to trade. Obviously they were not of Luis's tribe, but the Spanish did not understand that and only marveled at their innocence. Those who boarded were held at gunpoint, while last year's prisoner, who could now speak some Spanish, explained that they would be freed in exchange for Alonso. One of the hostages was sent as a messenger to Don Luis's people, who did decide to release the boy, but not to the tribe that was hoping to exchange him for their captive brethren. Rather, Luis's family sent Alonso straight to the captain of the Spanish fleet, whose ship lay at the mouth of the James River. They hoped, most likely, to convince the foreigners that they themselves were their friends, though other Indians might not be.

The Spanish holding the hostages upriver waited for two days, and when Alonso did not come, they blasted a round of shot at the assembled Indians crowding the shore, killing many who were undoubtedly relatives of their prisoners. Then they sailed back to the mouth of the river to discover that Alonso was already there—and that he had told all. One of the prisoners was released with the message that the renegade Luis must be turned over to them within five days or the others would be killed. But the captives were apparently Chickahominy, no friends of Luis's people. They would have known there was little prospect of Luis turning himself in. After five days a few men were released as "innocent"—perhaps Alonso had spoken for them—and the rest were hanged from the ship's rigging in full view of the shore. Years later the Chickahominy still remembered the Spanish with bitterness.[9]

It was the English, not the Spanish, who could have told Powhatan what he wanted to know about the Roanoke colony. It was their first attempt to settle this area, which they saw as being just beyond real Spanish control. Their tactics were in many ways comparable to those of their Catholic rivals. Sir Walter Raleigh, the force of energy behind Roanoke as well as numerous English explorations of the Caribbean, embraced the practice of taking Indian boys to England to be trained as interpreters. If they were to be effective, however, he thought that they should come by choice. Over the course of his life Raleigh brought about twenty Native Americans to

Durham House, his home in London, and hired tutors for them. Among his protégés were Manteo, a Croatan, and Wanchese, a Roanoke, picked up in 1584 on a reconnaissance mission in the Carolinas. When the two returned to Roanoke Island in 1585 with a group of English colonists, Manteo, whose home was several days distant, remained friendly, but Wanchese, like Luis, turned on the English and convinced his people to make war against them. He probably had never trusted the English, never even given them his real name: in Pocahontas's language, which was closely related to his own, *maro/wancheso* simply meant "young boy."[10]

The surviving Roanoke colonists, meeting hostility from the Indians and abandoned by their London suppliers for three years while the English faced the Spanish Armada, eventually fled the island. No European ever learned for certain where they had gone. They seem to have dispersed: most likely they were sold as slaves along a great inland trade route that followed the course of today's Interstate 85. Some scholars believe they went to the Chesapeake tribe, who had sheltered some of them earlier. They point out that, at about the same time as the Jamestown colonists arrived, Powhatan made war on the Chesapeakes and in a most unusual move chose to exterminate them all. It was said that he had no choice: a prophecy supposedly had it that he would otherwise meet his doom at the hands of a people coming from the Chesapeake Bay. But it was the self-satisfied English who wrote about this prophecy, fancying themselves the destroyers and pitying the chief for mistakenly imagining that the prophecy referred to the Chesapeakes. There may never have been any such prognostication. Or if there was, perhaps Powhatan's priests made it in order to justify their sovereign's politically necessary action. For whether they harbored any surviving Roanoke colonists or not, the Chesapeakes were, at that time, the only large tribe in the area that refused to pay tribute to Pocahontas's father. In ordinary times that just made them recalcitrant, but with the English on the scene it made them dangerous.[11]

Whatever plans Powhatan made after he received the news about the English ships, Pocahontas was not immediately affected. When she awoke the morning after she first heard of the exciting events, her life would have remained unchanged. The fire would have smoked as usual. It was the women's spiritual and practical duty to prevent it from ever going out, but by morning it always smoldered. She most likely removed her bedding from the low platform she slept on, bathed in the river, and breakfasted from the household stewpot of leftovers. It would be eight more months before she caught her first glimpse of a coat-wearer. She lived in the heartland of her father's chieftainship, surrounded by his personal army of at least forty warriors. Visitors came to him; he did not go to visitors.

Her father's power had not always been so immense. The idea that the coastal plain, the region of the four rivers running to the sea (or the Virginia Tidewater, as the maps call it now), should have one great governing figure was relatively new. Powhatan had fought many wars to make himself the paramount chief, the *mamanitowik*, with power over about thirty subordinate chiefdoms and perhaps twenty thousand people. When he was a young man named Wahunsenacaw, he had inherited from one or both of his parents six chiefdoms—the Powhatan, Arrohattock, and Appomattock on the James River, and the Pamunkey, Mattaponi, and Youghtanund on the upper York. This was an unusual circumstance but not incredible, as the noble families of most of the chieftainships were related by marriage. He had been born on the James River, but the northerners on the York had embraced his joint rulership, probably because the southerners had valuable trade ties to the tribes in the Carolinas, and because he was willing to establish his seat of power on the banks of their river rather than in his homeland. Since then, through peaceful alliance and intermarriage, as well as war and the forced resettlement of survivors, he had brought other tribes into submission. They paid tribute in corn, tanned hides, pearls, purple shell beads, and even valuable copper; and in exchange, he fought with them against their common enemies. In short, they recognized themselves as vassals of the man who had once been the Powhatan tribe's chief; he now took the political name "Powhatan" as his own, giving it as well to all the tribes who were tributary to him.[12]

The epidemics and migrations set in motion by the earlier arrival of Europeans in faraway Canada and Florida probably helped Powhatan gain power: when Iroquoian enemies closed in from the north (the Susquehannocks got as far as the Chesapeake), or microbes decimated some populations, the peoples of the region, who spoke closely related Algonkian languages, likely became more willing to work together. At the very least, these crises left temporary power vacuums that Powhatan deftly filled.[13]

In 1596 or 1597 Powhatan conquered the Kekoughtan in just this way. Fifteen years later the still-resentful losers of the war told the story to any white man who would listen: "Upon the death of an old Weroance . . . Powhatan taking the advantage subtilly stepped in, and conquered the people killing the [new] chief and most of them, and the reserved [i.e., those he spared] he transported over the River, craftily chaunging their seat [of residence] and quartering them amongst his owne people."[14] Was Pocahontas's mother one of the young women he brought home after that brutal war? It is certain that the child was born in or near 1597, and that her mother's family had no political significance.

When the baby girl was born, she was not considered particularly important, for by that time Powhatan had many other children by far more powerful queens. Still, she was the daughter of the mamanito-wik and so received presents and food in abundance. Like all children, she was given two names: she was called Amonute in a ceremony before the village, and she was probably also given a private or hidden name, which her parents revealed to no one else. Everyone assumed that her mother or father would eventually give her another name reflective of her personality. By the time she was ten, the child was known as Pocahontas, apparently meaning something like "Mischief" or "Little Playful One." It was understood that her deeds or experiences might cause her name to change again, just as her father's had.[15]

What did it mean for a girl to live as the daughter of the paramount chief? Many people in the modern world like to imagine that Native Americans were inexplicably and inherently different from Europeans—kinder, gentler, more spiritual—and that they instinctively chose not to deploy power in the same way. It is wishful thinking. The Indians were not essentially different from Europeans. Powhatan, who showed a sense of humor in his dealings with the newcomers, might well have laughed at our modern notions—if he did not use them to his advantage first. He knew how to wield power. His storehouses were full of goods produced by conquered tribes; he did not hesitate to dispense harsh justice when criminals were brought before him.[16] And as he managed his wealth and employed effective political stratagems, Pocahontas and his other children watched, reaping the benefits.

Realpolitik, not inherent egalitarianism, dictated the limits of Powhatan's power. Europeans later observed that he could not always make his subordinate werowances do his bidding. Indeed he could not. Even an absolute monarch at the head of a standing army must bargain to some extent with his underlings, spending symbolic capital on some occasions, real capital on others, threatening and practicing violence at some moments, giving way judiciously at others. And Powhatan was no absolute monarch. He was a brilliant strategist forging a new political unity out of groups that had lived separately for centuries. Those on the outskirts of his territory had least reason to fear his wrath and do his bidding. Even the Chickahominy, though surrounded by his followers, managed as a particularly large group to avoid having him name their werowances—though they made periodic tribute payments to help keep the peace.

Women and children were key players in these constant power negotiations. Many Algonkian groups were matrilineal, that is to say, the chieftainship was inherited through the female line. Men ruled, unless there was no male heir, but power passed through women. A chief was succeeded not by his son but by his younger brothers (his mother's other sons) and after them, in the next generation, by his sister's sons. They in turn were succeeded by their sisters' sons. If a suitable man was unavailable, then one of these sisters could herself become a female werowance, or *werowansqua*: before they ever saw Powhatan, for example, the Jamestown colonists would be awed by the stately queen of the Appomattock. There were clear advantages to the system: whole clans of brothers and sisters had an obvious shared interest in remaining united and maintaining their family's power.[17]

Powhatan incorporated matrilineality into his patterns of conquest. Viewers of twentieth-century movies may tend to think of women stolen in ancient wars as mere trophies, but when power passes through the female line, they are much more: they may be the source of legitimacy for a new dynasty. The Indians never explained this to the English, at least not in such a way that they could understand, but we see the principle playing out in the varying political arrangements that the Virginia Indians made. Powhatan placed his grown son Parahunt as werowance over the Powhatan tribe, but the young man ruled in his father's stead, not as his successor, and it was undoubtedly understood that he would not inherit. He was a "home-grown" child, and the Powhatan people would have had no resentments about the temporary arrangement. But the case must have been quite different when Powhatan deposed another tribe's own werowance and placed one of his sons to rule instead, as he frequently did. How could a people endure the disgrace of losing their kingly line? The answer is, they did not. Powhatan simply married a woman of their royal family. A son conceived by her would grow up to rule with loyalty both to his father and to his mother's people. When the English came, Powhatan's son Tatacoope was heir to the

Quioccohannock, the child's mother their werowansqua; his son Pochins, born to a Kekoughtan noblewoman before the conquest of that chiefdom, was placed in power after their werowance's defeat.[18]

The English made confused and scandalized comments concerning Powhatan's marriage practices. One boy who lived for many months in his village later wrote, "If any of ye Kings wives have once a child by him, he keepes hir no longer but puts hir from him givinge hir suffitient Copper and beads to mayntayne hir and the child while it is younge and then [it] is taken from hir and mayntayned by ye King, it now being lawfull for hir beinge thus put away to marry with any other."[19] John Smith and others told similar stories, less respectful in tone. Though it was undoubtedly an exaggeration that Powhatan "put away" *all* his wives (observers tell us that most of his wives were young, but by implication some were older), the story was probably largely true.

In context, the practice makes far more sense than it first appears to. For his political purposes, Powhatan needed many children by many different women. However, the lands of one village could not possibly provide the food and firewood necessary to keep all of them. In fact, he usually had only about twelve wives living with him. It made practical political sense for the women he married to be free to return to their people and remarry once they had borne a child of his. The children, however, were fated to return. To ensure their loyalty to their father and his people, they had to be raised with him. So after a child was weaned and no longer in need of constant care, probably at about the age of four or five, it came back to live with Powhatan's family. Other Native Americans, like some of the Aztecs, followed this sort of arrangement as a matter of course.[20]

Where did Pocahontas fit in this complicated web? Scholars do not know exactly. It is certain that she was not a carrier of political power: her mother was not a political pawn from a chiefly family but rather a young woman Powhatan simply wanted to marry. Did her mother live in the village with Pocahontas? Or had she returned to her own people, sending the girl back to her father only a few years before the English ships appeared? Perhaps she had died. It seems unlikely that she was present in the town. An Englishman who wrote with great interest about Pocahontas took the trouble to list the names of the wives residing with Powhatan in about 1610 and to explain which was the mother of two other children well known to the colonists, yet he merely noted in his list that living with Powhatan was "young Pocohunta a daughter of his." We do know that when Pocahontas was about six, a daughter was born to a favored wife named Winganuske. That child was known as "the great dearling of the king's" and later married a powerful werowance three days' journey away. It was almost certainly one of Pocahontas's jobs to help care for this daughter of daughters, as older girls always helped with their fathers' younger children.[21]

Pocahontas worked. Everybody worked. No exceptions were made for a king's daughter. And she worked with her father's other children and their mothers, negotiating her way successfully among them, earning or retaining her name, "Little Playful One." A love of solitude was not tolerated in a girl. In April, when the news of the ships first reached her village, last year's supply of dried corn and beans would have been gone or nearly gone. It was time to prepare for planting again, and to gather wild fruits. They would do it together.

Every morning the women divided into groups and set out on their self-appointed tasks. Their fields, already cleared by the men, were in walking distance from the village. When the land grew tired from overfarming after a number of years, the town would move. Each man's family planted corn, beans, squash, and fruits in their square of ground, intermingling the seeds so that the different species provided one another with what they needed—shade, varied nutrients, or trellises for climbing vines. The fields had to be small, as their only tools were digging sticks and wooden hoes, and each family had to provide all its own labor, with some of the women stopping peri-

"Ther was never seene amonge us soe cunninge a way to take fishe withal." *(Theodor de Bry, 1590)*

odically to nurse the babies suspended in cradleboards hung from nearby trees. At the end of the day young boys were left to practice their archery, proudly guarding the fields from ravenous birds and rodents. On the way home some women would stop to gather firewood, piling loose branches onto skins that they dragged back to the village; others gathered early spring berries and greens. There were eleven hundred edible species in the area, and Pocahontas was expected to learn them all from the older women.[22]

On certain days they had the more difficult—but perhaps more exciting—task of taking a canoe to gather tuckahoe root from the creeks. Tuckahoe was poisonous, but when processed properly, it could be ground into flour and made into bread. In winter, reeds had been sought to make sitting and sleeping mats as well as walls for the houses the women built, but now all the forays along the creeks were to collect tuckahoe. Canoe trips were not easy; at least three women were needed to handle the heavy dugout craft. Sometimes they had to pass through rapids roiling with spring rains, and they risked sudden squalls. The tuckahoe tubers grew under the icy water twelve to eighteen inches deep in the mud, with embedded root systems that were hard to dislodge without metal blades. The tide had to be at the perfect level if the women were to succeed in filling the canoe. And Pocahontas's people, in the center of Tsenacomoco, were the lucky ones: other women, living on the outskirts of the chieftainship, risked being abducted by a scouting enemy war party.

By late afternoon the women and girls had returned to the village. They busied themselves with the cooking that older women had already begun, or they started to gut and clean the animal carcasses their menfolk had brought home, or to scrape and tan the hides. They were indeed tired. Yet no Indian who saw them laughing and talking as they worked would have said they appeared beaten down or resentful. Skeletons from that time suggest that Indian women were as strong as many modern American men.[23] And their own men, who likewise worked hard, who waged war and brought home meat and fish as often as they could, knew their women's worth. Both sexes knew that neither could survive a month without the other.

Play followed work. Nearly every night after dinner there was singing and dancing or storytelling. The melodic, throbbing voices rose and fell, accompanied by rattlelike instruments in a range of pitches. If it was a special feast day or ceremonial event, Powhatan's family wore the clothing that other villages' tribute payments made possible. His honored wives were expected to make a grand showing.

Women always wore softened deerskin aprons, like wraparound skirts, fringed at the edges, and when they went to the woods, they also wore leggings and shoes (*mockasins*, they called them), like men. On special occasions—and when it was cold—the wives wrapped mantles around their shoulders and waists like blouses. The finest of these were embroidered with pearl and mother-of-pearl beads, or decorated with furs. Copper jewelry glinted from the noblewomen's necks and arms. Most beautiful of all were the feathered cloaks, made from the rarest and most beautiful plumes. "The cloak," an English visitor would later write of one queen's garment, ". . . [is] made of blew feathers so artificially [i.e., artfully] and thick sowed together, that it showes like a deepe purple Satten."[24]

If it was only an ordinary evening, Pocahontas might have sat in the flickering light of the torches and the central fire, hands busy twisting silk grass fibers into cordage. This was a skill so ingrained in all young girls that they could do it without focusing on the task, their minds intent on something else. At her age Pocahontas listened to the older people tell stories. She might have questions from time to time, but she would wait till the next day to ask them of some woman with whom she was intimate. She would never interrupt; it simply wasn't done. Later an English visitor would impatiently urge his young translator to interrupt the telling of the creation story with some clarifying questions, but the boy, though known for being saucy, would not do it. "[If they] had proceeded in some order, they should have made yt hang togither the better," fulminated the confused visitor, "but the boy was unwilling to question him so many things lest he should offend him."[25]

It is impossible to say with surety what Pocahontas learned about her gods and her history as she listened to her elders. We will never catch more than glimpses of what she was taught, for her people left no written records. The English who asked them about it later, like the Spanish before them in Mexico, claimed that the Indians believed in two great deities: a benevolent creator, and an evil force that plagued human lives. But there is no real evidence that they held such a dichotomized view. The Europeans were no doubt tempted to find evidence for a belief in God and the devil, but the discrepancies in their stories, combined with archaeological evidence and scraps of statements made by Indians and recorded in European writings, yield quite a different view. For the Indians, the universe was not so simple as to be divided between good and evil.

Every person, every chiefdom, even the cosmos itself, was a complicated entity in which good motivations and bad ones were inextricably mixed, and in which resulting actions and events could be interpreted in a variety of ways, depending on one's perspective. The people believed there was one great spirit who made heaven and earth, but infinite manifestations of that deity existed all around. The *manitous* or *manitos* of other Algonkian cultures, spirit beings, lived everywhere. Pocahontas's father was the *mamanitowik*, which apparently meant something like "keeper of many spirits." At the edge of every village was a temple in which an embodiment of that people's own deity, or *okee*, was kept, who seems to have been understood to protect the people even as he made demands on them.[26]

Pocahontas probably never saw the okee at her father's town of Werowocomoco, because only the priests tended to the gods and were privileged to enter their temples. When the priests prayed aloud, they sometimes spoke in a rarefied or formulaic style that ordinary people did not understand. But Pocahontas certainly heard the nightly stories—much more elegantly told than the English versions we have with us now—tales of love and pride, envy and competition, death and eternal rebirth:

> [The god] made the water and the fish therein and the land and
> a greate deare, which should feed upon the land, at which assem-
> bled the other 4 gods [of the four winds] envious hereat, from the
> east the west from the north and sowth, and with hunting poles
> kild this deare, drest him, and after they had feasted with him de-

parted againe east west north and sowth, at which the other god
in despight of this their malice to him, took all the haires of the
slayne deare and spred them upon the earth with many powerfull
wordes and charmes whereby every haire became a deare.[27]

Pocahontas was probably familiar with the tradition that her people had lived in Tsenacomoco for three hundred years. The Powhatans kept some pictoglyphic maps and apparently noted quantities
on notched sticks: they certainly could have kept such a historical
year count. Still, all the archaeological evidence indicates that the
culture developed there in situ, evolving from earlier cultures that
had been present for millennia. Both, in fact, may be true. About
three hundred years earlier an agricultural revolution, spreading from
the south, had changed the people's way of life. It began as early as
A.D. 900 but was not complete until about 1300. It is possible that
newcomers arrived, bearing the seeds of the Three Sisters—corn,
beans, and squash—or that the seeds arrived through trade, or both.
Eventually the groups that dedicated themselves most effectively to
farming the Three Sisters vanquished their enemies and established
their chiefdoms, and perhaps that was when the historical count began that would add up to three centuries in 1600.[28]

The fact that Pocahontas's people had been farming only for
something over three hundred years is crucial to understanding the
advantages that the Europeans had over them. Anthropologists have
long known that turning from hunting and gathering to sedentary
farming leads to an increase in population and the proliferation of
technological advances—involving not only tools and irrigation but
also weaponry, record-keeping, and transportation. What the field of
plant biology has recently been able to answer is why some ancient
peoples chose to farm, while others chose to remain in the Stone
Age. The answer, it turns out, lies in the constellation of suitable—or
protein-rich—wild plants available in a particular environment. Af-

ter all, it is at first a risky venture to turn from hunting and gathering to farming. Farming is time-consuming, and crops may fail or be stolen by enemies. If the plants available in one's environment include, for example, only such things as squashes and apples, upon which people cannot live, it makes no sense whatsoever to shift to farming, except perhaps on a part-time basis. On the other hand, it makes a great deal of sense to do it for the wheat, barley, and peas that were present in the Fertile Crescent (today's Southwest Asia, or Iraq and Iran). Unsurprisingly, it was in the Fertile Crescent that people began to farm eleven thousand years ago; their crops and budding technologies soon spread into Europe and Asia.[29]

In the case of the Americas, one rushes to ask, "What about corn?" Why didn't the Native Americans plant corn, while the people of the Old World were growing their barley and wheat? Corn is indeed a protein-rich plant, and the indigenous Americans did grow it, but they did not begin to farm nearly as soon as the people of the Fertile Crescent—for there was a catch. Unlike ancient wheat, corn eleven thousand years ago was not the same useful plant that we know today. After the millennia of part-time cultivation that it took to turn the nearly useless wild *teosinte*, with its tiny bunches of seeds, into something approaching today's ears of corn, the Central Mexicans did in fact become very serious full-time agriculturalists, but they could not do so before. And after several more millennia of long-distance trading, the precious seeds made their way up to Pocahontas's ancestors in the Virginia Tidewater, where her people immediately put them to good use.

In Pocahontas's time, her people were only just beginning to feel the want of iron that might eventually have driven them to mine it; they were only beginning to organize tribute payments that might eventually have caused them to work out a calendar or a writing system. At the time, however, none of that really mattered. The people were well fed, healthy, and happy. In fact, when white settlers found themselves marooned among the Indians, they often chose to stay with them even when an opportunity arose to return to their own kind. But when the two cultures met and entered a power struggle over land and resources, it would turn out that, unbeknownst to either side, they had been in something like a technological race for centuries. And the cultural heirs of people who had been full-time agriculturalists for eleven thousand years rather than a few hundred had already won.

None of this made an individual white man one whit more intelligent or more perceptive than an individual Indian—just better informed and better armed. Powhatan already knew that the strangers' boats, obvious navigational skills, booming weapons, metal blades, and armor were cause for serious concern. Most of all, he knew he needed to know more. After he first heard the news of the strangers' arrival, life in Werowocomoco continued normally, and he proceeded with his intelligence-gathering. The strangers settled on an island belonging to the Paspaheghs and called it "James-Towne." Several of his subject towns had dealings with them and reported everything back to him.

Spring gave way to hot summer. Pocahontas helped with the harvesting and the drying of the crops, preserving them for winter. The weather turned cold. The women put on their fur mantles and stayed in the village, weaving baskets and mats, tanning and softening hides, sewing and embroidering. The men were nearly always seeking game. They considered moving to a winter hunting camp. Then came important news. It was December, near the shortest day of the year. Powhatan's kinsman Opechankeno had caught the strangers' werowance and was bringing the bearded coat-wearer to the mamanitowik at Werowocomoco. If only Don Luis could have known. The tables were turned this time. No Indian prince had been taken hostage and dragged off to see the coat-wearers' king. Instead, the Indians had made one of the coat-wearers' leaders their prisoner, and he was coming to see their ruler. His name, they said, was "John Smith."[30]

What the English Knew

[That he had no interpreter] vexed [Hernando] Cortés exceedingly, because he lacked means of communicating with the [Aztec] governor and learning about the country, but he recovered from his vexation when he heard one of the twenty women given to them [by the Mayas] . . . speaking to the governor's men and understanding them very well. So Cortés took her aside . . . and promised her more than her liberty if she would establish friendship between him and the men of her country.

—Francisco López de Gómara,
Historia de la conquista de Mexico (1554)

John Smith opened the book and began to read. Peter Martyr's *Decades of the Newe Worlde* was a work he knew well. In 1606, as he prepared to join the newly formed Virginia Company's first expedition across the Atlantic, Smith often sought inspiration in Martyr's tales of Spanish exploits in the Caribbean:

The Lieutenant . . . sent for a bande of foote men, commanding them to lye in ambushe until such tyme as [the Indian prince] Guarionexius wente from the playnes to the mountaynes, and then soodenly to intrappe hym. They went as they were commanded, tooke hym, and brought hym awaye with them. And by this meanes were all the Regions nere aboute, pacified and quieted.[1]

In the pages of Martyr's book there were numerous examples of Spaniards kidnapping kings and so subjugating native tribes. The drama of Guarionexius, however, did not end there. A subtitle in bold print appearing in the margin hinted at what was to come: "A Bewtifull Woman," it said.

A certayne noble woman of nere kindred to Guarionexius, and wife to another kynge whose dominion was yet untouched, followed hym in all the adversities. They affirme this woman to bee the fairest and most bewetifull that ever nature brought foorthe in the Islande. Whom, when the kynge her husbande who loved her most ardently (as her bewtie deserved) hearde saye that shee was taken prisoner he wandered uppe and down the desertes lyke a man owte of his wytte . . . But at lengthe, he came to the Lieutenante, promysinge most faithfully that he wold submitte hymselfe and all that he could make, under his poure, soo that he wolde restore hym his wyfe.[2]

Like many of his countrymen, Smith seems to have liked racy stories about beautiful young island women being taken prisoner. The books written by scholars like Martyr were positively tame compared to the vividly illustrated broadsides and pamphlets passed from hand to hand among Smith's cohort. Starting almost one hundred years before, woodcuts had often represented America as a nearly naked Indian woman. Books and broadsides alike conveyed the idea that in taking an Indian woman, one took a continent, metaphorically speaking. Some authors even made the connection explicit: "Guayana is a country that hath yet her maidenhead," wrote Sir Walter Raleigh.[3] The vision of the conquest was enough to make a man's blood run warm. But if, on the other hand, one was squeamish enough not to relish the thought of taking a woman by force, to prefer in fact that she should desperately desire being taken, then "the Spanish decades," as Smith called Martyr's book, provided material for an alternative style of daydream:

> The [Indian] nobility, . . . men as [well as] women, repute it infamous to joyne with any of base parentage or strangers, except Christians, whom they count as noblemen by reason of theyr valientnes, . . . countynge it for a great matter and an honorable thing yf they be beloved of any of them. In so much that yf they knowe any Christian man carnally, they keepe theyr faith to hym.[4]

Martyr went so far as to insist that Indian women were insatiable, that those Christian men who had had carnal relations with them found it hard work to "satisfy theyr appetite." Perhaps the taking of the New World would be more thrilling than dangerous after all.

The book that Smith seemed to like even better than Martyr's was Richard Hakluyt's *Principal Navigations, Voyages, Traffiques & Discoveries of the English Nation*. Appearing immediately after the defeat of the Spanish Armada in 1588, it inspired hundreds if not thousands of English men. Offering a veritable encyclopedia of testimonial accounts regarding English explorations of the New World, in its pages readers learned that the English were well on their way to establishing an empire like the one the Spanish had already acquired. In 1497 John Cabot had purportedly explored the entire coast of North America, thus legitimizing British claims to the region. And as early as 1530 "one of the savage kings of the country of Brasil, was contented to take ship with [William Hawkins of Plymouth] and to be transported hither into England."[5] Hawkins brought him to see Henry VIII at Whitehall: "The King and all the Nobilitie did not a little marvaile, and not without cause." The English spent a year showing him off and teaching him their language, but when they tried to take him home, "the said Savage king died at sea." In the end, though, the unfortunate conclusion to their first effort at New World diplomacy did not matter much, as only Sir Walter Raleigh and a few of his followers continued to insist that the English attempt to make settlements in South America. Most acknowledged it was Spanish and Portuguese territory, and their attention shifted elsewhere.

The most useful parts of Hakluyt's book, from Smith's perspective, were the early reports on the country that the English had named Virginia, after their virgin queen, Elizabeth, stretching from today's Maine to North Carolina. The English wanted to believe that the women there would be as welcoming as the Spanish had reported the Caribbean women to be, and Hakluyt offered his readers material to feed their hopes. One Indian nobleman, who had welcomed the first English expedition to explore Roanoke Island, off the coast of today's North Carolina, reportedly had a "very well favored" wife. According to the Englishman who wrote the account, the Virginia Indians in general were "devoid of all guile and treason," and the lovely wife in particular wished the English men to feel comfortable, even if it meant embarrassing Indian men:

> While we were at meate [i.e., eating], there came in at the gates two or three men with their bowes and arrowes from hunting, whom when we espied, we beganne to looke one towards another, and offered to reach our weapons: but as soone as shee espied our mistrust, shee was very much moved, and caused some of her men to runne out, and take away their bowes and arrows and breake them, and withal beate the poore fellows out of the gate againe. When we departed in the evening and would not tary all night, she was very sory.[6]

There is no question that John Smith and his peers—those who wrote such books, and those who read them—embraced a notion of an explorer as a conqueror who strode with manly steps through lands of admirers, particularly admiring women. The stories never went the other way around: later, when women settlers went along, there emerged no tales of Spanish or English women being met by welcoming Indian chiefs who courted their favors. No, the colonizers of the imagination were men—men imbued with almost mystical powers. The foreign women and the foreign lands wanted, even needed, these men, for such men were more than desirable. They were deeply good, right in all they did, blessed by God. Hakluyt himself said that Psalm 107 had inspired his work.[7] "They that goe downe to the sea in shippes, that doe business in great waters, these see the workes of the Lord, and his wonders in the deepe."They were the heroes of legend, even of the Bible, alive now in the real world. No wonder twenty-seven-year-old John Smith was determined to be one of them.

In 1606, as the Virginia Company of London prepared three ships for sailing—the *Susan Constant*, the *Godspeed*, and the *Discovery*—investors buttressed their hopes with prayers. God willing, theirs would be the first English colony to survive in the Americas. If it did, all the unsuccessful earlier efforts would be vindicated. And they would be rich.

It was high time. The wealth arising from western Europe's century-long history of expansion had largely passed the English by. When they thought of how Columbus's request for funding had been turned down by Henry VII, they winced. "How many did condemn themselves, that did not accept of that honest offer of Noble Columbus?" lamented John Smith.[8] It had been the Spanish who fully recognized that they could only compete against the extraordinary power and wealth of the Muslim merchants if they could find a direct route to China and India, bypassing the Levant (as the English called the Middle East), the crossroads of international trade.

The big money of the era was to be made in trading for the textiles, spices, and gems of the Far East, and the Muslims, conveniently situated in the center of the known world, controlled that traffic. Chinese merchants obviously had no intention of coming to the Europeans: they had everything that they needed and that everybody else wanted right in their own backyard.[9] So the Spanish queen, Isabella, had funded Columbus to journey west, to see how long it would take to circle the world and dock in the land of silk and spices.

Columbus had, of course, been a fool to argue with the astronomers and mathematicians who told him it would take too long, that the earth was bigger than he believed. He was also lucky, however, and discovered a landmass that no one in Europe had known existed. Naturally, he did not then realize he had done so, and in his ignorance he called the native people he encountered "Indians," believing he was near India. But Amerigo Vespucci and others soon followed in his wake to explore and map, and they corrected his error. What Columbus had found was not the outskirts of Asia, but rather, a new world.

In less than thirty years the Spanish had launched a sufficient number of exploratory voyages from their base in the Caribbean to make it possible for Hernando Cortés to learn about and then conquer the Aztec emperor Moctezuma. Cortés was also a lucky man. An Indian woman he held captive, Malinche, turned out to be competent to translate between the Spanish and the Aztecs. Thus the Europeans were able to understand the country they had found, decapitate its government, and subjugate its people. The English learned about these compelling events from Spanish works translated into their own language by colonial enthusiasts. The most popular was the translation of a famous work by Cortés's personal chaplain, Francisco López de Gómara. The English edition was given the long and unusual title *The Pleasant Historie of the Conquest of the West India, now called New Spain, atchieved by the worthy prince Hernando Cortes, most delectable to reade.*[10]

In 1532, ten years after Cortés had conquered the Aztecs of Mexico, Francisco Pizarro began the process of bringing down the Incas of Peru. The silver mines of the two regions made the Spanish so rich that they soon indirectly ruled Europe. They lorded it over their once-feared Muslim enemies, and, in 1588, even attempted to invade England. In fact, until their Armada was defeated off Britain's coast that same year, Queen Elizabeth had hesitated to directly encourage any English attempts at settlement in the New World, lest she draw down the wrath of the Spanish.[11]

The English, however, had not been inactive by any means. In the 1560s they had launched a major offensive against Ireland, with the design of rendering an area that had been nominally theirs since the twelfth century an active, tax-paying entity. The war had been brutal, but Ireland's peasants were eventually brought into submission and placed under the authority of newly installed English landlords. The colonizers then moved farther west toward Newfoundland and Nova Scotia, parts of the New World so far north of Spanish interests as to be unlikely to raise a direct confrontation. In the 1570s Martin Frobisher announced he had discovered gold on Baffin Island, in today's Hudson Bay. It turned out to be fool's gold. In the 1580s Sir Humphrey Gilbert, who had earned his knighthood in conquering the Irish, attempted to establish a colony in Canada. But in 1584 his ship went down. His younger half brother, Sir Walter Raleigh, continued his work and launched the Roanoke colony. By 1590 all traces of the Carolina settlers had disappeared.[12]

How unjust, thought the young English enthusiasts, that the Spanish had meanwhile settled glowingly warm lands, rich in precious metals and valuable plants, and, best of all, peopled by sedentary Indians who could be made to work for their conquerors. Every year these subject lands sent the Spanish king silver in convoys of ships. The temptation to rob them was simply too great, and ambitious young men like Sir Francis Drake turned to piracy—or privateering, as they called it, as they held special licenses from Her Majesty Queen Elizabeth. They seized Spanish ships and made lightning-strike attacks on wealthy Spanish ports whenever they could. Eventually they even attempted to take over certain Caribbean islands on a more permanent basis. In the Spanish view of things, Drake and others like him were the terrorists of the seas: their names inspired horror for generations. The English justified their actions by insisting that when they attempted to take over an island or a port, they were only trying to free from bondage the wrongfully oppressed African slaves and Indians. With English masters, Drake reasoned, they would be infinitely better off.[13]

In 1583 a book very conveniently appeared detailing Spanish atrocities against the natives of the New World. Called *The Spanish Colonie, or a Briefe Chronicle of the Acts and Gestes of the Spaniards in the West Indies*, it was a translation of an earlier work in Spanish by Bartolomé de las Casas, a priest who, with passion and eloquence, sought to awaken his Spanish peers to their sins and change their course of action. Before the Roanoke disaster, Sir Walter Raleigh himself liked to cite Las Casas and claim that, once in possession of a colony, the English would treat the Indians quite differently than the Spanish had.

Despite their failed ventures, the English never gave up on settlement. After Roanoke, they gradually began to accept that they were probably not going to find gold and silver in the northern wilderness of Virginia. But from a settlement they could seek the still-elusive Northwest Passage to the Pacific; they could raid the Spanish with greater ease; and they could traffic in exotic plants, fish, and furs. And some hoped that they might yet become lords of vast tracts of farmable land, willingly worked by Indians. Furthermore, the New World might prove a sort of safety valve.

In England civil leaders believed they had a population crisis. It was true that between 1570 and 1600 the nation's population rose from 3.25 million to 4.07 million. The real problem, however, was that the enclosure movement occurred at the same time: land that cottagers had once worked was fenced off for wealthy men's sheep, whose wool supplied the burgeoning textile industy. People were uprooted to wander on the open roads, migrating toward the cities. Colonization, reasoned some, was the answer to unemployment and discontent.

For a number of years England's ambitious men were distracted: they fought the Spanish from the 1580s until 1604, and in 1603 Queen Elizabeth died. But as soon as the war was over and King James was settled on his throne, investors once again turned their attention to Virginia. One company received a royal charter to settle in the northern areas, and chose a spot at the mouth of the Kennebec River in today's Maine. But the colonists there were miserable, and they shortly abandoned their settlement and dissolved the company. Another venture, however, was assigned the southern regions. This was the Virginia Company of London, and its merchant backers were much wealthier. One hundred forty-four people set out in December 1606, and the eager John Smith was among them.[14]

Smith's thoughts, as the ship pulled away from the dock and the land disappeared over the horizon, went unrecorded. Glib accounts of history presume he felt only excited and confident. They cite the celebrations that took place a few years later, when the next batch of colonists sailed. Then the pastor Robert Gray, who admittedly went down to the sea in ships only in his dreams, called out to the colonists: "The preserver of all men preserve your persons from all perils both by sea and land; make your goings out like a host of men triumphing for the victories, and your comings in like an armie dividing the spoile."[15]

John Smith undoubtedly heard these tones with his inner ear, at least some of the time. But there were other moments, too: periods of fear, even panic, or of ordinariness, even depression. His journey was in fact just another in a century-long list of expeditions, all of them hazardous, most of them failures. There wasn't a man on that ship who did not doubt—some of the time. They knew that in large measure their fates rested in the hands of the Indians. For whatever the explorers might have been, most of them were not stupid: they

An engraving of John Smith based on a sketch taken from life. Published in Smith's *Description of New England*, 1616, and his *General Historie of Virginia*, 1624. *(Simon Van de Passe, 1616, courtesy of the New York Public Library)*

wanted to believe the prejudiced accounts of awed Indians, but there were already known instances of violent reprisals. On some level they must have known conquest would not be as easy as they wanted it to be. In fact, their future relationship with the Indians was already a matter of hot debate.

After all, the enthusiastic proponents of colonization were only some of England's people. Many others opined that no good could come of all this—that the Crown was too poor to support such projects, that America's northern lands were useless, that the Spanish would never let the colony survive if the lands in fact proved good, that past failures should teach them something. Many also argued that God would not look with favor on their dispossession of the Indians. Even Robert Gray, the same pastor who envisioned the colonists as the army of God, acknowledged: "The first objection [to colonization] is, by what right or warrant we can enter in the land of these Savages, take away their rightfull inheritance from them, and plant ourselves in their places, being unwronged or unprovoked by them."[16]

These words may startle people who assume that John Smith and his cohort lived in an era in which it never occurred to anyone that taking Indian land raised a moral issue. It is rare, though, that a great wrong is committed by one people against another without some among the perpetrators protesting the deed. Colonists made moral decisions, too. And some were adept at convincing themselves that whatever they wanted to do was indeed the right thing to do, whatever others might say.

How did they work it out for themselves? How did the pastor Robert Gray, for example, answer that question in his friends' drawing rooms, and then in his sermons? First, it is clear that nobody then envisioned eliminating the indigenous people. Up until at least 1620, as one historian has put it, "only madmen would have dreamed of extirpating the Indians."[17] Sane men could not think of it. Who but the Indians would tell the settlers what they needed to know—about navigable rivers, food crops, water supplies, and the like? No, killing or removing the Indians was not even discussed. Rather, the central question turned on how the English might colonize the New World and harness the labor of the Indians without cruelly oppressing them. They had always sworn they would not become like the Spaniards. What now gave them the right to "take away the rightful inheritance" of the Indians, who had never "wronged" them? The answer lay in the belief that, rather than make slaves of the Indians, as the Spanish had supposedly done, the English would give them the *opportunity* to work, to pay taxes to the

commonweal, to become Christian, and to learn how to make the
land more productive—so that they would ultimately be better off
than they were before. The Indians were castigated at every turn for
having failed to make the land yield more; they had thus forfeited
their right to keep all of it. With English neighbors and landlords
to show them the way, they would better manage the land left to
them.[18]

The more elite members of the Virginia Company aboard the
ships bound for America had literally been schooled in this notion.
As early as 1516, even before the discovery of the Aztec kingdom,
Sir Thomas More had rehearsed the idea in *Utopia*, and the work
had been translated from Latin into English and oft-reprinted since.
His fictional narrator was supposed to have sailed with Amerigo
Vespucci—whose work was "now in print and abroad in every man's
hands." In the idyllic society More's narrator described, land was for
those who worked it:

> If so be that the multitude throughout the whole island pass and
> exceed the due number, then they choose out of every city certain
> citizens and build up a town under their own laws in the next
> land where the inhabitants have much waste and unoccupied
> ground, receiving also of the same country people to them if they
> will join and dwell with them. They thus joining and dwelling
> together do easily agree in one fashion of living, and that to the
> great wealth of both peoples. For they so bring the matter about
> by their laws that the ground, which before was neither good nor
> profitable for the one nor for the other, is now sufficient and
> fruitful enough for them both. But if the inhabitants of that land
> will not dwell with them to be ordered by their laws, then they
> drive them out of those bounds . . . And if they resist and rebel,
> then they make war against them, for they count this the most
> just cause of war, when any people holdeth a piece of ground void
> and vacant to no good nor profitable use.[19]

The unproductive use of land was not the only reason the English insisted colonization was justified. Starting in the 1580s, even serious English writers—not just the producers of lurid broadsides—claimed that the practice of human sacrifice existed in Virginia, even though no one had observed it firsthand. There is in fact no evidence that human sacrifice occurred there. The writers were probably inspired by their readings about the Aztecs, among whom the practice did exist, and they interpreted male initiation rites—about which they had heard fearful stories—as ceremonies of death. They wanted to believe that it occurred, for they could then save the Indians from themselves. Sir George Peckham, for example, published a description in 1583 of the idealized feudal society in which willing indigenous serfs would not only benefit from their new knowledge of modern agriculture but would also abandon human sacrifice. "Over and beside the knowledge how to tyl and dresse their grounds, they shal be reduced from unseemly customs, to honest manners . . . Many of their poore innocent children shal be preserved from the bloody knife of the sacrificer, a most horrible and detestable custome in the sight of God and man, now and ever heretofore used amongst them."[20] Peckham's overarching theme was not that the natives were lost to all goodness, but rather, that they would be grateful once they had had the opportunity to mend their ways under English governance.

Almost every English commentator on the New World reiterated these themes; then in 1590 a book appeared that surpassed all others. It was more accurate and more widely circulated. The linguist and mathematician Thomas Harriot had returned from Roanoke with extensive notes and with some paintings done by John White—whose daughter and granddaughter would later disappear, along with the other settlers. Theodor de Bry published Harriot's *A Brief and True Report of the New Found Land of Virginia*, including his own engravings based on White's paintings. From a modern anthropological point of view, Harriot's work is indeed useful. He learned some of the language and noted details as accurately as he knew how; he clearly respected many of the people he met and understood that a lack of technology did not imply shortcomings in intelligence. His interpretation of Indian-white relations, however, ultimately served only to encourage the enthusiastic backers of colonization in their current perceptions:

> [T]hey are a people poore, and for want of skill and judgement in the knowledge and use of our things, doe esteeme our trifles before things of greater value: Notwithstanding, in their proper maner (considering the want of such things as we have), they seeme very ingenious. For although they have no such tooles, nor any such crafts, Sciences and Artes as wee, yet in those things they doe, they shew excellence of wit. And by how much they upon due consideration shall finde our maner of knowledges and crafts to exceede theirs in perfection, and speede for doing or execution, by so much the more is it probable that they should desire our friendship and love, and have the greater respect for pleasing and obeying us. Whereby may bee hoped, if meanes of good government be used, that they may in short time bee brought to civilitie.[21]

Similarly, in the illustrations the ingenuity of the people was showcased—in their houses, fishing weirs, archery. De Bry showed them embracing English education: a young girl danced about, holding a powder horn in one hand and an armillary sphere, a small instructional globe, in the other. The English could not know then that their faith in this pleasant prediction of future relations would not last: a century later, when the settlers had become disgusted with the Indians' failure to comply with their dictates, the book's illustrations would be redone, and the child would be left holding an ear of corn and an Indian rattle. One historian has commented, "It is as if the English had initially been eager to place European objects in native hands, but later they were just as eager to take these things away."[22]

In the meantime, however, Harriot's and de Bry's brand of arrogant optimism held sway and directly influenced the instructions given to the Virginia Company by King James:

> Furthermore, our will and pleasure is, and wee doe hereby determine and ordaine, that every person and persons being our subjects of every the said Collonies and Plantations shall from time to time well entreate those salvages in those parts, and use all good meanes to draw the salvages and heathen people . . . to the true service and knowledge of God, and that all just, kind and charitable courses shall be holden with such of them, as shall conforme themselves to any good and sociable traffique and dealing with ye subjects of us, our heires and successors, which shall be planted there, whereby they may be ye sooner drawne to the true knowledge of God, and ye Obedience of us.[23]

However, the possibility that the reality might well be more complicated was not ignored. About two weeks after the king's advisers released the instructions in his name, wealthy members of the Virginia Company presented the departing colonists with their own "Instructions by Way of Advice." They preached caution:

> Let [your Soldiers] never trust the Country people with the carriage of their Weapons . . . And whensoever any of Yours Shoots before them be sure that they be Chosen out of your best Marksmen for if they See Your Learners miss what they aim at, they will think the Weapon not so terrible and thereby will be bould . . . to Assailt you. Above all things do not advertise the killing of any of your men that the Country people may know it. If they perceive they are but Common men and that with the Loss of many of theirs they may Deminish any part of Yours they will make many Adventures upon You if the County be populous.[24]

Some scholars have argued that these instructions were written by Hakluyt. They bear the imprint of someone who knew the history of the Spanish campaigns very well: the writer knew that although steel armor normally made European soldiers relatively invulnerable, it would not work if the country was "populous." That is, it could not help them withstand the onslaught of thousands of enemies who had decided they could afford to lose a few hundred in making a rush. This careful thinking about what to do and not to do in facing Indian enemies makes it clear that consciously or unconsciously the English colonists knew they might not be as welcome as they hoped.

They had other worries as well. As part of the evolving belief that the Indians would be only too glad to become literal and figurative tribute-payers to the English nation, contemporary scholars had worked out an interesting theory: the indigenous Americans, they claimed, were very much like the ancient Britons—who had themselves been civilized by the Romans. This theory was both condescending and yet at the same time beautifully unprejudiced. On the one hand, it justified the English insistence that they were superior in every regard at the present time; on the other, it acknowledged that there were no inherent differences between English and natives. The idea made some people distinctly nervous: if Indians could become just like Englishmen, then could not Englishmen also become just like Indians? Alone in the wilderness, who was to say the colonists would not become "savages"? Many dire warnings were issued. And later English boys, when left with Indians, often did indeed become Indians. One man would write, "While I yet remained there [in Powhatan's village], by great chance came an Englishman thither, almost three years before that time surprised [and taken prisoner] . . . one William Parker, grown so like both in complexion and habite to the Indians, that I only knew him by his tongue to be an Englishman."[25] To some, William Parker was an awful specter.

As the *Susan Constant*, the *Godspeed*, and the *Discovery* plowed the seas following the usual route to the Caribbean, then bent their way northward and drew near the Chesapeake, each man on board entertained his own uncertainties. John Smith may well have been the one least likely to be trapped within unexamined expectations. He had lived as a prisoner of war in Turkey and had every reason to know that non-Christian men, however different they might be from him in some regards, were exactly like him in others. He does not seem to have entertained the belief that the Indians were likely to want to give up their sovereignty to the English. He apparently anticipated that they would have to be forced, and he may well have imagined that he was the man for the job. His later writings indicate that he saw Hernando Cortés as something of a role model, or that he at least saw himself as one in a long line of great conquistadors.[26] If he did already see himself as a latter-day Cortés, then he knew from his readings that his first step must be to find a way to talk to the Indians. The famous Spaniard had learned to his profit that nothing effective could be done until he understood something about the situation with which he was dealing: he had successfully used the polyglot captive Malinche. Smith's later writings indicate that he saw beautiful Indian women essentially as sources of information and advocates for him with their men. As the ships neared their destination, he likely wondered if such women waited for him in the green woods that looked so inviting to men who had been at sea for months. Another man who looked at the beautiful shore wrote home, "I was almost ravished at the first sight thereof."[27]

They made landfall in Virginia on April 26, 1607. It had been Captain Christopher Newport's assigned task to lead the three ships to Virginia, help the designated council members found a settlement, and then return to London to make a report and organize more shipments of supplies and colonists. By late summer 1607 Newport was back in London as directed, and fairly glowing with excitement. For the first time the Spanish ambassador to England became concerned about the Virginia project and wrote a coded letter to his sovereign. Unscrambled, the missive read: "They are mad about the location, and frightened to death that Your Majesty will throw them out . . . There are so many here and in other parts of the kingdom who are already arranging to send people there that it is wise not to regard it lightly, because very soon they will have many people, and it will be more difficult to get them out."[28] To the ambassador's frustration, his king ignored the warning.

Remarkably, even as more and more real information came back by boat to London, supporters of colonization managed to remain committed to their vision of awed and docile Indians for several more years. In 1610 William Strachey, who had just returned from a year in Jamestown, wrote a book that he hoped would win him the favor of the Earl of Northumberland, a good friend of Sir Walter Raleigh and Thomas Harriot. He was a university-educated man and had evidently been an avid reader of Sir Thomas More. He planned the future:

> [T]he trybute which they shall pay unto his Majestie shalbe far lesse then that which Powhatan exacteth from them, who robbes them as you have heard of all they have: but after such tyme as they shall submit themelves to the kings Majestie and consent to paie him a Trybute to be agreed upon, Powhatan shall lay no more his exactions upon them, but they shall freely enjoy all they can geather and have a peaceable and franck trade with the English for the Commodityes they can make of their owne exchaunging them for ours and that the English will take of their poorest into their families, as their better sort shall by patents and Proclamations hold their landes as free burgers and Cittizens with the English and Subjects to king James, who will give them justice and defend them against all their enemyes, whereas now they live in miserable Slavery . . . the Naturalls being thus constrained to paye duly this their Tribute will Clense double as much grownd as they doe [now].[29]

One element of this man's argument that was new in being explicit was that the English could gain more by following the example of the Spaniards' treatment of the Indians than by piously condemning it. Now that the English were themselves faced with bringing a population of Indians "into the fold," the Spanish might present the best practical model for success. How had the Spanish convinced the Indians to labor for them? They had prevailed upon the chiefs to make their people work. They had given the leaders certain advantages, in order to make them more willing to help: "The Cassiques or Comaunders [chiefs] of Indian Townes in Peru, whom the Virginians call Weroances, although they paie unto the king of Spayne great Tribute, yet because they make exchaunge [i.e., trade] with the Spaniards . . . they are rich in their furniture and horses and Cattell." In Virginia it would likewise be well worth the Europeans' time to cater to Indian royalty a bit. "The Spaniards were not able to make the Twent[i]eth parte of profit which they now doe but by the helpe of those Cassiques [chiefs], for they furnish out of their severall Territoryes . . . people to worke in the mines."[30]

These well-worked-out plans, however, still remained on the drawing board; Virginia's native chiefs had yet to embrace them. If only the English could find someone like the captive Mexican girl who had so aided the Spanish. "Surely," sighed the writer, "all this being delivered in fitt termes, by some perfect Interpreter, and to men that are Capable ynough of understanding, yt may begett a faire concept in them, of us and our proceedings, and leave them well satisffyed."[31]

The English knew a great deal as they approached Virginia. Thanks to their technology—their printing presses, ships, navigation tools, and maps—they knew a great deal more than Powhatan did about the state of the world. But they clearly did not know as much as they thought they did. Their misconceptions would almost prove their undoing.

THREE

First Contact

Now spying 8 salvages in a Canoa, we haled them by our worde of kindness; "Wingapoh," and they came to us. In conference by signes with them, one seemed to understand our intention, and offred with his foote to describe the river to us: So I gave him pen and paper (shewing first ye use) and he layd out the whole River from the Chesse[p]ian bay to the end of it so farr as passadg was for boates.

—"A Relatyon of the Discovery of our River, from James Forte
into the Maine[land]: made by Captain Christopher Newport; and
sincerely written and observed by a gentleman of ye Colony" (1607)[1]

When John Smith slipped in the mud, he gave up all hope. Until that moment, he later said, he had entertained the wild idea that he might be able to back away from the Indian bowmen who surrounded him, aiming his French pistol at an Indian hostage he held in a tight grip. He might somehow manage to get back to his canoe in the river. But now he just dropped his weapon and held his hands away from his body so his opponents could see he had no other. The man he had held, who had been his guide, moved away from him, telling the others that this was one of the white men's chiefs. His captors bound him securely. Perhaps it was fortunate that John Smith did not then know what often happened to Powhatan prisoners of war, or he might have lost heart. He was taken to the nearby winter hunting camp of Opechankeno, cousin[2] to the paramount chief and werowance of the Pamunkey, who emptied out his bag and asked him about his compass. Smith tried to sign how it worked. Opechankeno had something he wanted to communicate to Smith, too: he led him back to his canoe. One of the two English men who had been in it lay dead with twenty or thirty arrows in him. The Indian signed that the other one was dead as well. Smith then knew for certain that he was at his keepers' mercy; there would be no sudden rescue.[3]

That was in early December 1607. In the ensuing days Smith was taken from village to village as a curiosity: "At each place I expected . . . they would execute me, yet they used me with what kindness they could."[4] He had a list of Algonkian words, apparently compiled by Thomas Harriot, who had spent time among the people farther south at Roanoke and among the Chesapeakes. Some of the words worked here, and Smith tried to learn others. He persuaded his hosts that he should write a letter to be delivered to Jamestown, telling his people "how kindly used" he was, so that the English captain would not mount a punitive expedition. In his later report, Smith congratulated himself on having thereby reminded the Indians that the colonists might seek retribution if he failed to reappear.[5]

Opechankeno ordered that three messengers be sent with the missive—and they delivered it. Presumably Powhatan had already decided to spare the prisoner, as he would hardly have wanted to bring down future problems on his people by delivering a cheery letter from a man he planned to torture to death in the near future. But Smith had no way of knowing if the letter had truly reached its destination. He had read lurid Spanish tales about the Aztecs feeding their future victims in wooden cages, and so the more they fed him, the more he wondered if they meant to sacrifice him to their gods.[6] His life was indeed far from secure. He was taken to the Rappahannocks, who wanted to know if he was the same man who had kidnapped some of their own only a few years before. Their justice would have been swift, but they decided this man was much too short and sent him on his way with his captors. If Smith was counting the days, he knew that Christmas had just come and gone when they announced that he was to be brought before Powhatan at Werowocomoco.

When Smith and his Indian masters drew near the town, women and children ran out to meet the new arrivals.[7] Pocahontas would almost certainly have been among them, for this was no surprise visit that found only a few at home but rather a much-touted event. There is no knowing what she first thought of the short, stocky man past his youth, with an unkempt beard, bound as a captive. He was a prisoner of war, more property than person, trying to hide the fear behind his eyes. Yet he was also novel: in clothing, coloring, and physical type he looked different from any person she had ever seen. She did not yet know how much these strangers would affect the course of her own life, but she may already have learned from her father and his advisers how great their effect on the lives of the Powhatan people in general might possibly turn out to be.

If Smith looked worn-out as he faced what he thought would be his execution, he had every reason to. He had had an excruciatingly trying year. And Smith was not a man accustomed to soft living. His yeoman father died in the 1590s, when Smith was an adolescent apprenticed to a merchant in the seaport town of King's Lynn in Lincolnshire. He ran away to become a mercenary. After fighting with the English and Dutch against Philip II of Spain in the Low Countries, then traveling about Europe, he eventually joined the army of the Archduke Ferdinand of Austria to fight Muslim Turks in Hungary, near the Austrian border. He was taken prisoner on the battlefield, sold as a slave, and sent to work on a farm in Tartary. He escaped and made his way on his master's horse to Christian Russia, whence he was able to return to Europe and obtain an honorable discharge from the archduke. He retained the title "captain" ever after.[8]

Back in England, Smith found everyone talking about Virginia. His experiences in faraway countries and in the military apparently convinced people in high places to name him as one of the seven council members of the Virginia Company to travel to the colony: with his contribution of nine pounds, he certainly had far less money invested than any of the other council members. When he boarded the ship, Smith had every reason to believe the year 1607 would be a good one.[9]

Although Smith—and apparently his backers—believed he had seen everything, nothing, not even his research into the Spanish literature, had really prepared him for the voyage to the New World. By the time he stood before Powhatan, he had been away from England for a year and had faced death several times. It had taken the colonists almost four months just to reach the Chesapeake, first passing through the Caribbean, as ships then always did. Despite all his traveling, Smith had never been at sea so long and probably had never been so malnourished. On the way his attitude had caused him to be accused of insubordination by one of the well-born company members, and so, on first landing in Virginia, he had not even been allowed off the ship. He would not be free to roam for another month. From the water, he could see the sunlight falling into clearings between the cypress trees, bright green in spring, but he could not walk among them. Perhaps it was just as well, for the Indians of the Chesapeake tribe shot at them on that first April day; Smith heard the story only when the others got back to the boat, two of them wounded. Both the Chesapeakes and Powhatan's people had learned from their fathers' experiences with other Europeans that the best thing to do was to convince the strangers to move on.

The English saw no more Indians for four days, but they were watched in their reconnoiterings. On April 30 they landed in Kekoughtan territory and met a friendlier reception. Here the chieftainship had only recently been reconstituted under the son of Powhatan named Pochins. Perhaps he was under his father's orders. Powhatan probably wanted some information—a head count, a description of the weaponry, some sense of the newcomers' plans. After a pleasant repast the strangers moved on to Paspahegh territory, and the werowance, Wowinchopunk, also chose to meet with the strangers and provide them with a feast. In these encounters some of the white men always stayed on their boats, with their weapons trained on their hosts.[10]

On May 13 the settlers found a peninsula—virtually an island, the connecting neck of land was so narrow—in Wowinchopunk's territory that seemed a perfect place to establish their settlement: they named it Jamestown Island and began to unload the ships and cut wood to build a fort. It was uninhabited, so they chose to treat it as unclaimed, not attempting to learn what Wowinchopunk thought. Had he been consulted, he might have told them that the island was unsuitable for human habitation: after the rivers were no longer swollen with spring rains and melted snow, a swamp would emerge that bred disease-bearing mosquitos, and the water supply would turn brackish.[11]

The island's suitability, however, was not Wowinchopunk's uppermost concern. He did not want the well-armed white men to settle within his chiefdom under any circumstances. He requested aid from an allied tribe, and a few days later, when he had been able to gather a hundred warriors, he led all of them, fully armed, to the strangers' new camp. The chief brought a large fresh-killed deer and suggested that both sides feast together once again. He asked the white men to put down their weapons and eat, but they would not. Someone's temper flared in the taut environment, and a skirmish started. This may have been the first time the chief saw an Indian arrowhead shatter against English armor. Wowinchopunk immediately signed to his men to withdraw, and they left as quickly as they had come.[12]

Within a week, to Wowinchopunk's surprise, the 150-odd white men divided themselves, thus significantly reducing their strength. A number of them went exploring up the river, making friendly contact and trading with the Powhatan tribe, as well as the Weyanock, the Arrohattock, and the Appomattock. One Arrohattock mapped the river for them—accurately, they later discovered—first in the dirt, and then with pen and ink when they asked him to.

On May 27, when the locals suddenly became less welcoming, the English captain, Christopher Newport, decided the group should return immediately to the settlement. There they found that the day before, two hundred warriors had launched a concerted attack. They later learned which groups had been involved: the Appomattock, the Weyanock, the Paspahegh, the Quioccohannock, and the Chiskiak. Since the nearby Kekoughtan were a nonpower at that point, this list amounted to all the tribes on both sides of the lower James River who were united under Powhatan. Although they had more than enough men to overwhelm the force then at the settlement, especially with the element of surprise on their side, they had not counted on the boats' guns. The crew on the largest ship opened fire with cannon and musket, killing several Indians instantly and wounding many more. In less than an hour the warriors left, undoubtedly to report their defeat to their paramount chief.[13]

The English set about finishing their fort: whenever any of them ventured forth, skirmishes ensued. Several of the colonists were killed by arrows that struck places their armor did not cover. Tired of arguing among themselves and seeing the need for unity, the colonists decided that the upstart John Smith should be released from all restraint and sworn in as a member of the council.

On June 14 two Indians, probably sent by Powhatan, presented themselves unarmed. They explained which groups were dead set against the white men's presence and offered the paramount chief's help in bringing them to terms. Two days later two other Indians appeared who from a distance resembled those who had come before. From their boat they asked Captain Newport to follow them and speak with their king just around the bend in the river. Captain Newport set out in a barge, but when someone realized these were different men—they later turned out to be Quioccohannock, from the league of enemies—the captain turned around.[14] It is plausible that Powhatan was secretly behind the plan, trying to trick the newcomers with two sets of messengers in order to land himself a hostage English werowance, yet without appearing to be their enemy in case the plan failed. A few days later, having seen the fort finished, Newport set sail for England, taking with him two of the ships and about forty crew members. Powhatan knew his problem had just grown larger: he knew from the past that the departure of some but not all of the strangers merely meant that more would be coming.

The colonists, however, faced serious difficulties much more immediately. They argued violently among themselves about how to proceed in this alien territory where they were obviously unwelcome and the Indians were not behaving according to plan. Then in July they apparently ingested some sort of parasite in the water they drank and, in addition, began to suffer from salt poisoning, not having detected the increasing salinity. They began to get sick with "the bloody flux," a violent diarrhea. Initially someone died only every few days; the stronger men could still hope they would be left relatively untouched. Shortly afterward, however, the journal that one of them was keeping became a ghastly record of death. August 14: Frances Midwinter and Edward Morris. August 15: Edward Browne and Stephen Galthrope. August 16: Thomas Gower. August 17: Thomas Mounslie. August 18: Robert Pennington and John Martin, son of Captain Martin. August 19: Drue Piggase.[15] The list went on. "God (being angry with us) plagued us with such famin and sickness, that the living were scarce able to bury the dead," John Smith wrote later, ". . . myself having also tasted of the extremitie therof, but by Gods assistance being well recovered."[16] The stench was overwhelming; there was almost no one well enough to catch fish to eat, or to cook what food was on hand.

By the fall, the sickness had run its course, and migrating birds flew by in such numbers that even men in a weakened state could bring them down. But the surviving colonists needed grain if they were to last the winter, and there was no sign of Newport's long-overdue return. When they had less than twenty days of food supplies remaining, they drew lots as to who would take the small pinnace and a newly built barge upriver to try to trade for corn with the Indians: the task fell to Smith as leader and a few other men as followers.

Smith went up the as-yet-unexplored Chickahominy River, which drained into the James very near to their island. It was a fortunate choice. The Chickahominy were not part of Powhatan's paramountcy and were quite interested in these strangers who had the potential to be the enemy of their enemy—or more literally, the enemy of those with whom they had periodically strained relations. Three times Smith went up the river and filled the barge with corn in exchange for metal tools and beads. He became something of a hero at the fort. Perhaps he should have left it at that. In hindsight, it was obvious that Powhatan would learn that the strangers were forming some sort of alliance with the Chickahominy, whose territories touched on the lands of other independent inland tribes. Smith, however, knew nothing of the political configuration in which Jamestown was embedded. He was simply bent on finding the headwaters of the river and per-haps the long-sought Northwest Passage. So he went again. On his fourth trip, going farther upriver than ever before, he unknowingly headed into territory where the Powhatans hunted in winter along with the Chickahominy. The paramount chief seized the opportunity to gain control of the situation: he sent Opechankeno to capture the interlopers. Opechankeno and his men killed two of them as they slept in their canoe but took Smith alive, pulling him out of the mud and tying his hands.[17]

When Powhatan received Smith a few weeks later, he was reclin-ing in state on a low platform, with long chains of white beads and pearls around his neck, dressed in a gorgeous fur robe decorated with the extraordinary black-ringed tails of *aroughcun*, an animal no Englishman had ever seen before. He was symbolically surrounded by his subject tribes in the persons of his wives—though the political point was lost on Smith, who later referred to them only as "wenches." After some moments of silence, Powhatan made an elaborate speech.[18]

Years later John Smith painted a fanciful picture of what happened next. As the drums began to beat, Powhatan called for a great stone to be dragged forward, then had Smith's head placed upon it. Just as a warrior raised a club to beat his brains out and the shrill singing and chanting rose to a pitch, the young Pocahontas, who had been watching in horror, leaped forward and threw her body over Smith's. Powhatan smiled at the whims of his pretty daughter and signaled suddenly that the white man should be freed.

It is quite a story. But did any of it happen? There have been those who have wanted to believe it for four hundred years, starting with Smith's first audience and continuing right up to the present day. Yet the answer is unequivocally no. The truth, as it happens, is not only more complicated but also more interesting.

How do we know it did not happen? It is not enough to point out that Pocahontas was only about ten years old at the time. There is far better evidence against it than that. John Smith himself never wrote any such story until 1624, when as he knew quite well, there was no one left alive who could refute it, and Pocahontas had—for other, unrelated reasons—become a celebrity in London whose very name could sell books. He did not mention the story in the report he sent back to England shortly after the events. He did not mention it in either of the books he published on Virginia in 1612, which he directed to a London audience parched for tales about the region. Nor did he mention it when Pocahontas came to London. He only told the story seventeen years later, in 1624, in the wake of an Indian rebellion, at which point Powhatan's kindred were viewed as the devil incarnate, and Pocahontas was suddenly being interpreted as exceptional among all her people.[19]

Furthermore—and this is perhaps the clincher—in Smith's later accounts of his exploits around the world, he never failed to mention

This is a typical nineteenth-century romanticized version of the event that John Smith claimed had occurred while he was a prisoner at Werowocomoco. In this rendition, a nearly naked and adult Pocahontas with curling tresses appears to be European or Middle Eastern. The Indians look like nineteenth-century Plains Indians, even possessing ponies, and a nonexistent waterfall tumbles behind the scene. *(Edward Henry Corbould, 1815–1905, courtesy of the New York Public Library)*

that at each critical juncture a beautiful young woman had fallen in love with him and interceded on his behalf. It had happened, he said, in Turkey, where a young Muslim woman he identified as "Charatza Tragabigzanda" had purportedly begged her brother to treat the enslaved prisoner of war well, hoping to marry him someday. For the pleasure of speaking with him, "this noble gentlewoman . . . would feigne herself sick when she should go to the Banians [the Baths]."[20] (Not surprisingly, an account of such Turkish baths appears in Hakluyt's work, which we know Smith loved so well.) It had happened again on his escape route, when one "Callamata," the wife of a Cossack chieftain, supposedly came to his aid. In France, a "Madame Chanoie," Smith claimed, cared for him after a shipwreck; and elsewhere other

Standing at Werowocomoco, looking out at Purtan Bay, off the York River, the view appears much as it would have to Pocahontas and John Smith in 1607. *(Photo by Deanna Beacham, courtesy of Bob and Lynn Ripley)*

anonymous women provided him succor. Smith made these stories the toasts of his friends. Richard Brathwait, a well-known poet, wrote, "Tragabigzanda, Callamata's love, Deare Pocahontas, Madam Shanoi's too, . . . / Did what love with modesty could doe."[21]

Smith called his 1630 autobiography *The True Travels, Adventures, and Observations of Captaine John Smith in Europe, Asia, Africke, and America*. He had in fact been shipwrecked in Africa, and Turkey might in some ways be defined as Asian, so his reference to four continents was fair enough. But in general, how true were the "true travels"? Did anyone who read them then really expect them or even want them to be true? No, at least not literally true. Everyone then read travel narratives for the entertaining blend of fact and fantasy that they were. Of course, one might choose to believe that beautiful young women really did throw themselves at the short, stocky, cantankerous Smith everywhere he went, but the idea strains credulity to such a degree that different explanations of what actually happened must be sought.

It must be asked if anything remotely resembling what John Smith described could have occurred that December day in 1607. Unfortunately, the issue was thoroughly clouded by academics before it was eventually clarified by them. In the nineteenth century it became fashionable, amidst a certain circle of dignified white gentlemen scholars (several of whom were of Puritan descent), to denounce Smith as a braggart and a fraud. This caused those who loved him and his legend (a number of whom were of southern descent) to rally to his cause and insist on his absolute veracity in every particular. To this day there are scholars who seek to defend him by showing how biased his initial detractors were.[22] Only very recently have other scholars set aside the debate over John Smith's character and looked instead to the Algonkian culture to settle the question of whether a ritual such as Smith described could have taken place.

It is impossible to believe that Powhatan ever intended to "brain" John Smith. That was a punishment reserved for criminals; it was never meted out to captured warriors of enemy peoples. Captured warriors were ceremonially tortured, allowing them an opportunity to prove themselves before dying; it would later happen to other Englishmen. In 1607 and 1608 Smith probably did not even know about the practice of death by clubbing, but a few years later, back in London, Henry Spelman, an English boy who lived for a while among the Powhatans, published an account of the months he spent with them, including an oft-repeated description of the braining of criminals. In addition, the sequence of events in Smith's story is implausible. He claimed there was religious divining on the part of priests, followed by feasting, then negotiating with the political leaders, and finally the attempted execution. Culturally speaking, this makes no sense: Algonkians might have undertaken any activity on the list but, according to all the evidence that we have, definitely not in that order.[23]

For those who have liked the story, though, it may come as wel-

come news that there is a broad consensus among experts that Powhatan probably did in some way ritually adopt John Smith.[24] Pocahontas conceivably might even have played some small part in a vivid
ceremony, along with other wives and children. Adopting Smith
would have been in keeping with the Algonkian culture. The paramount chief, as we know, preferred actual sons to rule over subject
tribes, but he was certainly willing to work with ritually adopted
ones. Establishing kinship ties was the principal means of ensuring
his expanding control. Even ordinary prisoners of war were often
adopted rather than killed. Furthermore, later events prove that
Powhatan and Smith both believed some sort of special tie to have
been established between them at that time.

Some of the specifics of what happened emerge by looking at
what Smith had to say in each of his successive writings, placing each
statement in the context in which it was written and juxtaposing it
against confirming or damning external evidence. In 1608 Smith sent
a report back to one of his benefactors in England. It was published
almost immediately, without his knowledge. Most of what he wrote
there is corroborated by the letters and writings of other colonists:
there is less reason to doubt it than any of his other writings. Regarding his meeting with Powhatan, Smith wrote that he "kindly
welcomed me with good words" and that the first question he asked
was "the cause of our coming" to his lands. Indeed, this might well
have been the chief's first question: it was certainly what he most
needed to know.

By now Smith knew that the Indians did not want the English to
stay. He claimed that he managed to convey to Powhatan the following story: that in retreating from a battle with their enemy the
Spanish (whom Powhatan apparently knew of), the English sought
refuge in the Chesapeake, and since their pinnace was leaking, they
were forced to wait until Captain Newport returned from England
with another ship. Smith did not claim in this early account that
Powhatan was easily duped: very well, said Powhatan, but in that

case, why did the newcomers persist in traveling upriver in their smaller boats? Ah, said Smith, that was because they were looking for the great salt water on the other side of the mountains, where a child of the English king had been slain who needed to be avenged. They supposed the deed had been done by Powhatan's dastardly Iroquoian enemies. Would he, by the way, happen to know the way to the great salt sea? This exchange probably did take place: it was a relevant question on Powhatan's part, and Smith had every reason to suggest that the English king typically avenged any lost "children," that the English were willing to make common cause with the Algonkians against the Iroquoians, and that they would be generous to those who led them to the Northwest Passage.

Powhatan's unintelligible answer, as recorded by Smith, indicates either that he held only a vague notion of continental geography or that Smith did not understand him—probably more the latter. Smith then claimed to have said more—and what he claimed rings true, for the statement he attributed to himself is just the sort of thing that can be conveyed with signs and simple vocabulary: "In describing to him the territories of Europe, which was subject to our great King whose subject I was, and the innumerable multitude of his ships, I gave him to understand the noyse of Trumpets, and terrible manner of fighting."[25]

Pocahontas and the other children would have listened breathlessly to this exchange, watching the pantomiming and dramatic Smith. Then Powhatan made his prisoner a most exciting offer: he would take special care of the stranded English, if they would agree to become his tributaries. He would in fact give them the territory of Capahowasicke, near Werowocomoco. He would supply them with corn and venison if they needed it, and protect them from any enemies, in exchange for "hatchets and copper [that] wee should make him." Most of Powhatan's tributaries produced beads, clothing, and featherwork, but he could see that the English were more adept at making metal tools—and these would be most acceptable to him.

Would the English accept? Would they come to live there? Smith was in no position to point out that the English in fact had the opposite arrangement in mind: they expected Powhatan to become their vassal, not their lord. He said only that they would consider the arrangement.

In his first report Smith failed to state directly that Powhatan then promised to have him escorted to Jamestown in exchange for "two guns and a grindstone."[26] He mentioned it only in passing in an unrelated section toward the end of the account—and more openly in all his later versions. In 1608 he would have been eager to prove that his verbal adeptness had saved him, and eager to hide that he had promised to give weapons to savages, which he had been expressly forbidden to do in the "Instructions by Way of Advice." But when the Indians did return him to Jamestown a few days later, other colonists saw them demand their payment. Smith quite brilliantly offered them two cannons, which of course they could not move; he then offered them numerous smaller items (but not guns) that they could take immediately in lieu of the promised weapons. The Indians' demand for the agreed ransom in guns was undoubtedly generally known by the time his later works were published, and he then had to mention it openly.

Only in the 1624 version, after Pocahontas had purportedly saved him from certain death, did Smith explicitly claim to have been adopted as a son by Powhatan. He did not, however, connect the event to the obviously fictionalized story involving the beautiful girl. He said the adoption occurred "two days later" and described a separate ceremony.[27] So the adoption was not necessarily part of his fantasy of Pocahontas's rescue.

If the adoption occurred, it is logical that Smith had never mentioned it before. It was exactly that kind of thing that both Smith and company officials would have wanted hidden in the early years. Amidst the general fear of settlers "going native," it would have been extremely foolish for an English man who hoped to rise in the world to announce that the local Indian king called him "son." In 1624, though, in a different climate, Smith could safely assert that Powhatan said he would rule

Capahowasicke and be "as his son Nantaquoud." Maybe Powhatan meant that Smith would be as beloved as a favored son named Nantaquoud, or perhaps the word *nantaquoud* meant "my son."[28] Evidence that the story is true is embedded in earlier works by Smith, though it was never explicitly recorded there. His 1608 report mentioned the offer that the colonists should move to Capahowasicke as tribute-payers—and certainly anyone established as a werowance by Powhatan would have been in a symbolically filial position. That Smith was understood to be a werowance within Powhatan's matrix seems likely, given an oblique—and otherwise incomprehensible—statement in one of his 1612 books. Smith puts these irritated words in Powhatan's mouth: "Captain Smith, I never used anie Werowances so kindlie as your selfe; yet from you I receave the least kindnesse of anie."[29]

That John Smith got to know Pocahontas at least a little during his days in Werowocomoco seems beyond doubt. She lived there, and her later life proved her to be both outgoing and curious. She and the other children would have been the only ones without essential work to do during the daylight hours, and so free to spend time with the stranger. When she later made a brief appearance of only a few hours at the English fort, Smith called her "the nonpareil of her country" in the report he sent home immediately afterward. If she had been a gorgeous fifteen-year-old, he might—for obvious reasons—have needed only a few minutes to decide that was what he thought of her; but he would not have come to such a judgment of a ten-year-old so immediately without any previous acquaintance.

Whether Pocahontas had some minor role in any particular adoption ceremony is an open question. But it almost does not matter. Powhatan and his advisers, clearly, were making the policy decisions and were hardly under the influence of a ten-year-old girl. If she were not outside washing the dinner pots, as many girls her age would have been, and did participate, it was simply as the active, curious child that she was.

After four days Powhatan sent John Smith back to Jamestown in the company of four guides loaded with gifts. (Interestingly, between the original 1608 report and the more fanciful 1624 account, the escort mysteriously grew to twelve, just as the number of warriors needed to capture him grew to three hundred.) Most of his fellow colonists were elated to see Smith; a few, however, criticized the foolhardiness of the original venture, which led to the deaths of two men, and said he should be tried as a criminal. Fortunately for Smith, later that day, to everyone's inexpressible joy, Captain Newport sailed up to the fort, and all their differences were forgotten. The four Indian guides accepted the portable ransom and took the news of Newport's arrival back to Powhatan.

Their king had a great dilemma to consider. What was he to do about Jamestown? He obviously could not ignore it. He was not at all convinced that the English were there only in transit as Smith had claimed: they either intended to stay indefinitely or were planning on returning frequently. Should he destroy the settlement, rather than wait for it to upset the balance of power in the region and his own preeminence? He almost certainly already recognized that he could not: even if he could manage to defeat the current colonists by spending all his political capital and mustering every single warrior in all the tributary tribes, there would be an extraordinary number of deaths, and more English would probably come. His people's past experience with Europeans indicated as much, and Newport's reappearance proved the point. Recently, historians have been so eager to grant the Indian culture the respect it so richly deserves and to emphasize Powhatan's strength that they have often chosen to overlook certain facts that the paramount chief did not have the luxury of ignoring. He knew English technology exceeded his own and structured his strategies accordingly.

Powhatan was far from powerless. The white men were dependent on the Indians for sustenance in this early period. Indeed, they seemed so inept at providing for themselves that it must sometimes have seemed almost impossible for Powhatan to believe that they could ever really dominate him, technology notwithstanding. Very likely he surmised that they had come with the intention of extracting goods (much-needed food, in their case) and conceivably even lands from him. That was certainly why he himself conquered other tribes. Smith's story about their coming to avenge a fallen comrade on the other side of the mountains was hard to credit; Powhatan certainly knew there was no great salt water in his immediate backyard. He was aware, through the stories of Don Luis and Smith's own admission, that these foreigners were composed of warring tribes—of Spanish and English. That fact might be useful to him. Certainly his most dangerous foe up to this point had been the Iroquoians to the north and west. Perhaps the divided strangers could be made useful in his own battles.

Yet Powhatan was far from blind to the new peril; he was not locked within his traditional frame of reference. He knew he was facing a dangerously powerful entity. The weapons of the English were more lethal than his own, their metal coats fantastically protective; their boats could circle the oceans, bringing ever more men. Elsewhere, where the Indian population was larger and European determination to settle weaker, the indigenous held the upper hand longer.[30] But Powhatan was too intelligent, and by now had too much evidence, to imagine that he still had a multitude of options or that he was easily the stronger of the two parties. He would have to outmaneuver the newcomers in the best way he could.

He had begun well by making a friend of John Smith and through him, hopefully, of Captain Newport, whom Smith had described to him. The key to maintaining his power was the tribute he received from subject peoples, which he used to reward successful warriors and loyal werowances. If he could keep the coat-wearers isolated and contained, and then through trade with them gain a monopoly of access to the valuable weapons and metal cutting tools they brought, he could actually hope to turn these events to political profit. He would become more powerful relative to other Indian tribes and, as an even stronger leader, would be better able to render the newcomers vulnerable to his will. It was certainly worth making occasional gifts of corn to maintain good relations. (He ordered that some corn be sent to the fort almost immediately. It was delivered.) He would have to make sure that the strangers were prevented from trading with western tribes, or other groups not under his political umbrella. (He began to put pressure on various groups and probably ordered the annihilation of the Chesapeakes just about then.)[31]

Well-intentioned anthropologists have sometimes tended to ignore the political calculations made by this savvy prince, preferring to dwell on his cultural tendencies. They argue that Powhatan made decisions that were culturally appropriate "even in the face of a comparatively novel situation." In short, his traditional outlook blinded him to his peril and his opportunity. In looking with favor on trade and exchange, he is understood to have been trying to put the arrogant English in his debt, following the cultural norm of giving gifts to successful young warriors returning from a battle. He theoretically made decisions based not on political calculations but on what high-level priests told him the gods wanted. His culture allegedly dictated that he seek goods that were of ceremonial or spiritual value, like copper jewelry and glass beads; guns and metal supposedly trailed in second place. This kind of argument, however, seems a form of willful blindness based on a belief in the Indians' supposedly immutable way of being.[32]

The facts belie the belief. According to the original chroniclers, for example, Powhatan and his werowances expressed interest in guns and metal everywhere the English went, and only secondarily in pretty trinkets. In fact, a weapons demonstration was often the first thing they asked for. It is safe to presume the requests arose not from innocent wonder but from a desire for information. The captive Smith was asked to shoot something out of his pistol's range, so he, recognizing that they were testing its limits, claimed the piece was broken.

Up and down the eastern seaboard Native Americans used European goods ceremonially only at initial contact. Almost immediately they recognized what they really wanted: besides the ever-useful textiles, they wanted *metal*—hatchets, iron arrowheads, bodkins, swords, picks, knives, and kettles. They would also, of course, take guns whenever they could get them from the unwilling settlers. We know Pocahontas's people were no different. Less than a year later the women whom the girl accompanied to the fields wanted more European metal farming tools. Who, bending over the ground, trying to cut through a tough root, would not have wanted them? The Indians' love of their traditional culture in no way prevented them from seeing what might improve their lives and enable them to do what they had always done even better.[33]

One element is beyond debate: at no point did Powhatan, Pocahontas, or any of their people look on the strangers with wide-mouthed awe or consider them gods. Hernando Cortés never claimed that the Aztecs thought he was a god—as they almost certainly did not—yet the flattering notion became wildly popular in the after-the-fact accounts that appeared later in the century, several of which were widely available in England. The English waffled on the point in their early descriptions of Virginia: they tended to claim it only regarding tribes with whom they had not actually had much contact, or whom they had not seen in many years, or about whom they had only heard from other explorers. In fact, the farther removed the English were from the events they described, the more likely they were to report that the Indians had been virtually blown away in wonderment. John Smith, for example, who had only one brief encounter with the Susquehannocks, said several years later in 1612 that they had "adored" him and asked him and his men to accompany them on a raid against their enemies; in 1624 he added that they had wanted to "adore them as gods." Smith's friends, writing later about his captivity among the Powhatans, said he had convinced them he was a demigod, though in 1608 he himself had asserted no such thing.[34]

In 1608, when Smith asked his captors to let him write a letter, he did not profess them astounded at the concept of European writing. They probably were not. They had pictoglyphic symbols themselves; the Spanish Jesuits had left an entire chest of books when they died, and Don Luis probably explained what they were; Thomas Harriot had been working on a book when he lived among the Chesapeakes for a few months. When the English asked some of the first Indians they met to draw them a map of the James River, they complied easily. But in 1624 Smith embellished: when Indians delivered a note he had written to the fort and the colonists understood it, the Indians were supposedly stunned. It brought "the wonder of them all that heard it, that he [the reader] could either divine, or the paper could speake."[35]

Yet none of this answers the question of how the Algonkians explained to themselves the Europeans' clear technological superiority. It is a question that has been taboo until very recently. Before scientific analysis of the microscopic remains of plant seeds clarified why some early peoples chose to become full-time farmers, and thus developed writing and other technology, while others did not, the question seemed dangerous and divisive. In asking it, even well-intentioned writers might sound as though they were implying that Europeans were more intelligent. The Indians at the time, however, could probably talk about the question with greater ease, for they knew that unequal intelligence was not at issue: in fact, on the contrary, they were often stunned by the newcomers' marked inability to learn what they needed to know about their new environment. Like Algonkians up and down the coast, Powhatan's people were known to compose witty, mocking, even scornful songs about the English. No, they did not fear that they themselves were mentally inferior.[36]

So how were they to understand the discrepancies between the two civilizations? They did not leave written treatises to settle the question, but the fragments of evidence available do point toward a probable answer. They seem to have concluded, in keeping with their view of the cosmos, that the gods or okees whom they worshipped—who protected them and gave them corn and deer—simply were not as strong as the gods the Europeans worshipped—who protected them and gave them such enviable tools. Thomas Harriot, while living among the Roanokes and just beginning to learn their language, wrote that his scientific instruments seemed to convince the Indians that the Europeans were gods—"or," he added, as if to correct himself or be more honest, "at the leastwise they had been given and taught us of the gods."[37] In its greater specificity, the latter interpretation seems more likely to have been closer to what they actually said. In about 1610 an Englishman who spoke to a Virginia werowance through an interpreter said the Indian "believed our god as much exceeded theirs as our guns did their bow and arrow."[38]

The Algonkians had long believed in a universe revolving around struggle: unequal power, violence, domination, and tribute were a part of life. Recent events merely offered further proof of it. It was not fair, of course. They knew themselves to be just as deserving and just as intelligent as the newcomers, if not more so. For most of them, the Europeans' technological strength certainly did not mean that they should abandon the respected and beloved gods who had always done their best for them, and to whom they had committed themselves as young adults. An older brother-in-law of Pocahontas later told an Englishman wearily that he certainly would never do so. He advised his interrogator to try talking to the children, who were still free to choose their own paths and their own gods. He and his people faced a more difficult situation than most people ever have to face: their thoughts and feelings were necessarily complex.[39]

Without question, they knew about and actively discussed the Europeans' advantages. Also without question, they enumerated their own disadvantages. At present the strangers were few in number, constantly bickering, unable to feed themselves. What the Indians most clearly needed to know was exactly how great the technological advantages ultimately were. In all their interactions with the newcomers, the Indians sought information; what they gleaned must surely have been the subject of debate and conversation. Powhatan and his advisers spoke in council. The women working in the fields and in the village and at the riverside talked as they labored. Pocahontas, at age ten, heard all her elders had to say.

FOUR

Jamestown

Kekaten pokahontas patiaquagh ningh tanks manotyens neer mow-
chick rawrenock audowgh. (Bid Pokahontas bring hither two little
Baskets, and I will give her white beads to make her a chaine.)
        —John Smith, *A Map of Virginia* (1612)

Powhatan continued to send the colonists gifts of corn and
raccoon tails every few days. He frequently requested that
Captain Newport visit him at Werowocomoco. In late February 1608 the visit took place. The English were tense at every step.
When their guides asked them to cross a narrow fjord of stakes
driven into a creek, they suspected a trap. "I intermingled the Kings
sonne, our conductors and his chiefe men amongst ours . . . leaving
half [our men] at the one ende to make a guard for the passage of
[the others]," remembered Smith.[1] That is, he made it impossible for
the Indians to shoot at them from the banks by having each man
cross with an Indian in front and behind, and he left half his men on
the shore with their guns aimed at the Indians crossing. Then the

English who had already crossed turned and trained their weapons to protect those yet to come. For the rest of the visit, a portion of the English always stayed ready to shoot. This was to be a longstanding pattern. Powhatan complained of their lack of trust, but to no avail.

Newport brought Powhatan a red silk outfit, a large hat, and a white greyhound dog. The paramount chief professed to be delighted but also asked after the guns that Smith had promised in exchange for his release. Smith insisted that in offering the immovable cannon, he had fulfilled his part of the bargain—"whereat," said Smith, "with loud laughter, he desired me to give him some of less burthen."[2] The English were able to dissuade Powhatan from insisting on receiving guns by making an offer—long-planned on their part—to leave a purported "son" of Newport's in Werowocomoco, and to send a "son" of Powhatan's to London. The English hoped the boys might become their interpreters. Powhatan accepted: he stood to get essential information out of them as well, which would be more valuable than two guns. The English apparently thought they were deceiving Powhatan. Young Thomas Savage was probably either an apprentice or an indentured servant; he certainly was not Newport's son. Powhatan, however, most likely figured that out. He also deceived some of the English, for there is no reason to believe that Namontack, whom he sent to England, was really his biological son. Although some of the English believed he was, Smith did not.[3]

Over the course of the next few days in Werowocomoco, the Indians and English traded corn for beads and metal wares. Powhatan extracted a promise of some swords that he later did receive.[4] They discussed the possibility of mounting a joint attack on Powhatan's Monacan neighbors (Siouans, not Algonkians) living just to the west, though the project never came to fruition. The English eventually made an awkward exit: having missed the tide, they found they could not get their barge afloat, and they had to beg another night's lodging, with some of their number nervously standing guard yet again. Either to make a point or to express genuine sympathy, that night Powhatan gave them more food than they could possibly eat.

Watching them pull away from the shore the next morning, Thomas Savage, probably about thirteen or fourteen years old, must have felt a loneliness almost impossible to describe. Even if he had hated his English master, even if he had been having a wonderful time with the fun-loving Powhatan children—and either is more than possible—he stood now in a world where nothing was familiar, not even a word. It is possible that the adults encouraged the children to talk to him, that Pocahontas spoke to him, even taught him to say *netoppew*, "my friend."[5] Two months later she would apparently know some English. Thomas may well have taught her what she knew.

In April Captain Newport returned again to England, carrying the completely isolated Namontack away with him. Back in Jamestown the day-to-day work continued incessantly. There had been a serious fire, requiring some significant rebuilding of the settlement. Though the settlers put time into mending the bulwarks, the structures inside the fort were of the relatively primitive cratchet type: that is, a roof was raised up to ceiling height on four forked poles, and rows of sticks were stuck into the ground to make each wall, bearing no weight. One building was put just outside the fort, apparently so the colonists could trade with the Indians without necessarily giving them access to the inner sanctum. It included a fireplace so as to be functional in winter, and a cool cellar, probably to store food purchased from the Indians in the hot summer. Beneath the door on the side farthest from the fort, where the "devilish" Indians were to come and go, they buried a witch's bottle—a glass vessel containing sharp stones, instead of the nails used in Europe—which they believed would keep evil at bay. Eventually, for added protection, they decided to connect the building to the fort with a fence.[6]

It had not taken long for problems to arise. Apparently in an effort to cow the natives, the colonists began drilling and practicing their firing just outside the fort. Powhatan sent Thomas back to Jamestown with the request that he find out what was going on. According to Smith, they sent back a nonsensical answer, the gist of which was that they were preparing for a trip upriver to look for stones to make ax-heads. Powhatan sent young Thomas back to Jamestown; he did not want lies. Either Powhatan's displeasure was such that he actually issued an official statement that his people were free to harass the strangers, in an attempt to drive them away, or his disgust with them was simply so apparent that his people realized they were not likely to be punished if they stole from the fort. They began to molest stragglers found wandering outside the compound and to steal the much-valued metal tools.

In May, after one incident that the English found particularly egregious, they seized a number of Indian hostages. The next day the nearby Paspaheghs took two English men prisoner. The English wasted no time in retaliating: as darkness fell, well armed and well armored, they drew near to a Paspahegh town in their barge. They torched the nearest buildings and showered the village with shot— meaning not bullets, which must be aimed and can miss, but rather hundreds of tiny bits of lead flying everywhere. They withdrew unscathed. The next day the Paspaheghs sued for peace and released the two hostages. The English released one of theirs but continued to hold a number of others, whom they tortured. Under duress the Indians said that Powhatan planned to ambush them as soon as he had Namontack safely back.

On the third morning of the men's captivity, Powhatan sent Pocahontas to try to secure the prisoners' release. "He sent his Daughter, a child of tenne yeares old, which not only for feature, countenance and proportion, much exceedeth any of the rest of his people, but for wit, and spirit, the only Nonpariel [sic] of his Country," wrote Smith about three weeks later, in the report he sent back to England.[7]

It was Pocahontas's first visit to the fort. She walked in, straight-backed, head up. Like all Powhatan girls, Pocahontas wore her hair cut short in front. A long braid may have hung down her back. Accompanying her was a man whose Algonkian name the English heard as "Rawhunt." An adviser to Powhatan, he was in some way physically deformed and was held by his people to have special wisdom and powers of divination. Pocahontas saw the prisoners but pretended not to, looking straight ahead and maintaining a studied silence. Then Rawhunt began a complicated speech, which someone translated: it was almost certainly Pocahontas herself, possibly working with Thomas Savage, whom her father had sent back to Jamestown many days before. Powhatan, Rawhunt said, had not only affection but also respect for the English, in proof of which, he had trusted them so much as to send his dear child to see them and bring them presents. He asked that Thomas, whom he missed and regretted sending away, might return to him, and he asked that the prisoners be released, among whom were men he valued. Later, when other messengers arrived with gifts to serve as ransom and Pocahontas began to perceive that the English were feeling open to negotiation, she herself began to speak to the colonists and to greet and comfort the prisoners.

Why had Powhatan sent her? There were in fact other occasions on which werowances sent their daughters as emissaries: Opechankeno, for example, had done so once before. It may even have been a common tactic: it would have been a clear signal of a desire for mutual trust. What Powhatan's feelings were for this particular daughter we cannot be sure. Smith said Rawhunt called her "his child, which he most esteemed." Was she really the one then closest to Powhatan's heart, and did he believe that Smith would know this from his days of captivity and thus recognize her presence as a white flag? Or was she, as the daughter of a commoner and without claims to political power, among the children he could most afford to lose, and thus the one whose safety he chose to risk? Or did he as a shrewd statesmen simply choose the daughter in whose abilities he had most confidence? She was probably the best translator available. Possibly

all of the above were true. In any case, he certainly chose well: Pocahontas secured the prisoners' release. "In the afternoone," said Smith,
". . . we guarded them as before to the Church, and after prayer, gave
them to Pocahuntas, the Kings Daughter, in regard of her fathers
kindnesse in sending her."[8]

That visit was the first of many that Pocahontas made to the fort
over the course of the following year. Having returned home in triumph after her first one, it is small wonder that it became an appealing place for her. With her growing language skills, she became ever
more powerful—more welcome at the fort, and more important to
her father. She also had fun. William Strachey, who arrived the year
after she stopped visiting, was told of "a well featured but wanton
young girle Powhatan's daughter, sometimes resorting to our Fort, of
the age then of 11 or 12 years." *Wanton* then meant "frolicsome" or
"mischievous." He said she would "get the boyes forth with her into
the market place and make them wheele, falling on their handes
turning their heeles upwards, whome she would follow, and wheel so
her self naked as she was all the Fort over."[9] She was not shy; in fact,
she was bossy. She was quite an athlete—more so than the boys were.
"We can imagine," writes one historian, "a group of pale-faced
Jamestown boys, overdressed in wool, being goaded into turning cart-
wheels by a brown-skinned Indian girl, scantily clad by European
standards, whose acrobatic skills probably put them to shame."[10]
Yet they liked her. That is what comes through in all accounts. She
was energetic and fun-loving, open and interested, adventuresome
and smart. They liked "Mischief" just as much as her own people
apparently did.

It is only possible to glimpse her character, impossible to study it
thoroughly. Historians would give a great deal to find a letter or di-
ary written by Pocahontas, something in her own words, about her
aspirations and opinions. With such crumbling papers in our hands,
we could gain new insights into her personality and thoughts. Instead, she is visible only in the comments left by the white men who

knew her and wrote down their impressions. What we glean comes from reading between the lines. The colonists make clear how little they cared to find out what the girl who admittedly fascinated them was herself thinking. In the words of one scholar, "The documents written by Englishmen display a remarkable indifference to her opinion of them."[11] This is a classic dynamic, of course: it is always the less powerful who must learn to gauge the thoughts of the more powerful. The servant or slave considers the master's reactions; the subservient wife considers the dominant husband's; the courtier must know the king's mind better than he knows it himself. But the master, the husband, and the king are not in the habit of pondering the thoughts and feelings of those beneath them. So, too, the English colonizers gazed at Pocahontas and judged her, but did not ask her what she thought.

The problem is exacerbated by the fact that Pocahontas's language is largely lost, unlike numerous other American Indian languages. In the case of Malinche, for example, the Aztec woman who translated for Cortés, we may not have her own writings, but we do have those of innumerable other Aztecs who wrote about their traditions as soon as they began to learn the Roman alphabet in the 1530s. Even today there are at least a million speakers of the Nahuatl language in Mexico. The Powhatan language—or perhaps we should say languages—met a very different fate. The Indians in the region spoke closely related dialects that were mutually intelligible, varying from village to village. This is a normal pattern in a world where nation-states have not yet developed. An apt comparison would be to the lands in medieval Europe between Paris and Rome. Walking on foot many centuries ago, one would have passed through territories where people spoke at certain points what we recognize today as French, Catalan, Spanish, and Italian, but the shift would have occurred gradually, the people in any one village understanding perfectly what those in the neighboring villages were saying. Only a few people—Thomas Harriot, William Strachey, and John Smith—

recorded lists of Algonkian words or phrases, and they almost never mentioned from which tribes their informants came. What results is a hodgepodge of words from all dialects and almost no sense of the grammar. Thus we cannot even gain insights into Powhatan categories and assumptions by studying texts in their own language.[12]

Pocahontas, interestingly, offers one ray of light in this darkness. Formally or informally, she participated in a course of mutual language instruction with John Smith, and it is probably thanks to her that the only full Powhatan sentences that we have were recorded. "Because many doe desire to knowe the maner of their language, I have inserted here these few words," wrote Smith in 1612. In the midst of his lists of numbers and trade goods, he suddenly included several whole sentences. *Mowchick woyawgh tawgh noerach kaquere mecher.* "I am verie hungrie, what shall I eate?" And then: *Kekaten pokahontas patiaquagh ningh tanks manotyens neer mowchick rawrenock audowgh.* "Bid Pokahontas bring hither two little Baskets, and I will give her white beads to make her a chaine." Smith referred elsewhere to giving Pocahontas presents, so one can imagine them enacting an actual exchange as they taught each other the necessary words. Apparently Pocahontas did not want an English-style trinket as a gift, but rather, white beads—such as all Powhatan noblewomen were privileged to wear once they passed the age of about twelve and attained womanhood. Perhaps the eager child did not want to wait for the luxuries due to adults.[13]

Sometimes the topics of conversation were more serious. "In how many daies will there come hither any more English ships?" was the very first full sentence Smith recorded. *Casa cunnakack, peya quagh acquintan uttasantasough?* This clearly was a very early question, for the speaker, whoever he or she was, used the word *acquintan*, literally meaning "canoe," though within only a few years the Powhatans widely adopted another word that had apparently existed in certain dialects—*messowt*, indicating a particularly large watercraft. The word *uttasantasough* for "English" was probably something borrowed from the Indians farther south who had contact with the Roanoke colonists, for the word was still in use in North Carolina in 1701.[14] At any rate, that question conveyed what the Indians most wanted to know.

The English had other concerns. Smith recorded a short dialogue, carefully translating each part:

> Where dwells Powwahtan?
> Now he dwells a great way hence, at Orapaks.
> You lie, he stayed ever at Werowocomoco.
> Truly, he is there. I do not lie.

It may well have been Pocahontas who uttered these words. "Truly, he is there. I do not lie." Regardless, she clearly participated in conversations very much like this one, revealing something of her interesting and interested self, and demonstrating the strategies each group was attempting to adopt toward the other.

We have some direct evidence as to what John Smith was thinking while Pocahontas cartwheeled, laughed, posed questions, and gave answers. She was a child, probably ten years old, when she began to visit, and eleven or twelve when she stopped coming—a year older at most.[15] She would be considered marriageable by her own people after she had passed puberty and was at least twelve; in fact menarche probably did not usually occur until at least thirteen. Once she spent her first time apart in the women's menstrual hut just outside the village, she would have stopped cartwheeling and cavorting. So we know that she was only a girl. But John Smith loved the books that represented America as a forthcoming young and naked virgin. In 1612 both Smith and William Strachey, back home in England, represented Pocahontas as nubile and sexy in the books they published, years *before* she became famous to the London public as a beautiful (and adult) Indian princess—after which any market-oriented writer might well have been tempted to make retroactive claims as to her alluring qualities. (Indeed, in the 1624 book, when his audience was primed, and envisioning a grown woman, Smith went so far as to claim that she and thirty other naked young women once virtually attacked him in a dance, demanding sexual favors.) Smith's 1612 reference is thus particularly interesting, as it reveals that he thought in sexual terms about a ten- or eleven-year-old prepubescent child.[16]

The comments appeared in a book of testimony collected from friends of his who had been in Jamestown; some of their contributions were in reality written by him, and all were edited under his hand. A segment purportedly by Richard Pots and William Phettiplace reveals that Smith's relationship with Pocahontas had brought him criticism, in the form of innuendos that he was trying to form close bonds with the Indians in order to dominate the other colonists more effectively:

> Some prophetical spirit calculated hee had the Salvages in such subjection, hee would have made himself a king, by marrying Pocahontas, Powhatan's daughter. It is true she was the very nomperell of his kingdome, and at most not past 13 or 14 years of age. Very oft shee came to our fort, with what she could get for Captaine Smith, that ever loved and used all the Countrie well, but her especially he ever much respected: . . . but her marriage could no way have intitled him by any right to the kingdome, nor was it ever suspected hee had ever such a thought, or more regarded her, or any of them, then in honest reason and discretion he might. If he would, he might have married her, or have done what him listed. For there was none that could have hindered his determination.

There had even been a Virginia Company investigation of Smith's behavior toward the girl, orchestrated by his enemies in the corporation:

Some that knewe not anything to say, the Councel instructed, and advised what to sweare. So diligent were they in this businesse, that what any could remember, hee had ever done, or said, in mirth, or passion, by some circumstantiall oath, it was applied to their fittest use . . . I have presumed to say this much in his behalfe for that I never heard such foule slanders, so certainly believed, and urged for truthes by many a hundred.[17]

These paragraphs give away a great deal—not just that Smith had made many enemies by the time he was finished in Jamestown. On the one hand, they reveal that Smith was a more attentive student of Powhatan culture than most colonists were: he was conscious of the fact, for example, that in a matrilineal polity, his marrying Pocahontas would in no way make him a king. At the same time, the comments reveal his arrogance toward the Indians—or at least toward Indian women. He claimed that if he had wanted to marry Pocahontas, or to sleep with her, he would have done so, as absolutely no one could have stopped him—including Pocahontas herself, presumably. His own—or his friends'—summary of the council's investigation openly acknowledged that he had made lewd comments about her—or had even done things to her—in jokes ("mirth"), or in moments of sexual arousal ("passion"). Perhaps that is why, even as he reminded the people to whom he was defending himself that she was only a child, not yet fit for marriage, he raised her age by a good three years. Suddenly she was "no more than thirteen or fourteen" at the time, instead of her actual ten or eleven.

Did Pocahontas know that Smith viewed her in a sexual way and recognize his overtures as lascivious? Probably. Hers was not a prudish culture. But we cannot know what it meant in such matters to say that an eleven-year-old knew and was apparently not put off. She might, for instance, have said she found it funny or flattering at the time but been pained by memories later. That, indeed, is the most frequent scenario in such cases, then and now. Or she might have found Smith overbearing and troublesome, a pest in her otherwise happy visits to the fort. It is impossible to know. But to imagine that Smith's thoughts reflected her own would be unthinkably presumptuous.

Smith, in any case, took a more and more prominent role in the colony during the time when Pocahontas frequented Jamestown. In the late summer of 1608, a few months after her first visit, he led two exploratory trips. He met with friendly reception in most places. Once when he did not, in the country of the Nansemond, his men opened fire and began to destroy a village's laboriously constructed dugout canoes; the people sued for peace immediately.[18] In the early fall the council members elected him president. It was a rare tribute to a man of his relatively low social rank.

Then Captain Newport returned once more with supplies. Namontack was onboard. Newport sent a message to Powhatan that he should come to Jamestown to swear loyalty to the British king and receive some presents sent by him, including a crown. Powhatan sent back a disdainful reply that they should come to him—and that he would wait for them in his present location only eight days. Newport went, bringing Namontack with him. The young Algonkian must surely have told the paramount chief something about England. Yet he did not say enough: Powhatan would seem only marginally more versed in English plans and capabilities in his later dealings with them. Unfortunately, the well-traveled Namontack was killed less than two years later, eliminating whatever insights he might have offered.[19]

Namontack convinced Powhatan to accept the gifts of a metal basin and pitcher, a cloak, and a bed. "But a fowle trouble there was to make him kneele to receave his crowne." Smith asserted that this was because the Indian did not know the "meaning of a Crowne," but in fact he probably understood only too well the gesture of kneeling to receive a crown at the hands of another. He himself, after all, liked the practice of anointing tributary werowances who were bound to do his bidding. "At last by leaning hard on his shoulders, he a little stooped, and Newport put the Crowne on his head."[20]

After the ceremony, for the rest of the autumn, President Smith made it his business to collect as much corn as possible from the natives. The Indians, however, were beginning to realize that English demands for corn might well be insatiable.

> Arriving at Chickahamina [the Chickahominy villages], that dogged nation was too wel acquainted with our wants, [therefore] refusing to trade, with as much scorne and insolence as they could expresse. The President perceiving it was Powhatan's policy to starve us, told them he came not so much for their corne, as to revenge his imprisonment, and the death of his men murdered by them, and so landing his men, and ready to charge them, they immediately fled, but then they sent their ambassadours, with corne, fish, fowl, or what they had to make their peace.[21]

Smith said, in effect, that he did not care if they did not want to trade: if they would not give him corn in exchange for the trinkets he chose to give them, he would just take it and call it his revenge for their having allowed him to be captured in their territory the previous year.

The settlers' cold reception proved to be the same everywhere. The harvest had been poor that season, and the Indians did not want to turn over their major source of sustenance. In village after village, muskets and steel convinced them they had no choice. Generally the English congratulated themselves on their own cleverness in taking all that they needed, but occasionally a writer admitted to painful memories: "The people imparted what little they had, with such complaints and tears from the women and children; as he had bin too cruell to be a Christian that would not have bin satisfied [that is, refrained from taking any more] and moved with compassion."[22]

In December 1608 the English went to see Powhatan at Werowoco-moco. Powhatan played his hand as well as he could. Knowing the English were hungry, and believing that they would be loath to attack his town as quickly as they had attacked others, he said he would certainly trade with them. But he wanted swords and guns—lots of them: "For 40 swords he would procure us 40 bushels." They showed him other "commodities." "But none he liked without gunnes and swords." Smith complained loudly, and then Powhatan answered, demonstrating that his knowledge of the English had improved somewhat—either through observation, or conversation with Namontack, or both—"Captain Smith, some doubt I have of your comming hither, that makes me not so kindly seeke to relieve you as I would; for many do informe me, your coming is not for trade, but to invade my people and possesse my Country." If he hoped that the English would protest their innocence and give him guns, he hoped in vain.[23]

To end the business, Powhatan gave them ten small units of corn in exchange for a large copper kettle. That was expensive corn, and it was all he would do for them. He made a long speech, in which he warned that if the English continued to attack his people and demand more corn than could be spared, his people would remove themselves from the rivers' edges and retreat deep into the woods, where the English could not find them. "What can you get by war, when we can hide our provision and flie to the woodes, whereby you must famish?" He said that he, too, hoped to avoid this. In essence, he promised an annual tribute, though in the form of unequal trade, not overt offerings: "Let this therefore assure you of our loves and everie yeare our friendly trade shall furnish you with corne, and now also if you would come in friendly manner to see us, and not thus with your gunnes and swords, as [if] to invade your foes."[24]

The English were tense during this visit, fearing that in his frustration and anger, in his sense of having few alternatives left, the paramount chief would order an ambush. Smith and the others later described various incidents they believed were foiled attempts on their lives. Smith even said that at one point Pocahontas warned him of one of the plots, coming alone in the dark and the rain. It is possible that she really did it. It is also very possible that she did not. It was not until 1624, when she was dead and he was embellishing, that Smith specifically connected her warning to this period. In 1612 he did refer to such an event, but not in this segment of the narrative, rather only in a vague subordinate clause in another chapter where he detailed her goodness to the colonists—in the same section, in fact, in which he tried to defend himself against the accusations that he had adopted the lifestyle and manners of the natives. Even supposing for the sake of argument that Pocahontas did want John Smith to escape death more than she wanted her father to gain the upper hand, she would have known that the English did not really need her warning. Their implacable suspicion, combined with their arms and armor, had protected their lives thus far.[25]

In fact, it is unlikely not only that Pocahontas fled through the night to warn her English friends but also that Powhatan seriously intended to kill Smith at this point. He knew his warriors could surprise small groups and pick them off—they had done so before. But he also knew that it would do no good. It would only bring more, angrier coat-wearers. Reading the English accounts of these days spent up the York River from start to finish, it seems apparent that the Indians created skirmishes to prevent the English from finding out, until after the event, that Powhatan was quickly moving his entire town and most of his corn supply. After a brief corn-gathering foray into Pamunkey territory farther upriver, the English returned to Werowocomoco a few days later to find the large town completely abandoned, as Powhatan had threatened might happen. Pocahontas had gone with her people, and John Smith did not see her again—until she came to England years later. There was no tearful good-bye in the dark.

The frustrated English soon kidnapped a Paspahegh werowance whom they believed was working with some newly arrived Dutchmen to plan an ambush. With the help of his people, the werowance escaped from Jamestown under cover of night. In retaliation, Smith sacked a village: "Six or 7 salvages were slaine, as many made prisoners." Their werowance then sent a messenger who drove home the point that Powhatan had already made:

> We perceive and well knowe you intend to destroy us, that are here to intreat and desire your friendship, and [ask] to enjoy our houses and plant our fields, of whose fruit you shall participate, otherwise you will have the worst by our absence, for we can plant any where, though with more labour, and we know you cannot live if you want [i.e., do not have] our harvest, and that reliefe wee bring you; if you promise us peace we will believe you, if you proceed in reveng[e], we will abandon the Countrie.[26]

Smith took the deal. He had learned the hard way that this was as good as he would get. If he pushed these people too far, they would, in Powhatan's words, "fly to the woods." And then there would be no tribute in corn at all. Only when the Indians were clustered around rivers and creeks could the English descend on them and defeat them handily.

These were nothing like the Indians of whom Smith had read in the great epic adventure stories of Hernando Cortés and Francisco Pizarro. Smith, indeed, was among the first of the English—perhaps the very first—to gain a clear understanding of the vast difference between the Aztecs and the Incas on the one side, and the North American Indians on the other.

Most North Americans today have lost sight of this distinction, but it was crucial. The Spanish had found indigenous people who had been farming, although not as long as Europeans, for at least several millennia. They were sedentary; they could not possibly fly to the woods. They lived in permanent villages, with schools and temples. They paid taxes. They had roads and fixed long-distance trade routes. Some of them had causeways, small aqueducts, and running water. They knew no more of life in the woods than most modern urbanites do. When the Spanish came, with their superior arms, it soon became clear to the Aztecs that they had no choice other than to offer allegiance to this new government and pay their taxes in goods and services into new coffers.

The Powhatan Indians, however, were not going to settle for that. They were seminomadic. They had moved before, and they would move again. Under no circumstances would they become serflike tributaries. Smith came to understand this quite clearly, but he refused to accept it gracefully. In explaining the greater difficulties he and the Jamestown settlers had faced in comparison with the Spanish, Smith and his friends found it satisfying to insult the Powhatans, to blame them for the English misfortune in having conquered the "wrong" Indians. Wrote Smith:

> It was the Spaniards good hap to happen in those parts, where were infinite numbers of people, whoe had manured the ground with that providence, that it afforded victual at all times: and time had brought them to that perfection, they had the use of gold and silver, and the most of such commodities, as their countries afforded, so that what the Spaniard got, was only the spoile and pillage of those countrie people, and not the labours of their owne hands. But had those fruitfull Countries beene as Salvage, as barbarous, as ill peopled and little planted, laboured and manured as Virginia, their proper labours (it is likely) would have produced as small profit as ours.[27]

Armed with this new understanding, which had yet to make its way back to the theorists in London, Smith made sure there were no more serious skirmishes with the Indians while he was president. But resentful colonists—especially the wellborn—continued to rail against his autocratic style of management. They were mutinous on several occasions, and when he accidentally suffered a serious burn in October of 1609, he used it as an excuse to resign and return to England. Those remaining managed but poorly without him and without Powhatan. They starved.

The new president sent a pinnace up the Pamunkey River carrying, in his words, "Powhatan's son and daughter" to try to convince the Indian king to give them some corn. Was this Pocahontas, who had made a final visit to the fort at a bad time? She certainly had some type of communication with the colonists around then, for someone wrongly told her in this period that Smith was dead. Still, it seems likely that the president writing the report would have called her by her name, as she was well known to him. It was probably a half sister of hers, appearing suddenly in the record and disappearing as quickly. Was the boy in fact Henry Spelman, another English adolescent who had been living with Powhatan as a son? Spelman later admitted that he was there—though he disclaimed any responsibility for what happened next.

The captain of the pinnace, a man named Ratcliffe, let the girl and boy go once they found Powhatan's new village, and some of the men wandered off in small groups to beg for food. Powhatan wanted to make it clear one last time that he would not give corn on demand and that he had withdrawn his settlement for a reason. He had the men killed: Ratcliffe was captured and tortured to death as an enemy warrior. Only one man managed to escape and make it back to the pinnace to travel back to Jamestown with those who had had the wisdom to remain onboard. That winter other colonists who approached Indians demanding food were also killed. Warriors lost their lives in these skirmishes, but Powhatan's policy had changed. He clearly wanted to convince the English to leave, or at least not to pursue his people inland.[28]

It nearly worked.

That horrible winter eventually gave way to spring, and in May 1610, two ships arrived at the settlement's crude port. They had been built in Bermuda by Englishmen who had wrecked there on the way to Jamestown. The new arrivals found that only about 100 English people were left alive in Virginia—some 60 in Jamestown, 40 in other camps. This was out of a total of about 550 who had migrated thus far. Of the lost 450, an unknown number had returned to England or fled, but most had perished over the course of three years, more than 100 in the last winter alone.[29] Within days the leaders decided to evacuate the colony and go home. They organized the voyage and boarded the ships. On the crowded vessels, they could make it to Newfoundland, and there they would disperse themselves among the fishing boats that came and went. Jamestown, it seemed, was to be added to the list of failed experiments in the New World. English colonization would have to wait a few more years, until the lessons from this venture had been digested and a new scheme developed. Powhatan's people would have some breathing room. And Powhatan's daughter would live out her days with her people in Virginia.

But as the fleeing colonists made their way down the river, they met a grand flotilla. Lord De La Warr, their new governor, had arrived with a new charter, at least 150 additional people, and substantial provisions meant to last. And so they stayed. English technology was to triumph now, not later. A messenger brought Powhatan the devastating tidings.

FIVE

Kidnapped

Now Naaman, captaine of the host of the king of Syria, was a great man with his master, and honorable, because by him the Lord had given deliverance unto Syria. He was also a mighty man in valour, but he was a leper. And the Syrians had gone out by companies, and had brought away captive out of the land of Israel a little maid, and she waited on Naaman's wife. And she said unto her mistresse, "Would God my lord [Naaman] were with the prophet that is in Samaria, for hee would recover him of his leprosie." And one went in, and tolde his lord, saying "Thus said the maid that is of the land of Israel."

—King James Bible, 2 Kings 5:1–4

The English man whom Pocahontas would later marry, and who would be the father of her child, was one of the new arrivals at the fort. So was his wife. Pocahontas, however, did not then know that either of them existed. That same year, when she was twelve or thirteen, she married a man called Kocoom. He was a warrior, not a chief; she married him by choice, not to cement a political alliance. Most young Algonkian women were free to choose their partners, but not if they were from a noble line on the mother's side. Then they were often expected to bear a political burden. Pocahontas's royal younger sister would be promised to a hereditary chief even before she turned twelve, but her own mother's lack of political significance left her free to choose her partner. She may have been pleased, or perhaps at the same time pained by her own lesser importance.[1]

Kocoom was called a "private captain" by an Englishman who used similar language to talk about the forty or fifty young men who served as Powhatan's personal guard, or army. Kocoom, then, may have been one of these. Or he may have lived at a distance from Werowocomoco and met Pocahontas only by chance. Like so many participants in Pocahontas's story, he recedes into the mists.[2]

If their courtship was like that of their peers, Kocoom began to pay his attentions to Powhatan's pretty, outgoing daughter before he knew how she felt about him. She was free to respond or not, without fear of being called "cold" or worse if she felt no interest. There is no reason to believe Pocahontas would have lacked for suitors, so she must have liked Kocoom very much indeed. Before they were wed, he and her father needed to agree on the bridewealth, the goods the groom's family would pay the bride's to compensate them for the loss of her labor. Then he and his family would work hard to gather together whatever had been agreed to. On the arranged day the two families met at the home of the groom to feast and make merry. The bride and groom clasped their hands together. Then the man's father—or another relative, if he was dead or could not be present—raised high a great string of beautifully worked shell beads, showing it to be as long as the span of both his arms, and brought it down forcefully over the couple's joined hands, so that the string snapped and the beads flew. In other ceremonies, the scattering of such beads symbolized the fertilization of the earth. Later, they were all gathered together again and given as a gift to the woman's father. And the merrymaking continued into the night.[3]

Within a few years Kocoom seems to have disappeared. Did he and Pocahontas find themselves quarreling or drifting apart, and choose divorce? That was an acceptable option among her people. Did he die? Since he was an active warrior, that is certainly possible. It even seems likely, given that the English, who knew of her earlier marriage, never seem to have given Kocoom a second's thought when they later contemplated Pocahontas's marrying one of their own.[4] Granted, they wanted the marriage and were motivated to overlook impediments, but it seems unlikely that the evangelical pastors and scholars in Virginia who were so eager for the union would have been willing to risk its being exposed that she had a living "common law" Indian husband. It would have invalidated all their efforts and left them looking like fools. They, who gave away their insecurities on so many issues, never introduced even a subordinate clause's worth of doubt on this point.

Did Pocahontas have children by Kocoom during the one, two, or three years in which she was married to him? It is certainly possible. But it is unlikely. She was very young when first married and, like other girls, unlikely to have been as fertile as she later would be when her cycle had regularized. And though it is possible that Pocahontas chose to remain silent on the subject, it is hard to believe that the assertive, sensitive, and keenly intelligent woman whom the English later came to know was willing to leave behind a child or children and never mention their existence in any context ever again, apparently not even to her husband. Still, if Pocahontas was married to Kocoom for three years, it would have been unusual for there to have been no child at all. One reasonable possibility is that there was a pregnancy (or even more than one), ending either in miscarriage, stillbirth, or infant death.

There is a strong possibility that Kocoom was from the Patowomeck (or Potomac) nation. A few years later Pocahontas went on a long visit there as her father's representative, and Powhatan certainly favored the exploitation of kin ties. Long visits to family were also common for social reasons.[5] One might think that she was visiting her mother's people, except that the Patowomecks later treated her so poorly that such a possibility seems doubtful. Interestingly, the young English boy Henry Spelman, who had been left among the Indians to learn the language, found himself less welcome in the period after the killing of Ratcliffe—that is, about the same time as Pocahontas was married—and she seems to have seen to it that he was taken to the Patowomecks, where she was apparently going herself.[6]

Wherever in Tsenacomoco it happened, in about 1610 Pocahontas became a young married woman. She grew out the hair that had been cropped in front, then cut it all to a common length, either long or shoulder length, as she chose. She probably had tattoos applied to her arms or legs (none that were visible outside the English clothes she later wore). She would have sported finer garments than before, and worn the white beads she once coveted. She worked for her own and her husband's welfare, gathering, carrying, planting, and harvesting. The English would have intruded on her daily consciousness only in the form of news of increasingly frequent skirmishes.

DURING THE TIME of Pocahontas's courtship, across the sea in England, another young couple had launched their adult lives as well. The groom was John Rolfe, who would one day be Pocahontas's second husband. In some ways he is as much of a mystery as Kocoom: no one knows for certain who he was. He was *probably* the son of another John Rolfe, a small landholder near the village of Heacham, in Norfolk, whose epitaph still reads, "He increased his property by merchandise. By exporting and importing such things as England abounded in, or needed, he was of the greatest service."[7] If Jamestown's John Rolfe was the son of this ambitious man, then he had a small twin brother who died when the boys were three, and he was twenty-four and newly married when he decided to migrate to Virginia in 1609 to try to pursue merchant trade from there.

The thought of migrating had crossed the minds of many young people in the early months of 1609, for the nation was in the throes of a great enthusiasm for the Jamestown project. One might simply say the time was ripe, but in fact the backers of the Virginia Company were doing their best to fan the flames of the excitement. They had just orchestrated a great reorganization of the corporation. Rather than continuing as a private company in the hands of a few citizens who had a charter from the king, it became a public joint-stock company whose shares were open for purchase by any and all. Men might buy shares (at a rate of twelve pounds, ten shillings, each, or about $2,500 in today's terms), or they might "adventure their persons" (that is, be given a share in return for traveling to Virginia at their own expense); or they might do both. Poorer men could travel at company expense in exchange for signing away seven years of their labor.[8]

It had become clear that the Virginia Company might yet do well by growing valuable crops, but it would require a great outlay of capital and many more settlers. Thus it was that the backers had made the change and were now in the process of recruiting colonists. They published numerous pamphlets extolling the possibilities of Virginia; pastors preached and scholars discussed. Petty merchants, cloth-workers, fishmongers, and other tradesmen participated in fund-raising to buy shares, the leaders castigating those few of their fellows who "utterly refused to pay at all." In letter after letter to his king, the Spanish ambassador agonized: "I am sending Your Majesty an announcement which was issued to all officials, and [which contains] what they are given to go, and they have collected in 20 days an amount of money for this voyage that frightens me. Between fourteen of them, the earls and barons have given 40,000 ducats; the merchants give much more; and there is no fellow or woman who does not go offering something for this enterprise." And one month later: "The preparations they are making here are the most urgent they know how to make, for they have seen to it that the ministers, in their sermons, stress the importance of filling the world with their religion, and of everyone exerting themselves to give what they have to so great an undertaking."[9]

Not long after the ambassador penned his complaint, in April 1609, Reverend William Symonds preached a sermon at White-chapel "in the presence of many honorable and worshipful, Adventurers and Planters [bound] for Virginia." It ran two hours long and covered every inch of ground, attempting to relieve those shortly to depart for the New World of any lingering doubts and to make others envious. Symonds used colorful, attention-grabbing language, even humor, as well as scores of biblical references.

First, the pastor dealt with the usual objection that the land in question belonged to the Indians. This, he said, was a ridiculous objection, since the English intended to plant "a peaceable Colony in a waste country, where the people doe live but like Deere." He scathingly told the objectors that they would see this "if they had any braines in their head." And if the doubters meant that the Indians might nevertheless perceive themselves as being robbed and respond with violence—well then, let them: "We should be worse than mad, to be discouraged by any such imaginings of this place . . . A mat is their strongest portcullis, a naked breast their Target of best proofe: an arrow of reede, on which is no iron, their most fearefull weapon of offence."[10]

The second objection, Symonds admitted, was more considerable: "Divers are the difficulties into which a man is cast when hee liveth among barbarous people." It was all too easy to lose the blessing of the Lord in such a situation. But a man might be extra zealous in his efforts to remain devout in a heathen land and so protect himself. And this did not mean simply going to church and reading the Bible. It meant casting out of one's mind the naked Indian girls that appeared in all the travel books: "Then must Abrams posterities keep them to themselves. They may not marry nor give in marriage to the heathen, that are uncircumcised . . . The breaking of this rule, may breake the good successe of this voyage."[11]

By now the listeners had heard, of course, of sundry problems with the Indians and understood that the natives were not, after all, eager to become tributaries to the English. They might well have to be forced, and if so, the colonists would have to do the forcing. Yet when contemplating the violence entailed, they need not struggle with their consciences, for they were going to bring Christianity to the heathens: "The summe is, what blessing any Nation had by Christ, must be Communicated to all Nations: the office of his Prophecie to teach the ignorant." They could employ the old trick of capturing some young people and using them to win over their elders. There need be nothing shameful in it. Symonds rose to a crescendo: "Go on courageously . . . Suspect not the blessing of God." He ended:

A captive girl brought Naaman to the prophet. A captive woman, was the means of converting Iberia, now called Georgia. Edesius & Frumentius, two captive youths, were the meanes of bringing the gospel into India. God makes the weake thinges of the worlde confound the mighty, and getteth himselfe praise by the mouth of Babes and sucklings. Be cheerfull then, and the Lord of all glory, glorifie his name by your happy spreading of the gospel, to your commendation, and his glory, that is Lord of all things, to whom be power and dominion forever. Halleluiah.[12]

No one seemed to consider the fact that in the Bible the powerful Naaman's slave girl converted him, not her own people. It was enough that the Bible said that captives could be key to conversion.

This idea of putting abductions to better use in Virginia than the English previously had was not merely the brainchild of an exhausted pastor seeking suitably dramatic closing lines. The notion was in fact quite widespread and even appeared in the formal instructions prepared for those listening to the sermon who were about to set sail for the New World. Company officials specified that the abducted children should be of royal blood and preferably next in line to rule their people:

> If you perceive that [the Indians] upon your landinge, fly up into the Countrey and forsake their habitation, you must seise into your custody half there [sic] corne and harvest and their Werowances and all their knowne successors at once whom if you intreate well and educate those which are younge and to succeede in the government in your Manners and Religion, their people will easily obey you and become in time Civill and Christian.[13]

This was no passing fad. The succeeding year the idea of kidnapping would appear again, in the set of instructions prepared for the next departing flotilla:

> Yt is very expedient that your Lordship [the Governor] with all diligence endeavor the conversion of the natives and savages to the knowledge and worship of the true God and their redeemer Christ Jesus as the most pius and noble end of this plantation, the better to effect, you are to procure from them some of their Children to be brought up in our language and manners and if you think it necessary . . . by a surprise of them and detaining them prisoners and in case they shall be willful and obstinate, then to send us some 3 or 4 of them into England, [so that] we may endeavor their conversion here.[14]

The young John Rolfe was surely exposed to these ideas as he made up his mind to go. He probably heard the sermon at Whitechapel and may even have read the official instructions. (He was an educated man, even traveling with a signet ring to seal his letters.) Did he and his wife look at the promised violence from the Indians' point of view? Possibly. Did they believe they were fulfilling God's will? Probably. Did they hope to become great merchant traders? Most certainly. When they boarded the flagship of the flotilla, a great vessel holding at least 150 people, young Mistress Rolfe was in the early weeks of pregnancy, harboring hopes for her child.

They were part of the first fleet to depart since the company's restructuring. Thirty-three-year-old Thomas West, the third Lord De La Warr and a privy councilor to James I, had been given wide powers as governor of the reorganized colony. He himself was not ready to leave the country, however, and instead sent Sir Thomas Gates, a fellow veteran of the wars against Spain in the Netherlands, to act as his deputy in Virginia until he himself should arrive. The Rolfes sailed with Gates on the prestigious lead ship, the *Sea Venture*. On board with them were also Christopher Newport, the ship's experienced captain, and Sir George Somers, the admiral of the fleet. Remarkably, among the travelers there were ten women and children, for whom accommodations had been made.

They left Plymouth on a beautiful June evening in 1609, and for the next seven weeks the seven ships and their two pinnaces never lost sight of one another. All was going splendidly when they reached the Caribbean and turned north, following the usual route. But on July 23 they were introduced to the Caribbean hurricane: "A dreadful storm and hideous began to blow from out the northeast, which, swelling and roaring as it were by fits, some hours with more violence than others, at length did beat all light from Heaven." William Strachey later described the horror of attempting to come to terms with imminent death when the body is so racked by agonizing nausea and the mind so disoriented that even the simplest of thoughts seems nearly impossible: "It worketh upon the whole frame of the body and most loathsomely affecteth all the powers thereof. And the manner of the sickness it lays upon the body, being so insufferable, gives not the mind any free and quiet time to use her judgment." After twenty-four hours the storm was so strong, the passengers could not even imagine greater natural violence. It quieted suddenly, then grew yet more terrible: "Fury added to fury, and one storm urging a second more outrageous than the former." Strachey did not preach to his readers. He only said that he had been in many severe storms before and had thought he understood how frightening a tempest could be; he knew now that he had been wrong.[15]

On the second day of the storm they discovered that the ship's hold was five feet deep in water. Strachey could see on the faces of even the bravest and most experienced of the sailors that this news nearly destroyed them. Yet the crew took candles and conducted a search for leaks. The news was bad. There was no single hole to stop up: the caulking seemed to have been washed away almost everywhere. In retrospect, what Strachey found most strange was that in this extremity, when it seemed clear that they would die, they all continued to struggle to ward the end off, if only for a few more hours.

John Rolfe joined the 140 other men, who divided the ship into three sections and themselves into three groups: "Thereunto every man came duly upon his watch, took a bucket or pump for an hour, then rested another." There was not one who refused, no gentleman born too high: "[Those who] in all their lifetimes had never done an hour's work before (their minds now helping their bodies) were able twice forty-eight hours together to toil with the best." They threw off luggage, and barrels of beer, oil, and vinegar. Rolfe's wife and the other women tried to keep a fire lit to cook some meat, but they could not do it in the dampness and the wind. They brought what biscuits they could to the laboring men. The storm was abating, but that would not save them now; the water gained on them. It was ten feet deep in the hold, and there were far, far too many of them to fit on the tiny lifeboats. And then George Somers, sitting up on the poop, where he had been for three days, cried "Land!"[16]

Their luck turned. The ship stuck in an upright position in some rocks off the coast of one of the Bermuda islands. They used their rowboats to ferry themselves and then their remaining goods to land. The isle appeared to be uninhabited. They slept.

They spent August searching for fresh water, building cabins, planting gardens, gathering fruits, fish, and tortoises, and learning how to trap the pigs that roamed wild over the island. (They learned afterward, reading the work of the Spanish explorer and historian Gonzalo Fernández de Oviedo, that he had left hogs there over a century ago, for later use. They had rare reason to bless the Spaniards.) They held church services every Sunday. Some of them conducted a more thorough study of the archipelago in which they found themselves, and others began to build two small ships. Later in the fall— or what they considered the fall, though the leaves did not drop—the people began to argue among themselves. The memory of the storm, which had bound them together thus far, had begun to fade. Those who did not expect to receive social accolades and high stature when they reached Virginia or London preferred to remain on this plentiful island and not take to sea again. The arguments and threats became violent.[17]

But John Rolfe's wife had other concerns. In early February 1610 she withdrew to her cabin and, for the second time in a few months, endured such pain, fear, and nausea that her thoughts lost coherency. She gave birth to a baby girl. John Rolfe held the child. On February 11, they christened her Bermuda and gave thanks to God for having seen them safely through. The child, however, did not have the strength to continue. She stopped breathing, and they buried her there on the island. It was God's will, they said. Yet it is impossible to believe that the baby's mother and father did not entertain the thought that it probably would not have happened if they had stayed at home in England.[18]

On the tenth of May, having made the decision to continue on, the entire company set off on their newly built little boats, the

Patience and the *Deliverance*. On the twenty-first they reached the James River. The good news was that all but one of the other boats in their fleet had made it to Virginia through the storm. The bad news was that there was no food in Jamestown, and the Indians were hostile and attacked those who went outside the settlement.

It was a year since John Rolfe and his company had left home. They had arrived at their dreamed-of destination to find it literally in ruins. "Viewing . . . [Jamestown] we found the palisades torn down, the ports open, the gates from off the hinges, and empty houses (which owners' death had taken from them) rent up and burnt, rather than the dwellers would step into the woods a stone's cast off from them to fetch other firewood."[19] They decided to leave, and were prevented from doing so only by the sudden arrival of the governor, Lord De La Warr, who had at last managed to put his affairs in order and come to Virginia himself. Sometime not long after that, John Rolfe's exhausted young wife died. We do not know exactly when, or of what. We do not even know her name.

POCAHONTAS'S PEOPLE and John Rolfe's people were at war. There was no official declaration; to describe the situation as one of low-intensity warfare, though anachronistic, would be quite accurate. Life in the Jamestown vicinity under the company's second charter reflected the changed circumstances. It was now something of a military state. Under the newly issued "Lawes Divine, Morall and Martiall," even a relatively minor crime might incur the death penalty. Gone was any expectation of voluntary participation on the part of the Indians. Instead, interactions between colonists and Indians were strictly controlled. Individual settlers were not to molest the Powhatans or trade with them: all dealings with the enemy would be controlled from above.[20] Powhatan also made his intentions clear. He could not force the settlers to leave, but he could withdraw his people and his corn and attack settlers who strayed beyond the confines of their forts. The message was clear: he wanted them to abandon the site.

Powhatan knew he needed some European weapons to hold this line, and he instructed his warriors to bring him what they took from the English dead. "Seizing their arms, swords, pieces, etc., . . . he hath gathered into his store a great quantity and number, by intelligence above two hundred swords, besides axes and poleaxes, chisels hoes," wrote one disgruntled colonist. Lord De La Warr sent a party of messengers to promise peace and friendship if Powhatan ceased his hostilities and returned all prisoners and English weapons, or an open confrontation if he did not. Powhatan answered with a direct statement of his policy, and what was probably a bit of sarcastic humor:

> Powhatan returned no other answer but that either we should depart his country or confine ourselves to Jamestown only, without searching further up into his land or rivers, or otherwise he would give in command to his people to kill us and do unto us all the mischief which they at their pleasure could and we feared; withal forewarning the said messengers not to return any more unto him, unless they brought him a coach and three horses, for he had understood by the Indians which were in England [that is, Namontack] how such was the state of great werowances and lords in England.[21]

Incensed, Lord De La Warr, whose grandmother had been Queen Elizabeth's first cousin, had the hand of a captured Paspahegh Indian cut off, and sent the man back to his chief with a final warning. There was no answer.

On August 9, 1610, the governor sent George Percy and some seventy men to the Paspaheghs' largest town, home to about forty able-bodied adult men. The colonists ran fifteen or sixteen through with swords and apparently shot others. They burned the houses, cut down the corn, and made prisoners of the wife and children of the werowance, Wowinchopunk, the same man who had feasted the colonists when they arrived in 1607. Once safely back on their anchored boats, the officers called a council: "Itt was Agreed upon to putt the Children to deathe the wch was effected by Throweinge them overboard and shotinge owtt their Braynes in the water." George Percy was troubled by his memory of that day: "Yett for all this Crewellty the Sowldiers wre nott well pleased And I had mutche to doe to save the quenes lyfe for thatt Tyme." The queen's remaining time proved brief. Back at the fort, Percy convinced the governor not to burn her; she was put to the sword instead. The Paspaheghs who escaped never recovered as a political entity: they dispersed, finding shelter with friends and relatives throughout the region, spreading their story with them. Wowinchopunk was killed in a skirmish a few months later.[22]

The English began to do exactly what Powhatan had most hoped to prevent: they established other forts and settlements up and down the James River. Indeed, having finally concluded (quite rightly, if a bit late) that the Paspahegh island they originally settled was extremely unhealthy, they began to prioritize these other settlements. They fenced land for farming, and by the fall of 1611 brought in a passable if not stellar crop of corn. When the Indians harassed them, they launched raids against villages, killing and burning houses and crops.

De La Warr had not forgotten the injunction to send a royal hostage or two back to England. Just before the attack on the Paspaheghs, as a small fleet was being prepared to take Sir Thomas Gates back to England to report on the state of affairs, the English went to trade with the Warrascoyaks, who lived just across the James River. Ostensibly there to buy cedar and walnut wood, they also took the opportunity to kidnap the chief, one of his advisers, and his son, Tangoit. The adults were later released, but Tangoit was to be sent to England. The chief struck a bargain: if they would take his nephew in lieu of his son, he would, when his crops came in, exchange five hundred bushels of corn for some minor trade goods. As it turned out, the boy who took Tangoit's place, whoever he was, jumped into the sea before the ship departed, leg irons and all. The Indians later taunted the English that he had made it home, but the colonists did not know whether to believe it.[23]

Not surprisingly, the Warrascoyaks did not make the promised payments at harvest time. So shortly after the attack on the Paspaheghs, De La Warr sent one of his favorites, Captain Samuel Argall, "with lyke commission ageinste the Wariscoyans." Their own recent experiences, however, and their knowledge of the fate of their Paspahegh neighbors left them better prepared: when the English boat drew near, they disappeared into the woods. All Argall was able to do was burn down their houses and destroy the crops that were still in the field. He left no Indians dead and returned without hostages.[24]

Captain Argall was related to the governor by marriage. The eighth and last son of a Kentish landowner, he was another veteran of the wars in the Netherlands and in the pay of the Virginia Company. In 1609, while the great fleet of Sir Thomas Gates was yet in the planning stages, the company sent him in a fishing boat to test the viability of sailing from London to America straight across the North Atlantic, rather than traveling first south to the Caribbean, then north. He arrived without mishap in Virginia, met John Smith, sold him supplies, and returned to England, arriving after the great fleet had sailed. The voyage straight across, he reported, was safe and would take seven to nine weeks.

When Lord De La Warr himself set off for Virginia in April 1610, Argall was the captain of his ship. After they arrived and De La Warr established his government, he sent Argall and George Somers off to Bermuda to obtain some of the island's wild hogs and other edibles for the Jamestown colony. Somers died on the trip, apparently of a stroke, but Argall eventually returned. Upon his arrival, he received an update on the failed kidnapping of Tangoit and the colony's current relationship with the Warrascoyaks, and was sent to destroy them. His incomplete success in that regard was more than made up for in December, when he took a small boat up the Potomac River to trade for corn with the friendly Indians there. In Potomac country he found young Henry Spelman, apparently well looked after but anxious to return to England. Argall bought the boy's freedom and used him as a most effective translator, enabling him to obtain more corn than he had expected. He returned to Jamestown—and to the favor of Lord De La Warr, who mentioned his name to key people in London the following year. Argall was a man with a future, if he would live up to it. He had learned that managing the Indians was the key to success.[25]

He returned to England—carrying the ecstatic Henry Spelman with him—but came back to Virginia in the fall of 1612. This time he had instructions to find and root out a rumored French colony on the New England coast. Entrusted with the 130-ton *Treasurer*, with a crew of sixty and bearing fourteen heavy guns, he found the Jamestown colony surviving relatively well, despite the recent departure of Lord De La Warr, who had gone home sick. Sir Thomas Gates was again acting governor, and Sir Thomas Dale, another veteran of the Netherlands, was military commander. Argall apparently made the decision not to attack the French settlement until the end of the winter—when, presumably, they would be at their weakest. Instead, he spent his time that fall helping to extract corn from the Indians and to organize fishing expeditions.

He set off for the Potomac River on the first of December to seek the Patowomeck village of Pasptanzie, where Henry Spelman had lived and where Argall himself had been well entertained. He found the people he sought. Through trade he obtained fourteen hundred bushels of corn—three hundred for the men of his ship, eleven hundred for the colony. He had, he said, "likewise given and taken Hostages." A young ensign named James Swift and a boy named Rob Sparkes were left with the Paspatanzies, and an Indian boy or two (no one specified how many) went with Argall, who had learned the value of such an arrangement from his experience using Spelman as a translator.

At the end of March 1613, after directing the building of a frigate in Jamestown, the ambitious Argall returned to Patowomeck country once again. With commerce in mind he hired Indian guides to show him the most remarkable plants, animals, and minerals they knew: they showed him some sort of bison (a few bison may have existed in Virginia at that time, or they may have been some remarkable male deer), a spring of medicinal waters, and some mineral deposits. He took samples to bring home to England for study. The best—from his perspective—was yet to come.[26]

"While I was at this business," Argall later wrote to a friend, "I was told . . . that the Great Powhatan's daughter Pokahuntis was with the great King Patawomeck." This was news indeed. Since his attack on the Warrascoyaks—if not before—he had been well aware of the Virginia Company's desire to see royal hostages taken. The tactic had, they believed, worked very well for the Spanish. Why shouldn't it work for them? Argall was excited: he would seize Pocahontas and present her to the governor as the perfect pawn for getting what they wanted in their conflict with Powhatan. "[To Patowomeck] I presently repaired, resolving to possesse my selfe of her by any stratagem that I could use, for the ransoming of so many Englishmen as were prisoners with Powhatan, as also to get [back] such armes and tooles as hee, and other Indians had got by murther and stealing . . . with some quantitie of Corne, for the Colonies reliefe."[27]

When he got to the village of Pasptanzie, he weighed anchor, manned the guns, and sent for the werowance and the English hostages. When he had at least one of the English boys back in his custody—he mentioned Ensign Swift but said nothing about Rob Sparkes, who apparently had no social position—he "broke the matter" to the king. He wasted no time: "If he did not betray Pokohuntis

This illustration of Pocahontas's abduction was made in London a number of years after the fact, when the story became well known in the metropolis. *(Attributed to Georg Keller, reproduced by Theodor de Bry's family in Americae Pars Decimae, c. 1634, courtesy of the New York Public Library)*

unto my hands, wee would no longer be brothers nor friends." The werowance, Yapassus, said the thing was impossible; Powhatan would declare war on him. Argall was unmoved and said the English would declare war on Yapassus if he did *not* do it, and that the English could defend him from Powhatan.

Argall's young translator apparently did his job well. What Argall next reported in his letter to his friend matches perfectly with what is known of Algonkian politicking. The werowance said he was only a minor chief and would have to consult with his older brother, the great king of the Patowomeck. He went. The Patowomeck king called his council together, and they deliberated for many hours. "They concluded," said Argall, "rather to deliver her into my hands, than lose my friendship."[28]

Argall probably had the gist of their conclusion quite right. The Patowomeck were the most distant northern members of the loosely bound coalition of peoples who paid tribute to Powhatan. As such, they were probably among the most recalcitrant of his subjects. Despite paying the taxes, they often had to deal with non-Algonkian enemy peoples in or near their territories and so experienced the least degree of security of any tribe in the network. In addition, their contact with northern peoples meant that they had access to a wide variety of unusual trade goods, such as furs, which were in growing demand. If they could strengthen an alliance with the English and become the local purveyors of European goods, they stood to become wealthy indeed. Freedom from the paramount chieftainship might have looked appealing. They also knew enough about the English to realize that Argall meant it when he promised English vengeance: even now, seven shipboard guns were aimed at the village of Yapassus.

Pocahontas had been among the Patowomeck for about three months. She may have been visiting her husband's people. She definitely was acting as an envoy representing her father, charged with trading a consignment of goods. Possibly it was understood on both sides that the trading was to be unequal—that in essence, she was there to supervise the collection of tribute. As Powhatan's daughter, she frequented the homes of nobles: she was probably even a guest of the chief of the Patowomeck, as Argall was apparently told. They had to act quickly: not only was Argall growing impatient, but it was crucial that the deed be done before any gossip reached her.

Yapassus and his wife invited her to come and see the great English ship riding at anchor before their village. Once on the beach the wife said she wanted to go aboard and see the inside of the vessel. Yapassus pretended to be angry with her, saying that it would be wrong for her to proceed on such a venture without any women attendants. But would Pocahontas go with her? Pocahontas was no fool. The English later reported, "Now was the greatest labor to win her, guilty perhaps of her father's wrongs, though not knowne as she supposed to goe with her."[29] These words meant that Pocahontas knew the history of European kidnappings of those unwise enough to venture onto their boats; and she knew her father was at war with the English and considered by them to have committed great wrongs. Her hosts reminded her, however, that Argall had no way of knowing who she was or even of recognizing a king's daughter when he saw one, and that he was friendly to the Patowomeck. Surely there would be no danger. She boarded.

Captain Argall gave them a tour and provided an excellent repast; he then suggested that the women take a nap in the gunner's room. Pocahontas did not sleep long on the swaying boat, if she did at all: she soon reappeared and told Yapassus that she wanted to be gone. Then Argall pretended to tell Yapassus for the first time that he was taking Powhatan's daughter prisoner, to be offered in exchange for the English men and weapons that the chief held. He told him to send Powhatan a message to that effect immediately. James Swift or perhaps Rob Sparkes, both of whom Pocahontas had probably socialized with in the preceding months, apparently translated it all as best he could.

At first she said nothing: "She began to be exceeding pensive." It was the diplomatic way in her world, to begin with a meaningful silence. Her father used the tactic. She had used it as a ten-year-old visitor to Jamestown, come to ransom prisoners. She would use it again in England, and werowances who ruled her people after she was dead would, too. Perhaps she used the time to think, to sort out all that she knew, to pray. Perhaps she was merely waiting for the others to grow silent and wait upon her words. For Pocahontas's silences were never self-effacing; they were always preliminary to a rush of speech. So it had been in Jamestown. So it would be in London. And so it was now. As the English recorded it, "Much adoe there was to perswade her to be patient, which with extraordinary curteous usage, by little and little was wrought in her." What did she say? The one clue that she was as enraged at Yapassus as at Argall is an Englishman's statement to the effect that Yapassus repeatedly proclaimed his innocence and his sorrow at the turn of events. Then he and his wife left the ship.[30]

Argall waited where he was for the messenger sent to Powhatan to return. He came "without delay"—it would have taken between twenty-four and forty-eight hours for the runners and rowers to do their job. He said that Powhatan was deeply grieved, that he desired the English "to use his daughter well." They should bring their ship "into his river," and he would give them what they demanded in exchange for her. Satisfied, on April 13 Argall drew anchor and went straight to Jamestown to bring his prisoner to Sir Thomas Gates.[31]

When Pocahontas disembarked from the cramped ship for the first time in days, it is doubtful she felt anything other than fear. She could no longer pretend to herself—if she ever had—that it was all a horrible misunderstanding, that Argall would be prevailed upon to change his mind, or that Yapassus intended to rescue her. She stepped off the wooden planks into the dismal-looking sandy dirt that the foreigners created wherever they stripped the land. The principal gate of the fort opened onto the river near where they had docked. She walked through. Rather than the visitor of old, she would be a prisoner in Jamestown now. With one exception, none of the boys she had once played with were still there: almost all had died or left. English men were not known for their kindness to Indian women. Rape had been common. They had even killed the queen of the Paspaheghs to teach Powhatan a lesson. They could do anything they wanted to her, alone as she was.[32]

The women in Pocahontas's world grew up knowing they might be kidnapped by enemy war parties, forced to change their allegiance and their identity. It had almost certainly happened to girls known to her; some of the women living in Werowocomoco had not originally come by choice. The event was always horrifying, always traumatic, but the women also understood that they would be treated kindly, that the shift would be made as easy as possible under the circumstances, that they might hope to become wives rather than slaves. But these English men, Pocahontas knew, were different. They had different agendas.[33]

She remembered Jamestown's three streets, still laid out in a triangle, surrounding the open area where the market and the chapel were. She used to give her cartwheeling lessons there. But the houses looked different now: they were covered with tree bark, Powhatan style, to insulate against both winter cold and summer heat, for the colonists had finally learned that plastered walls, so effective in England, made the rooms inside "like stoves." Her captors led her into one of the better houses. In the dim light she saw that the walls were lined with the finely woven mats made by her people.[34]

The young woman's arrival was not a quiet, unnoticed event. Argall crowed. The colonists stared. They had wanted a royal hostage, and the name of Pocahontas was already well known to them, old-timers and newcomers alike. Even before they quite knew what they were going to do with her, they were writing letters home to England that they now had in their power the daughter of the "king that was theyre greatest ennemie." One young man literally took notes: he was planning the book that he would write. The English were more than a little excited: God had given them what they needed. Did any of them look at her with sympathy behind their eyes? John Rolfe, for one, was almost certainly not there.[35]

And Pocahontas? She must have struggled, in her exhaustion and her tension, to recall the English she once had known, trying to understand what the men said to her that first night. She probably ate little, slept less. She was fifteen, sixteen at the most.

SIX

Imprisonment

Until now I had hoped to go in this ship of Captain Argol, but now they tell me it sailed [for London] two days ago . . . From this may be seen the want of truthfulness in these [English] men; and that they only mean to deceive us . . . Although I am badly treated and endure much suffering, I reflect that my sins have been great and that I have deserved it all.

— Diego de Molina, prisoner in Virginia (1614)[1]

Reverend Alexander Whitaker's Bible showed extraordinary workmanship when Pocahontas examined it. Embossed words stood out from the smooth leather of the cover, which disappeared in neat, tiny tucks under the painted endpapers inside. The pages were of the finest-quality paper, just thin enough to crinkle slightly when turned. The letters, so full of meaning to those who knew the code, were draped over the whiteness like a black net. Maps and pictures were scattered throughout. Unsurprisingly to Pocahontas, animals figured prominently in most of them; powerful horses dominated the battle scene on the front page. Reverend Whitaker wanted her to study it, and she had had plenty of time to do so. She had heard nothing from her family for the first three months, and then her father had sent seven captive colonists back to Jamestown with some damaged muskets in exchange for her. Sir Thomas Gates, the governor, had said it wasn't good enough. So here she was still.[2]

Gates relied heavily on his second-in-command, Marshal Thomas Dale, and tensions ran high in the colony under Dale's military rule. Around the time Pocahontas was taken, a Spaniard, who had been arrested as a spy over a year earlier, gave a letter describing the place to a Venetian sailor. The latter promised to sew the missive between the soles of his shoe and take it to the Spanish king, who would surely reward him. The imprisoned Diego de Molina painted a bleak picture of the English settlement: "Little food and much labor on public works kills them, and more than all, the discontent in which they live seeing themselves treated as slaves with cruelty. Wherefore many have gone over to the Indians, at whose hands some have been killed."[3] Hoping to convince the Catholic monarch to invade, Molina emphasized the weakness of both men and fortifications but acknowledged that there was one especially propitious new settlement: "Twenty leagues further up [beyond Jamestown] is another colony strongly located—to which they will all betake themselves if occasion arises, because on this they place their hopes—where are one hundred more persons and among them there are women, children and field laborers."

This was Henrico, which Pocahontas knew well, for it was here that Dale decided to send the Indian hostage. It was an eminently reasonable choice from his point of view. In Jamestown, the settlers, who were all male, cohabited with Indian women. If Pocahontas remained there, she would simply end up spending her days with her own kind. But in Henrico there were white women and children present to socialize her. The settlement was highly defensible, in case her

Sir Thomas Dale (d. 1619) was the first marshal of Virginia and served as deputy governor at different points between 1611 and 1616. He took an active role in Pocahontas's imprisonment, Christian education, and marriage. This painting was probably commissioned during Pocahontas's visit to London in 1616 in the company of Dale. *(Artist unknown, Virginia Museum of Fine Arts, Richmond, The Adolph D. and Wilkins C. Williams Fund. Photo by Ron Jennings)*

people entertained any ideas of a rescue, and perhaps best of all, there was an eager young pastor who wanted the job of educating the girl in hopes of converting her.[4]

So they rowed her upriver to the new settlement, a distance of about fifty-five miles. It took at least a full day. The town was situated on a peninsula that dropped in steep bluffs down to the water. From the river Pocahontas could see five blockhouses keeping "continual sentinel for the town's security." A great fence with watchtowers protected the landward side about two miles in, closing off land for farming. The town itself consisted of three small streets of well-built houses and a church the people thought "handsome" indeed; this place was to be the colony's pride and joy.

Pocahontas was to live just across the river, where the town had recently expanded. There five small forts and another fence protected about twelve square miles of ground, mostly for hogs to roam and feed in. Near the construction called Fort Patience, the well-to-do Reverend Whitaker had built a parsonage called Rock Hall and fenced off from the general land about a hundred acres for the church. The house was a simple wooden frame structure with shutters over the windows, a bit more ornate than the others she had seen.[5]

The prisoner was turned over to Whitaker's servants, for he had no wife. At least one was a woman, functioning as a housekeeper, perhaps married to one of the menservants, as was typical. Once in the household Pocahontas's clothing had to be altered, permanently and immediately. They took away her deerskin apron and gave her instead a long white undergarment or "petticoat," a stiff bodice, and a colored overskirt, along with socks and some sort of shoes, although perhaps these were Indian moccasins. The clothes were hot in the thick summer air; the hemp of which the linen was made scratched her skin; the bodice was laced tightly over her breast.[6]

At mealtime they used metal knives and poured liquids from glass flasks, items that she had previously seen only as prized trade items. They sat at a table and ate from pottery that glistened in a way that her own clay pots at home did not. The meat was mostly of the kind she knew—wild turkey or deer or fish—but except for the corn, the plant foods were strange to her, grown in English-style gardens. Later she would learn their names: peas, onions, turnips, cabbage, cauliflower, carrots.[7]

These drastic changes in Pocahontas's world, however, were as nothing compared to her confusing relationship with the Reverend Alexander Whitaker, a man whose intensity was bewildering even to many English people. In the reverend she found a jailer who was determined to treat her with such kindness that her gratitude would be infinite, and who wanted at the same time to control her hopes, her thoughts, her very life. He gave her regular lessons in English and Christianity. Little by little, incident by incident, and sentence by sentence, she pieced together what she could about him.

Whitaker was no impoverished emigrant or second son come to make an otherwise elusive fortune. He had grown up in a prosperous, prominent household, with expectations of a brilliant career. William Whitaker, his father, was Master of the College of St. John's and Regius Professor of Divinity at Cambridge University, and his mother, Susan Culverwell, was related to some of the wealthiest men in London. Alexander's childhood was not easy, however: his mother died when he was four, his father when he was ten. When he was old enough, he attended Cambridge, just as his father had. It was an exciting moment to be a student of religion: the professors were in the midst of the agitating and inspiring work of debating the nature of Protestantism and writing the King James Bible. Alexander was ordained as a minister in 1609, and his family connections secured him a good living in a parish in the north of England.[8]

But he stayed only two years. After lengthy internal debate and "notwithstanding the earnest disuasions of many of his nearest friends," he decided to go instead to Virginia to serve for a period of three years. This, he felt sure, was his chance to prove his worthiness, to perform a great work in converting the Indians. He would not follow the life of ease that had been laid out for him: "Why then hath God made thee rich, and commended to that thy liberalitie [that] which was not thine own, but that thou shouldest bee bountifull to those whom he hath made poore?"[9] And who in all the world was poorer than the benighted Indians of America, who had never yet even had a chance to hear the word of God as delivered by Protestants rather than Papists?

He traveled in the spring of 1611 and immediately helped Sir Thomas Dale establish Henrico. His first letter home at the end of the summer was that of a credulous boy, who said the Indians seemed to have the power to bewitch the settlers and send them stumbling about in a haze.[10] His tone, however, evolved considerably over the next year, and he turned his hand to helping the colony fund-raise.

In July 1612, almost a year before he met Pocahontas, he wrote the finishing touches on a religious tract that he planned to send back to London for publication. It was called *Good News from Virginia*. He spoke of the Indians who lived in darkness, whose nakedness was emblematic of both their spiritual and material poverty, and his message was that it was the duty of his countrymen to give liberally to the naked: "We are all members of one mysticall bodie, most unseparably united to our head Jesus Christ, by the power of the Holy Spirit. How then can we see our fellow-servants, our deare brethren, yea the members of our owne bodie to passe us by, hungry and naked, unfed, unclothed?" He had specific advice for those in England who wanted to save their own souls: "Those men whom God hath made able in any way to be helpful to this Plantation, and made knowne unto them the necessities of our wants, are bound in conscience . . . to lay their helping hands to it, either with their purse, persons or prayers." God had saved the colony over and over for a reason, as a sign to them of what he wanted: "Let the miserable condition of these naked slaves of the divell move you to compassion."[11]

When Pocahontas entered Whitaker's home, she was perhaps in his mind not so much a person as a long-awaited opportunity to demonstrate his precepts. If her relative nakedness elicited any other thoughts, he likely did his best to repress them. He had no patience with men who had kept women; indeed, "whoring" was one of the crimes he most abominated in his writings. The Spanish prisoner living downriver heard that young Whitaker was making himself few friends because of his tendency to criticize the colonists for their liaisons with Indian women.[12]

Pocahontas would soon have found that Whitaker was not at all surprised by her quick intelligence; he did not expect her to be stupid. In fact, Whitaker was well schooled in the idea that the Indians were exactly like the ancient Britons before the Romans and then the Christians came: "One God created us, they have reasonable souls and intellectual faculties as well as wee; we all have Adam for our common parent . . . What was the state of England before the Gospell was preached in our countrey?" Whitaker said even before he began to tutor Pocahontas that he knew for a fact the Indians were quick learners and would respond well to Christian education: "If any of us should misdoubt that this barbarous people is uncapable of such heavenly mysteries, let such men know that they are farre mistaken." He continued:

> Let us not thinke that these men are so simple as some have supposed them: for they are of bodie lustie, strong, and very nimble: they are a very understanding generation, quicke of apprehension, suddaine in their dispatches, subtile in their dealings, exquisite in their inventions, and industrious in their labour.[13]

Whitaker, in short, was invested in believing that Pocahontas would absorb what he had to say quickly and easily. When she did, she must have seen his joy at being proven right.

If, as might be expected, Pocahontas ever raised any doubts as to the virtuousness of English people, she might have been surprised to learn that Whitaker appeared to agree with her. Indeed, he ascribed all of the colony's former ills to his own people's erring ways, even making indiscreet public statements to that effect: "Some of our Adventurers in *London* have been most miserable covetous men, sold over to Usurie, Extortion and Oppression. Many of the men sent hither have bin Murtherers, Theeves, Adulturers, idle persons, and what not besides, all of which persons God hateth even from his very soule."[14]

At the end of each week Pocahontas was relieved somewhat from her tête-à-têtes with the intense Whitaker, but she then had to face the English in large groups, and increasingly she was expected to perform for them by conversing and reciting what she knew. On Saturday evenings the nearby colonists gathered for prayer at the plantation of Sir Thomas Dale, just a few miles downriver from Henrico. On Sundays Whitaker and his household spent the day in the town itself, so he could preach in the morning and teach a catechism class in the afternoon. These would have been the occasions when Pocahontas and the twenty-eight-year-old widowed John Rolfe met and talked. John Smith would later assert that Rolfe had been one of those who helped with Pocahontas's English lessons. Perhaps. Regardless, by the end of that winter, John Rolfe would write that Pocahontas was she "to whom my hart and best thoughts are and have byn a longe tyme soe intangled & inthralled in soe intricate a Laborinth, that I was even awearied to unwynde my selfe thereout." John was in love, and had been for months.[15]

He eventually covered both sides of four sheets of foolscap paper pouring out the history of his love in a letter to Sir Thomas Dale, whose permission he needed if he was to ask Pocahontas to marry him. It is a remarkable document, written in the heat of passion, when, according to the writer himself, Pocahontas was still staunchly unconverted.[16]

Rolfe says much that is honest and self-revealing, even airing his doubts about Pocahontas and her background. Some have quoted from the letter to prove his love was lacking, a stunted, grudging thing, with the implication that Pocahontas should have steered clear. All lovers have doubts about their partners, though. For Rolfe to have incorporated none of the fears and prejudices of his era would have been impossible. What seems more remarkable is that, given those fears and prejudices, he rose to the task of announcing to his social peers that he loved her. He asked, "[What] should provoke me to be in love with one, whose education hath byn rude, her manners barbarous, her generation Cursed, and so discrepant in all nutriture from my selfe?"[17] The epithets, it is true, are insulting. He was not saying, though, that the woman herself was inherently rude or evil, only that her education and acculturation, the customs taught her, were not what his had been—and certainly he thought his had been superior. Despite all that, apparently, he admired her for herself. He published to the world that he was in love with her anyway.

Rolfe's feelings passed through several stages. He voluntarily admitted what he knew all others would guess—that lust had been there from the beginning. He had struggled "to cure so dangerous an ulcer." He knew that he must not mistake the devil's importunities for love: "I forgatt not to sett before myne eyes the frailtie of mankynde, his proneness to ill, his indulgency of wicked thoughts, with many other imperfections, wherein man is daylie insnared and often tymes overthrowen, and then Compared them with my present estate."

He also turned to the book of Nehemiah in the Bible and read of the prohibition against "strange wives," which the Reverend William Symonds had brandished before them all on the eve of their sailing from England. He was reminded that there was a reason mixed marriages were disastrous: "Their children spoke halfe in the speech of Ashdod, and could not speake in the Jewes' language."[18] He thought of his own children yet unborn. Often before Rolfe retired to bed he would decide, "Surely theise are wicked instigations hatched by him whoe seeketh and delighteth in mans destruction." He concluded he had no choice but to push the beautiful Pocahontas from his mind.

He tried going away. Out of sight, out of mind. Probably he went down to Jamestown for a while and stayed away from Whitaker's church. It didn't work. He thought of Pocahontas constantly: "Daylie, howerly, yea in my sleepe." Then comes a statement that at first reads like a kick in the teeth: "These many passions and sufferings . . . have happened to my greater wonder, even when she hath byn farthest separated from me, which in Common reason (were it not an undoubted worke of god) might breede a forgettfullnes of a farre

more worthy creature." A far more worthy creature? Why directly insult the woman he loved? Thinking of the man's immediate history,
though, the statement does not have nearly the same ring.

Not so many years before, he had married a "good English girl"
who had accompanied him when he had decided to go to America,
who had braved the worst of shipwrecks at his side, given birth to
his child in a wilderness, withstood the gruesome first sight of
Jamestown—and then died. Since then he had begun to forget her.
In fact, he had begun to care wildly, passionately, for another woman
whom his wife—to whom he thought he owed his allegiance—
would have feared, perhaps even scorned. What could possibly cause
him to forget a woman whom all his social peers would have viewed
as a worthier creature than Pocahontas? Rolfe did not have modern
science's view of the psyche, had no idea that the human mind does
begin to forget someone who has been irrevocably removed from
reach; he could not excuse himself on that basis. Instead he added in
parentheses that the phenomenon simply proved that God did not
want him to separate himself from the captive girl.

That thought became Rolfe's lifeline. The question that was
thenceforth with him night and day was, "Why doest not thou en-
deavour to make her a Christian?" He said he conferred with "honest and religious persons." Surely one was Whitaker himself, for
Rolfe echoed the preacher's very thoughts: "Shall I be so unnatural
not to gyve bread to the hungry, or soe uncharitable not to Cover the
naked?" And this was not just any naked soul. This was a soul who
wanted to be saved, thus rendering it a greater sin to ignore the plea.
"Her great appearance of love to me, her desire to be taught and instructed in the knowledge of God, her Capableness of understanding, her aptness and willingness to receive any good impression"
determined his course. "What should I do?" he demanded. "Shall I
be of so untoward a disposicion to refuse to leade the blind into the
right waye?"[19]

Rolfe had even dealt with the obvious objection as to the fate of the children. All would be well, he insisted, as they would be Christians, even if the mother was not. Whitaker had apparently helped him do some research: "I hope I do not farre erre from the meaninge of the holy Apostle, . . . upon which place Master Calvin in his Institucions lib. 4. Cap. 16; Sect. 6 . . . The Children of Christians are accompted holye, yea although they be the yssue but of one parent faithfull." He still hoped, however, to make Pocahontas a Christian. "I will never cease (god assisting me) until I have accomplished and brought to perfection soe holy a worke, in which I will daylie praye God to bless me to myne and her eternall happiness."[20] That would be the point of undertaking the marriage, he told himself. And when he found the courage to give his letter to Dale, it was the line he pursued in attempting to get permission to marry.

If we know many of the thoughts of Master Rolfe, we know little of the mind and heart of Pocahontas. Unfortunately, she left no ink-covered sheets of paper declaring her feelings. Moving slowly and thoughtfully through the facts, however, we can glean a great deal. She took a series of steps that are in and of themselves significant: she said she loved John Rolfe, and she later accepted Christian baptism and married him. But what were her *motivations* for taking these actions? In such a case, motivations are critical for understanding meaning. Anthropologists offer the clearest insights, providing a cultural context that helps to explain the decisions made by the young Powhatan woman.[21]

It is now increasingly obvious what *wasn't* a motivation. It was once commonplace to assert that the Indian girl had adored white men, English culture, and the Christian God. She turned away from her supposedly violent, backward, and narrow-minded people, hoping to become a bridge of peace as she herself embraced a better way of life and helped Jamestown to flourish. Just as she had once placed John Smith's needs above her own safety and her family's harmony, she later desperately hoped to please John Rolfe and accepted all that he had to teach.

This view of events sheds more light on the people who advanced and embraced it than it does on Pocahontas. Most powerful people, like other humans, see their own point of view as being the most reasonable, and if they pressure others to bend to their will, it is often important to them to believe that those being forced to bend do so, if not willingly, at least for their own betterment. Very few people wish to envision themselves as hurting others. It is therefore not at all surprising that the symbolic if not literal descendants of the English colonists have liked to imagine that Pocahontas was delighted, even entranced, by the settlers. They have preferred to ignore that she was undoubtedly pained and angered by the colonists' behavior, at least some of the time. Looking back objectively, however, it is impossible to believe that Pocahontas had no independent agendas and desires of her own and that she worshipped unquestioningly the white male figures of our legends. Such a view demeans and objectifies her, in that it deprives her of the full range of human feelings and reactions.[22]

Unfortunately, the recent corrective to this misrepresentation has often failed to grant Pocahontas any real control over her own behavior. In the politically sensitive 1970s and 1980s it became popular in some quarters to focus almost exclusively on the fact that she was a prisoner and a hostage. The conclusion was that, rather than running forward to accept all that white culture had to offer, she had been forced—virtually at gunpoint—to convert to Christianity and marry a white man. But while Pocahontas had been a hostage for over a year when she married John Rolfe, she clearly retained some control over what happened to her. Certain facts make this evident. First, after two of her brothers later spoke to her alone, her father decided to send three male relatives to her marriage ceremony. He would not have done so if she were being forced to wed. Second, John Rolfe gives no evidence of having been that rare, brutal kind of man who would want to force a woman who disliked him into marriage. He might well have had sexual fantasies about such a woman. But unless a transfer of wealth is involved, the unexceptional man does not promise to spend his life with a woman who says from the outset that she has no interest in him—especially when the rest of the man's social world has little or no respect for the woman. And finally, after the marriage, Pocahontas appeared so happy that the Virginia Company officials wanted to bring her to London to show her off: advertisers do not want models who are working at gunpoint, who feel violated and demonstrate no interest in what they are purportedly promoting. It is clear that Pocahontas was doing, at least to some extent, what she wanted to do.

Why? Why would an Algonkian noblewoman who had lived happily among her people want to throw over what she knew and cross into another world? For starters, she was keenly intelligent and had been living with the English long enough to have begun to grasp the resources they had at their disposal. If her people were to survive, they needed the English as allies, not as enemies. How did an Algonkian noblewoman build an alliance? In a time-honored custom, she married with the enemy and bore children who owed allegiance to both sides. Later in her imprisonment Pocahontas's father sent a message that she should remain with the English as part of Thomas Dale's family; he quickly and easily gave his approval that she should marry Rolfe. Clearly father and daughter were thinking alike.

In a changed world, one proactive strategy could be intermarriage not just with other tribes but also with Europeans. It did not have to be a sign of self-effacement or of dismissal of one's own people; rather, it could indicate the Indians' age-old desire to incorporate strangers into the political family: "Through her, the English and the Powhatans became fictive kin, and the ceremonial, political and economic basis for peace, as the people of Tsenacommacah understood that concept, became possible."[23]

It is illuminating to look at the situation from Pocahontas's particular angle. At home she was not truly royal: her mother had been no one important, so no chiefly line was vested in her person. Normally she would not have been considered eligible for a politically significant match—unlike the younger sister she had helped to raise, for example. These English people, though, thought she was a princess and were willing to treat her accordingly, thus raising her status in her own people's eyes as well. She may have felt a bit triumphant, particularly under her current circumstances. In her world, a female prisoner of war often had some hope of being ransomed, but her father had not met the English demands. We will never know what she felt about that fact, but Thomas Dale claimed she was out of countenance because her father seemed to "value her less than olde swords, peeces, or axes," and that she said she would therefore "dwell with the English men, who loved her."[24]

What Pocahontas's feelings were for Rolfe is an open question, but it is clear that she was fond of him at the very least. Any Algonkian woman who was a prisoner of war hoped to become a wife rather than remaining a servant, and if she was sensible, she hoped to catch the eye of someone who was a good hunter, a strong warrior, a respected figure in the community. It is not difficult to see why, in this context, Pocahontas preferred John Rolfe. He was a well-dressed gentleman, a favorite of Dale's and of Whitaker's; he read from their ceremonial tome, and servants listened to him. He loved her and was willing to defend his love for her before a hostile community. She let her preference show: Rolfe believed she loved him back.

She probably truly found him interesting. She had been culturally encouraged as a child to pay attention to her dreams, to seek out what her own name or names should be. We have every reason to believe that she saw marrying John Rolfe as a way of keeping her own nature alive and well. Every documented action that she took indicates a curious mind. "Like Smith, she was an explorer," writes one author.[25] She may possibly have found certain elements of English culture fascinating; what is certain is that she wanted to know more about other people. If Reverend Whitaker's ardent nature did

oppress her—and that is definitely possible—then John Rolfe offered a way of exploring the strange new world on terms more to her
liking.[26]

Her feelings, whatever they were, should not be dismissed or
taken for granted. They were undoubtedly complicated. Rolfe ea-
gerly promised her many things. The patterns of English courtship
implied an appealing egalitarianism between two souls standing before God; she could have had no way of knowing that English marriages were generally very different from the period of courtship. If
Pocahontas, like John Rolfe, was in part simply lonely and seeking to
find a way out of a present predicament, that fact did not make her
affection for him any less real than his was for her, or in any way in-
validate their feelings. Deep love can be born in just such circumstances. Pocahontas may have loved John Rolfe. If so, it was not
because she was dazzled by his English ways but rather because she
wanted to, because he answered her needs as they were then. She
alone knew what she saw in him.

It is perhaps as well that Pocahontas seems to have experienced at
least some moments of joy and empowerment in her relationship
with John, for there were to be stretches of agony as well. Their two
peoples, after all, were still at war, and Powhatan had not given a sat-
isfactory answer to the English demands concerning his daughter.
Spring was around the corner, and Rolfe had not yet spoken to the
colony's leaders, however often he opened his heart to Whitaker.
Captain Argall and his deadly ship had spent the cold months
searching for and destroying the fledgling French colony in modern-
day Maine.[27] But in March 1614, when Pocahontas had been with the
English nearly a year, Governor Gates departed, and Sir Thomas
Dale, the former marshal, succeeded to his position. Argall immediately put the *Treasurer* at Dale's disposal for war against the Indians.

The governor put 150 men onboard the frigate, loaded up the
other, smaller boats present in the port as well, and prepared to move
against Powhatan. Pocahontas once more was forced to board the

ship that had stolen her from her people; she was to be used in a battle against her father and her kin, threatened with death if they
would not comply with the colonists' demands. The English traveled
up the York River toward Werowocomoco to insist, once again, on
receiving tribute in corn and their lost weapons.

The Indians on the riverbanks extended little goodwill toward
the expedition. One Englishman later remembered:

> A great bravado all the way as we went up the River they made,
> demaunding the cause of our coming thither, which we tould
> them was to deliver Pocahuntas, whom purposely we brought
> with us, and to receive our Armes, men and corn, or else to fight
> with them, burne their howses, take away their Canoas, breake
> down their fishing Weares, and doe them what other damages we
> could. Some of them to set a good face on the matter, replied,
> that if we came to fight with them we were welcome.[28]

The English earned the enmity. At one point they went ashore and
sacked a village as Pocahontas watched. They burned about forty
houses, took the goods they found, and killed five or six men. This
was the first time she had seen the English attack; coming from the
heartland of her father's chieftainship, it was probably the first time
she had seen any warfare at all.

They went farther upriver to Werowocomoco, where the king
had once lived. There they demanded to speak with Powhatan. The
Indians said he was over a day away, but they could send a message.
They waited for a while, but negotiations stalled, and there was some
skirmishing. The English sailed farther upriver, to the village of
Matchcot (elsewhere called Manskunt), which they understood was
closer to where the king was. Here many of the English went ashore
en masse, taking Pocahontas with them. Dale later wrote that she insisted on speaking with none but nobles; Ralph Hamor said she
spoke only to her two brothers who came to see her.

She must have told her brothers of the possibility of her marrying John Rolfe, for they suddenly proposed that they remain on the ship as hostages, while John Rolfe and young Rob Sparkes—the same one whom Argall had left for a while with the Patowomecks and who thus knew something of the language—went to speak with the king. At about this point in the negotiations, Hamor gave Dale the long letter that Rolfe had put so much time into, declaring his love for Pocahontas and asking permission to marry her. Rolfe put his fate in Dale's hands and deferentially reminded him that the marriage would be for the good of the colony as well as the glory of God: "To your gratious providence I humbly submytt my selfe." Dale assented.[29]

Pocahontas would have watched as John Rolfe and Rob Sparkes followed their guides into the woods. Surely she would have told them what to say. They were taken to see not Powhatan but rather Opechankeno. On Powhatan's behalf, he gave permission for Pocahontas to remain with the English, as part of Dale's family ("his child," symbolically speaking). He declared that of the two remaining English prisoners, one had run away, and the other was dead. He promised that Powhatan would collect all the English weapons his people had in their possession within fifteen days and send them to Jamestown with a load of corn. When the much-looked-for messengers returned with this news, Dale pronounced himself satisfied, and the English withdrew to their vessels. Pocahontas said good-bye to her brothers and sailed away with her soon-to-be-husband's people. The war was over. It had been an extraordinary week.

SEVEN

Pocahontas and John

And they said, Wee will call the Damsell, and enquire at her mouth.
And they called Rebekah, and said unto her, Wilt though go with this
man? And she said, I will goe ... And they blessed Rebekah, and
said unto her, Thou art our sister, bee thou the mother of thousands of
millions, and let thy seed possesse the gate of those which hate them.
—King James Bible, Genesis 24:57, 60

The dizzying pace of events in Pocahontas's life did not abate. In the first week of April 1614 she publicly declared herself a Christian, accepted baptism with the new name Rebecca, and married John Rolfe. It is significant that Pocahontas did not make any public declaration as to religious principles until after she was sure she had the political agreement she sought well in order: when she converted, she was probably living up to her implied part of the treaty, or at least doing her best to make the agreement a lasting one. At the very least, it is notable that after living in the household of a zealous minister for over a year, with baptism always a possibility, she chose a particularly important moment to make a public conversion.[1]

Whitaker, Dale, and others all avowed that Pocahontas publicly renounced her country's idolatry, confessed the faith of Jesus Christ, and was baptized, at her desire. The language they used in referring to the events suggests that Whitaker stuck closely to the ceremony prescribed in the Book of Common Prayer, as might be expected: "Dost thou forsake the devil and all his works, the vain pomp, and glory of the world, with all covetous desires of the same, the carnal desires of the flesh, so that thou will not follow, nor be led by them?" And Pocahontas would have given the prescribed answer: "I forsake them all." "Dost thou believe in God the Father Almighty, maker of heaven and earth? And in Jesus Christ his only begotten Son our Lord, and that he was conceived by the Holy Ghost, born of the Virgin Mary . . . ?" And she would have responded, "All this I steadfastly believe." "Wilt thou be baptized in this faith?" pressed the minister. "That is my desire."[2]

Whitaker, of course, thought this was his moment—though in public he deferentially gave credit to Dale, who thought it was his. They both thought they knew all that was passing in Pocahontas's mind. But they didn't. Pocahontas left no secret diaries, but numerous other converted Indians throughout the hemisphere wrote or spoke of their experiences, and many pastors who came to know them better than Whitaker ever did analyzed the situation thoroughly. These other texts tell us that Indians who converted in the first months of contact were virtually always incorporating the Christian God into their previously existing pantheon. Even the story of a god's spirit impregnating an unsuspecting woman was an old one in many of their cultures. Pocahontas almost certainly was agreeing to set aside her village's okee in favor of Jesus Christ; she would have had to do something similar if she had been carried off by Iroquoian Indians or any other enemy. But nothing she said that day is proof that she was in fact renouncing all that she had previously known and loved, or that her own personality had been obliterated. In her conversion and in her married life she continued to assert herself.[3]

The baptismal name Rebecca was almost certainly Whitaker's choice. They would have read her the relevant passages from the Old Testament, or pointed them out to her if she was already reading for herself. When Abraham was old, he told his servant to go and seek a wife for his son Isaac from the lands where he had been born. The servant waited outside the walls of a city by a well. Rebekah came: "And she said, Drinke, my lord: and she hasted, and let downe her pitcher . . . and gave him drinke." [4] Her generosity was such that the visitor asked her parents if she might come with him to the land of Canaan and marry his master. And she was willing to go.

Whitaker probably had another metaphor in mind as well, however, involving the question of the future. By Isaac, Rebekah conceived twins: "And the children struggled together within her, and she said, 'If it be so, why am I thus?' And she went to enquire of the Lord." He answered:

Two nations are in thy womb,
And two manner of people shall be separated from thy bowels;
And the one people shall be stronger than the other people;
And the elder shall serve the younger.[5]

In due course, the twins were born. "And the first came out red"; they called him Esau. "And after that came his brother out, and his hand tooke holde on Esau's heele; and his name was called Jacob." Rebekah favored the pale son over the red one and, when they were grown, helped him to trick his father into giving him the blessing and birthright of the eldest son. It is more than likely that Whitaker thought the parallel perfect. Pocahontas's children would be by nature both Indian and Christian, both red and pale. But if she was like the Rebekah of the Bible, she would devote herself to a next generation whom she envisioned as the heirs of Jacob, who were younger in this land than their red brethren.

If Whitaker read the story this way, however, Pocahontas likely did not. She could easily have focused her attention on the passages narrated from the perspective of Rebekah's people, in which the great decision is left to the young woman herself, and her siblings bless her for being willing to go and bear children among the enemy. It was, they knew, a means to end that enmity. The parallels with her own people's worldview were striking.

She who grew up listening to stories may also have focused her attention on the almost lyrical beauty of the narrative itself. Rebekah played a starring role in a great drama. At her desire, she and her servants traveled to the land of Canaan: "And Isaac went out to meditate in the field, at the eventide: and hee lifted up his eyes, and saw, and, behold, the camels were coming. And Rebekah lifted up her eyes, and when she saw Isaac, she lighted off the camel."[6]

Pocahontas became Rebecca. She would not have found the idea of a renaming traumatic: it was in keeping with her culture for her to change her name as she proceeded through her life and had new experiences. Men, in fact, said that they aspired to earning many names, and women may well have, too.[7]

This woman certainly did not accept the proceedings mutely: she told the English for the first time that day that her name was not really Pocahontas but rather Matoaka, which may have meant "One Who Is Kindled" or "One Who Kindles."[8] Apparently, her English audience was stunned and asked why she had never mentioned this fact before. Samuel Purchas later recorded her answer secondhand, apparently having gotten the story from Rolfe: "Her true name was Matokes [sic], which they [i.e., the Indians] concealed from the English, in a superstitious fear of hurt by the English."[9]

It has become commonplace to assert that Matoaka must have been Pocahontas's secret name, but no other colonists who described Powhatan naming practices ever mentioned the existence of private names. The Powhatans may have had them—other Native Americans certainly did—but this incident seems rather to indicate that Matoaka was simply the name that the person once called Pocahontas (Little Mischief) went by as an adult, probably since her marriage to Kocoom. She didn't say that no one else had ever known the name, just that she had not felt like sharing it with her English captors. Purchas labeled her reserve "superstitious." It was more likely to have been a subtle form of defiance. If Matoaka was truly her secret name, in the same way that other Native Americans had secret names, she would have been unlikely to reveal it to anyone under any circumstances and certainly would not have selected it to be used in an advertising brochure for the Virginia Company, as she later did.[10]

On April 5 Pocahontas married John. She stood before the pastor in fine clothes made of fabric brought from England and responded to the words in English. John promised only to love, honor, and keep her; she also promised to obey and serve. "Wilt thou have this man to thy wedded husband, to live together after God's ordinance in the holy estate of matrimony?" the pastor asked. "Wilt thou obey him and serve him, love, honor and keep him, in sickness, and in health? And forsaking all other, keep thee only unto him, so long as you both shall live?" She answered, as had been rehearsed, "I will."

Then the minister asked, "Who giveth this woman to be married unto this man?" Opachisco, "an old uncle of hers," was there as a senior male in her family—to represent her father, according to her people's custom, and to give her away, as the English saw it. Two of her brothers stood with him as well; the other guests were all English.[11]

IN THE DAYS THAT FOLLOWED, the couple set up housekeeping on John's property. He had land granted to him from the Virginia Company on Hog Island, directly across the river from Jamestown. (It had, not so long ago, belonged to the Quioccohannock.) Later he would gain more land on Mulberry Island, a peninsula downriver from Jamestown.[12] Previously, as a widower, Rolfe had probably lived in someone else's household in Henrico, while he conducted some agricultural experiments in the fenced-in lands. Now, married again, he could have a household of his own, and with Pocahontas as his wife, he no longer had to work within territory barricaded against Indians.

His agricultural experiments, in fact, were what made him enough of a player in Jamestown to hobnob regularly with men like Whitaker and Dale and thus come to know Pocahontas so intimately. By 1611 he had somehow obtained tobacco seeds of the species grown in the Spanish Caribbean, and he had recently sent the first tobacco shipment to London. In short, he was turning the financial situation of the colony around.

European merchants had seen a wild demand for Spanish tobacco grow in the sixteenth century. Nowhere, however, was the smokable New World plant more popular than in England; this was problematic, as the English had to purchase all that they consumed from their archrivals. The Powhatan Indians grew tobacco for smoking as well, and Thomas Harriot had mentioned the plant as a possible commodity as early as the 1580s. (He was an avid smoker and later died of a disease that was probably cancer of the throat.) The species that was native to Virginia, however, was very different from the one that so appealed to Old World consumers. Early on William Strachey, Ralph Hamor, John Rolfe—and probably others—attempted to smoke it, gagged, and quickly came to understand why the Indians used their variety largely for ceremonial purposes. They would need to try growing the Spanish variety.[13]

Whether Rolfe arrived in Virginia with the precious seeds in his pocket—bought in London for a hefty price and preserved through shipwreck and travel—or whether he somehow obtained them from one of the sailors who came and went from Jamestown in the early years, he never let on. He placed them carefully in the Virginia ground.

They sprouted and survived, and by 1612 he had his first small crop. In 1616 he would write, "The esteemed weed . . . thriveth there [in Virginia] so well that no doubt but after a little more triall and expense in the curing theeof, it will compare with the best in the West Indies." In 1617 the company exported twenty thousand pounds of "the esteemed weed," and in 1618, forty thousand pounds. The Spanish monopoly was broken. The plant was to make the English colony's fortune.[14]

The most important of Rolfe's "trialls" or experiments concerned "curing" or drying the plant. To dry the crop, the colonists gradually shifted from piling up the leaves, covering them with dried grass, and then letting them sit in the sun, to the much more time-consuming—but more effective—method of carefully hanging each leaf on a rack—just as the Indians did with theirs. It has been suggested that Pocahontas may have pointed out the technique to John Rolfe.[15] Certainly she would have been helpful to him in the cultivation of the product, for the Caribbean and Virginian species, though somewhat different, shared certain traits. She could have told him, for example, that the plant would do best in a recently burned woodland field, with a southern or southwestern exposure, on land sloping down toward a creek or river. And that he would do well to pile up dirt around the base of each stalk, and to remove the seed head at the top so that all nourishment would go to the leaves. In fact, Pocahontas would have considered it within her purview to do such agricultural work herself.

Whether Rebecca told her husband what she knew or not, she was there on the plantation with him, working every day to maintain an English-style household. Within a few months of marriage, she began to experience her own version of the trials and joys of pregnancy. If anyone wondered whether she carried the biblical twins, they soon found that she did not. She gave birth to a son. To what must have been the relief of John, given his last experience in the matter, both mother and child seemed to thrive. They named the baby boy Thomas, almost certainly after the governor, Sir Thomas Dale, who had permitted them to marry and was essentially their patron.

The Rolfes clearly had people in the household working for them. John was made secretary of the colony shortly after his marriage, a position that entailed a salary and special privileges.[16] No man of John's social rank would have expected that his wife could do all the water-hauling, wood-carrying, fire-tending, soap- and candlemaking, laundering, ironing, cooking, cleaning, sewing, darning, and gardening necessary to maintain a household fit for a governor and pastor to visit. In addition, there was more agricultural work to do than they could accomplish alone.

A number of the people who worked for them must have been Indians. Eight years later, when there were far more immigrants available and John was financially better off, he had only three white indentured servants laboring with him in the fields, and they were recent acquisitions.[17] Within the house itself, it is difficult to imagine the roughly seventeen-year-old Mistress Rebecca, who was still learning English, supervising an entirely white workforce, especially since only a handful of white women were present in the colony. As Pocahontas later took numerous Indian companions with her to London, who were acculturated enough to wear English clothes and function on a basic level in the language, it seems certain that some of these were with her at her home in Virginia. They probably were the ones who aided her in her childbirth, using the more sanitary and helpful Indian techniques; they would have spent the days chatting away with her in their own language whenever John was not present.

Rebecca may even have suggested the possibility of bringing one of her sisters to Jamestown to marry another colonist, to further cement the peace. Someone, at any rate, told the colony's leaders about Powhatan's favorite daughter—the one who had been born about six years after Pocahontas. In May 1614, Ralph Hamor, speaking through the interpreter Thomas Savage, made the proposal to Powhatan, first noting that Pocahontas was well and happy and hoping to have her sister near her. Hamor may have been speaking without any authority from Pocahontas, however, for what he asked, very specifically, was that the girl be given as a "wife and bedfellow" to Governor Dale. And Dale had a wife in England, as Pocahontas would have known. Hamor might not have expected the polygamous Indian chief to be surprised by the request, but Pocahontas, knowing what she knew about English culture, would not have backed any such offer. Of course, Pocahontas might have spoken of her sister as a "child" for Dale, politically speaking, just as her father had once termed her, and the Englishman might have found it amusing to put the request another way. If Hamor was making a sexual joke with his readers at the expense of the supposedly naïve Indians, he did not have the last laugh.

Powhatan refused him in no uncertain terms, not even waiting to let him finish speaking. He said he could not possibly part with another daughter, and that she was betrothed to a great chief anyway. Then, when the two were negotiating for the freedom of one more English captive and Powhatan was listing the metal tools he wanted in exchange for him, the chief turned suddenly and insisted that Hamor use his beloved alphabet to write it all down, lest he forget anything.[18]

In that same interlude, Powhatan reiterated his threat to take his people deeper into the woods and out of reach of the English if they demanded too much. But he said he himself wanted the peace to last. And indeed, it seemed that it would. Not only had the war stopped, but some Indians were being taught to shoot by the now-confident English. The populous Chickahominy nation, which had always managed to remain independent of both Powhatan and the English—engaging in hostilities with either or both—took the situation seriously. Perceiving Powhatan and the English to have become friends, they suddenly sued for peace themselves, accepting a treaty in which they agreed to pay the English a yearly tribute in corn of two bushels per adult male.[19]

The colony began to thrive. For a time, at least, the settlers tried not to trespass on the lands of the Indians or demand too much from them, as they, too, wanted the peace to last. Laws guaranteed that the settlers planted not only tobacco but also corn and other food. Cows, oxen, goats, hogs, and chickens multiplied steadily. When Rolfe wrote of Jamestown in this period, he alluded to Eden: "The great Blessinges of God have followed this Peace; and it . . . hath bredd our plenty: every man sitting under his figtree in safety, gathering and reaping the fruites of their labors with much joy and comfort."[20]

Rolfe, for one, was content. He reflected that he had been through many trials, but that it had all turned out to be worth it. God had rewarded him. The faithful, he said, "daily attend and marke how those blessings (though sometimes restrained for a tyme) in the end are powred upon the servauntes of the Lord at his due pleasure."[21]

In these happy days Rolfe was living with Indians. He and Pocahontas often talked: later, in London, he gave the scholar Samuel Purchas several correctives to his information on Powhatan religion, offering perspectives that could have come only from someone who really knew. Rolfe's writings even give evidence of there having been some arguments in his household: "They [that is, Indians he had known] doe runn headlong, yea with joy, into distruccion and per-petuall damnation." He told Purchas with some irritation that Indians often contradicted one another on the subject of religion, "either not knowing, or not willing that others should know, their devilish mysteries."[22]

On some points John apparently accepted Pocahontas's arguments, for in a public report he said what no other settler would say at the time: "The Indians hold a just and lawful title [to their lands]." If the lands were "purchased of them" in a lawful manner, they would be willing to sell, and there would be no need for brutalities. But then, a few pages later, his other way of thinking triumphed, and he asserted that the English were "chosen by the finger of God" to possess Virginia. "Undoubtedly He is with us."[23]

In his dealings with Pocahontas and her companions, Rolfe seems to have fallen back on a brand of condescending tolerance that got him through the difficult times when they chose to ignore his teachings. He reiterated that all people were ultimately one: "[The Indians] bear the Image of our heavenly Creator, & wee and they come from one and the same moulde." If they were stubborn sometimes, it was because they were "nursed and trained from their infancies" in their old beliefs.[24]

It is impossible to know exactly what Pocahontas thought. Rolfe's writings prove, however, that she was not a blank slate upon which he could write: clearly she was not always doing just as he wished. His soul-exploring tendencies likely were difficult for a woman from an Algonkian village to accept: in her world, people survived in such close quarters because of their ability to respect each other's privacy on the deepest levels. His belief that sexual relations were potentially fraught with evil would certainly have been mystifying to her. His conviction that he was always right, and that he needed to be patient with her errors, could only have been galling. He was obviously happy; it is unlikely that he was living with a miserable partner. "She lives . . . lovingly with him," wrote Dale. She probably knew joy, too. But in a thousand ways, she must have found Rolfe's thoughts as alienating as he sometimes found hers.[25]

The days passed. Pocahontas lived and labored on her Virginia plantation for two years—bearing and raising her son, working with her Indian companions, learning English ways. There were happy weeks and bleak ones. The winter of 1615 was bitter cold, worse than any she could remember.[26] At some point in that period, John came home one day with a question: the Virginia Company's leaders wanted to know if she would like to go to London. Would she cross the sea?

EIGHT

In London Town

Picklock: *A tavern's as too unfit for a princess.*
Pennyboy Canter: *No, I have known a princess, and a great one,*
   come forth of a tavern.
Picklock: *Not go in, sir, though.*
Pennyboy Canter: *She must go in, if she came forth: the blessed*
   Pokahontas, as the historian calls her, and great king's daughter
   of Virginia, hath been in womb of a tavern.
      —Ben Jonson, *The Staple of News* (1626)

On the voyage over, beneath the all-encompassing sky, they hanged a man named Francis Lymbry from the yardarm. The body continued to twitch for some moments. They left him hanging for a while, to be sure that he was dead. Then they cut down the corpse, laboriously slid it into a sack, and threw it overboard. Pocahontas may have watched. If she turned away her face, the close quarters of the ship still ensured that she experienced the execution's intended impact. Sir Thomas Dale was on board, heading back to England after five years as marshal and sometime governor of the colony. Many a man had already complained—and would continue to complain—of his draconian laws. But Pocahontas had previously been somewhat sheltered from his policies, living as she did in the homes of Whitaker and Rolfe, two favorites of the evangelical marshal.

It was April 1616. They were sailing with Captain Argall on the *Treasurer*, of which Argall was now a proud part-owner. The ship, though it had been familiar to Pocahontas since that fateful spring day in 1613, was more crowded and uncomfortable than it had been the first time she traveled in it. There were about one hundred people on board. Besides the crew and Dale and some other English passengers, there were Pocahontas; John Rolfe; their young son, Thomas; an adviser and son-in-law to Powhatan named Uttamatomakin; and at least six native attendants. Of these, some were nobles and some servants, one of whom was to act as Uttamatomakin's interpreter. There had also been, at the start, two Spanish prisoners who had been held as spies since 1611. One of them, Diego de Molina, had sent his scathing report about the colony to his monarch in an Italian sailor's shoe. The other, called Francisco Lembri, was whispered to be in truth a renegade Irishman who had been working for the Spanish, his real name Francis Lymbry. Something happened on shipboard that convinced Dale of it. He summarily tried the man and ordered him hanged.[1]

Nothing in their river-based experience had prepared Pocahontas and her party for life on that boat. Uttamatomakin acknowledged the disorientation he experienced when he realized that they would not stop at night, that all the many coasts he had heard of had been left far behind.[2] It is a rare person who does not experience extreme seasickness for the first several days of travel on the open ocean. There is no respite from it. One-year-old Thomas would have fared no better than the adults, and there would have been almost no one equipped to tend to the sick child. The ship offered no private place to hide one's suffering. Argall undoubtedly shared his captain's quarters with Dale, or simply gave them over to him. Pocahontas and her women may have slept in the gunner's room, a dry place where the ammunition was stored. The others slept where they might, on deck in drizzling rain or in cramped, fetid storage areas where insects swarmed in the dark. By the end of the seven weeks that their voyage took, it was to be expected that the dried food would be infested, and the drinking water dangerously low.[3]

Why had the Indians come? The Virginia Company was prepared to make only a limited contribution toward the Rolfe family's travels, so the presence of so many created a financial problem. Someone must have insisted. That there were ten or twelve Indians along, including not only Pocahontas and some servants but also some female relatives of comparable rank and an adviser to the paramount chief, certainly proves that this was not the honeymoon of a giddy girl eager to visit London. This was a fact-finding mission more than a pleasure trip. Powhatan had already complained of not learning enough from the first Indian sent to observe England: "Namontacke . . . I purposely sent to King James his land, to see him and his country, and to returne me the true report thereof, he as yet is not returned, though many ships have arrived here from thence." The English reporter of his speech had the story partly garbled, for Namontack had of course returned and been part of negotiations for a brief period. But he had since been killed, and Powhatan did not yet know that.[4] Powhatan knew he needed more information—and perhaps not the kind that one could get from a returned captive. With Pocahontas's marriage, he had the opportunity to send a veritable delegation, people who would be accorded respect and be allowed to ask questions. Later, Londoners were given to understand that the Indians were indeed there to gather information.[5]

The passengers, whatever language they spoke, would have sensed the crew's excitement as they drew near to England. The coast of Cornwall showed itself first, and then Argall guided the vessel into the

Channel and straight to Plymouth. Pocahontas would have watched from the deck as they pulled into the port, taking in the city's dirty drabness—and its extraordinary size and bustle. It would not have taken many moments for the discrepancy between her people's position and that of the English to hit her full force. She must have spent the rest of the trip thinking, on some level, of how to warn her father. Even with all his experience and insight, he had had no idea of what he was up against. Now she knew. Uttamatomakin did, too. They all did.

The crew lowered the sails and anchored as quickly as possible. Some of the passengers were rowed to the docks. They went into the town and bought food and drink. Dale hired an express messenger to take a letter to the Virginia Company in London: "I shall with the greatest speed the wind will suffer me present myself unto you."[6] He was home, he thought. Home, thought Rolfe as well. Perhaps after seven years it was a strange feeling for him, as he now envisioned spending his old age elsewhere. Pocahontas's thoughts must surely have turned to her own home, whose future she read in this teeming port. They waited on the ship for as many days as it took for the wind to be right to carry them through the channel. When it was, they left immediately, skirting the southern coast of England, passing through the Strait of Dover, sailing around Kent, entering the mouth of the Thames, and continuing on up to London as the tide rose.

In the port, John Rolfe and his household hired carriages to take them to their hotel. The streets they passed through were home to over 200,000 people, more than almost any other European city held at that time. A century earlier the Aztec capital had been larger—and infinitely cleaner—but Pocahontas, knowing nothing of the Aztecs unless she had heard stories from Don Luis, could take no comfort from the comparison. She could never before even have imagined so many people. London had not yet passed the threshold to modernity in the way that great cities on the European continent had. Here were no wide avenues lined by monumental buildings. Instead, Pocahontas saw a warren of one- and two-story buildings made mostly of wood, the streets generally of mud. London Bridge was covered with so thick a growth of shops and awnings that, looking out of a carriage window, she might not even have realized she was on a bridge. But the lack of marble fountains and splendid views would not have diminished the city's most salient trait: throbbing trading and movement. These ships, cannons, buildings, roads, bridges, horses, vehicles, construction projects, trade goods, and hurrying people were enough. They added up to power.[7]

The carriages stopped before the Bell Savage Inn. Servants appeared to unload the boxes and bags—and, most probably, to stare at the Indians. The inn's name was a trick of history: the choice of lodging probably was not even made as a joke by a member of the Virginia Company. The Bell Savage was simply a very well known hotel—and this was, after all, a publicity tour. The inn took its name from the Savage family that ran it. *Bell* probably stemmed from *bail*, meaning "boundary," for the hotel stood off of Fleet Street, just outside the archway in the old city wall called Ludgate. Recently a well-known Scottish showman had stayed there, then with much fanfare taken a silver-shod horse up the steps of St. Paul's. Strolling players performed at Savage's with some frequency. Near the time of Pocahontas's stay, Christopher Marlowe's *The Tragical History of Dr. Faustus* played there. One commentator had praised the Bell Savage as a place "where you shall never find a word without wit." It seemed the perfect place for the company to display the witty and beautiful Indian "princess."[8]

Sir Edwin Sandys, a member of Parliament and a rising star in the Virginia Company, took the Rolfes under his wing. He arranged for the company to pay the Lady Rebecca, as she was to be called, a stipend of four pounds a week to defray the cost of her stay in the expensive city. If the tour was to be a success, she would have to dress like a Jacobean grande dame and feed her attendants decently. Word had already spread that she was here: mention of "Pokahuntas" appeared in numerous diaries and letters within days of Thomas Dale's message from Plymouth arriving in London. The company, however, was not satisfied with that. The officials wanted everyone to hear of the Indian princess who promised friendship to the settlers.[9]

The Virginia Company's standing was precarious. Even as Sandys prepared the Lady Rebecca to meet London society, the company was involved in several lawsuits. It had sued various investors who had promised certain sums of money but then failed to deliver after reading some of the more dire reports coming back from Virginia. The organization's financial situation would remain shaky until the general public became convinced that Virginia was truly a land of promise. Naturally, tobacco shipments would be critical, but to raise a significant crop the company first needed to convince potential settlers and investors that the Indians were not bloodthirsty savages.[10]

At Sir Edwin's request, John Rolfe set about writing a report that contained the kind of data he needed. Rolfe directly addressed the colony's detractors: "'Tis true," he acknowledged, "Virginia is the same as it was." And that, he said, was wonderful. He gloried in the peace that now reigned; the only thing needful, he argued, was more labor, "good and sufficient men." Those who crossed the sea would be well rewarded, far more so than if they struggled on with their drudgery-filled lives in England.[11]

One wonders if John told Pocahontas, working in the other room, exactly what point he was engaged in making. She herself had set about the daunting task of ordering clothes for herself and her people. In London she would have to go beyond anything she had worn in Virginia, with canvases to hold out her skirts, sleeves so large they nearly immobilized her, and a wooden board placed along her stomach and the lower part of her breast to ensure a certain shape once she was dressed.

Most of the romantic paintings of Pocahontas testify to their creators' desire to envision her as adoring European culture in general and white men in particular, but an occasional artist has demonstrated quiet sympathy. *(E. Boyd Smith, 1860–1943, courtesy of the New York Public Library)*

The invitations began to come in. Samuel Purchas, an enthusiastic pastor and scholar who made it his business to meet every returning colonist he possibly could—and who was busy collecting testimonies from any and all—socialized with the party on several occasions. He was predisposed to find the lovely Pocahontas fascinating. Before she herself had even been captured, he had called Virginia a "virgin . . . not yet polluted with Spaniards' lust" and the colonists her "wooers and suiters" bent on making her "not a wanton minion, but an honest and Christian wife."[12] Pocahontas was, then, to be the personification of his vision.

But Purchas found reality more complicated. In his account of the social gatherings, he mentioned Uttamatomakin first, identifying him as the one who spoke publicly about Powhatan's kingdom: "With this Savage I have often conversed at my good friends Master Doctor Goldstone, where he was a frequent guest; and where I have both seen him sing and dance his diabolicall measures, and heard him discourse of his Countrey and Religion, Sir Tho. Dales [Indian] man being the Interpretour." Purchas quickly moved on to praise Pocahontas, offering her genuine tribute:

> [She] . . . did not onely accustome her selfe to civilitie, but still carried her selfe as the Daughter of a King, and was accordingly respected, not onely by the Company . . . but of divers particular persons of Honor, in their hopefull zeale by her to advance Christianitie. I was present, when my Honorable and Reverend Patron, the Lord Bishop of London, Doctor King, entertained her with festival state and pompe, beyonde what I have seene in his great hospitalities afforded to other Ladies.[13]

These gatherings were often within walking distance of the hotel. Samuel Purchas's church was just up Ludgate Hill, on the other side of the city wall that the inn lay outside of, and not far beyond that was the palace of John King, the bishop of London, who made so much of the Virginia princess as the first convert. This section of the city became the place to be in the evenings. One man indicated that the course of his life was changed by meeting with the Virginia Indians and participating in the heady conversation about converting the people of the New World that ensued within his social set.[14]

But despite—or perhaps because of—the welcoming whirl of social activity, Pocahontas wanted to move. She was tired and sick. She had no way of knowing that she was being attacked by thousands of foreign microbes, against which she had no built-up immunities. They blamed the smoky air instead. Chimney smoke was unlikely to have been the real problem, since she had lived in smoky Indian homes, but urban pollution more generally may have been an exacerbating factor. In London in 1616, great houses and the stinking alleys of the poor lay side by side. Nearby "Fleet Valley" had been famous for its noisome lanes for decades. Even industrial production was substantial enough to be problematic. Blue dye, for example, not yet made from Virginia indigo, was still produced by mixing the English plant woad with household urine and letting it ferment for nine weeks, creating an odor so vile that the usually rational Queen Elizabeth had once forbidden woad processing within a five-mile radius of her person.[15]

Rolfe found lodgings in Brentford, Middlesex, nine miles up the Thames, still a clean country suburb. The area was the ancestral home of the Percy family. George Percy, back in London now for several years, had known Pocahontas when she was a child; he may have been instrumental in making the transfer. Strolling the country lanes, Pocahontas improved in spirits. By that time little Thomas must have been walking and talking, mixing the Algonkian words of his caretakers with the English he heard everywhere. Or perhaps, like many young children in bilingual worlds, he trotted about quietly, listening to everything in relative silence longer than usual, then suddenly bursting into full sentences in either tongue. Pocahontas/ the Lady Rebecca watched him work it out for himself.

There may have been another reason for the need to retreat from the heart of London. Pocahontas may well have been exhausted by the mental strain of presenting the perfect "princess" facade, and at the same time swallowing the anger that necessarily results from being insulted and objectified as someone unreal. It would not have taken her long to realize that friend and foe alike held at least one notion in common: she was to them a model, a stick figure, representing a race that was either barbaric or charming, or both, depending on their perspective, but never simply human.

It would be too simple to say that she faced hatred. The British were fascinated by her, adored her exoticism. At first it probably seemed flattering. Only later would she have begun to experience the psychological costs of being a symbol rather than a person. All things Virginian were indeed the rage, as England struggled to become a colonial power, to dominate the mysterious world whence Pocahontas came. Shakespeare had written *The Tempest* within months of first reading the accounts of the wreck of the *Sea Venture*, which Rolfe had sailed on.[16] And in Shakespeare's *Henry VIII*, written in 1613, a man sarcastically asks for an explanation of a gathering mob: "Have we some Indian with the great tool come to court, the women so besiege us?" Londoners regularly came to gape whenever captive Indians, or even Indian artifacts, were displayed. The men's fashion in London of wearing one lock of hair long seemingly traced to the first group of colonists who had returned from Roanoke, and Uttamatomakin, who wore his hair that way, brought the "savage" fashion to life for London society. In George Chapman's masque of 1613, the marriage of King James's daughter was set in Virginia, and the royal family participated as dancers representing "Virginian princes." Now here was a genuine Virginia princess come to visit, a character from a play or a dance come to life.[17]

Pocahontas left no written record of how she felt, but we can at least dissect the treatment she received at one particular event: the annual Twelfth Night masque at the Court of King James, at the end of the Christmas season, which she was invited to attend. She had been to Court before, having had a formal audience with the king. She would have curtsied before him, as she had been taught, then raised her eyes to exchange the necessary pleasantries, at which she apparently excelled. She may also have seen the queen. John Smith later claimed to have written to Queen Anne the moment he heard that Pocahontas had landed in Plymouth, but it is likely that someone more highly placed, like Sir Edwin Sandys, actually got the message through to the royal couple that they should treat the young woman well. Those who had actually been in Virginia knew that Pocahontas's father held real power, and they did not want to risk alienating her in the process of using her to improve the company's prospects: "If she should not be well received, seeing this Kingdome may rightly have a Kingdome by her meanes; her present love to us and Christianitie, might turne to such scorne and furie, as to divert all this good to the worst of evill."[18] Besides, if she was well received by royalty and nobility, it would only add to her fame and thus enhance the company's future. It should come as no surprise, then, that Pocahontas and her party—which included not only John Rolfe but also Uttamatomakin—were considered to have been extremely well placed at the Twelfth Night masque. That is, their seats were prominent, visible, and near to King James.[19]

In no way, however, was Pocahontas the ceremonial or political focus. When Christian of Denmark had visited on Twelfth Night ten years earlier, the masque had revolved around him. The Lady Rebecca, however, did not rate in the same way. In this case, the event was dedicated to the remarkably long-legged George Villiers, the king's latest lover, who the day before had been created Earl of Buckingham—the first person outside of a royal family to receive the title in more than four hundred years.[20]

Despite some puritanical critiques and percolating political tensions, the Jacobean court was one of extraordinary sumptuousness and self-congratulation. The black-and-white-clad Elizabethans, with their ruffs and laces and embroidered garments all made in England, were gone. In their place moved a cosmopolitan people dressed in foreign silks and satins and softly draping brightly colored wools, made up in the latest Continental fashions. Protestantism was still strong, but side by side with it grew merchants' pride in their own accomplishments. Industrial breakthroughs had helped: whereas once drab English wools had been considered by the moghuls of India to be fit only for their horses and elephants, now England's softer, bright-colored productions could be sold almost anywhere. The defeat of the Spanish Armada had also been key: as English naval power grew, so did that of her merchant marine. Asian cloths were brought back to London in quantity now; they were no longer available only from Muslim and Spanish middlemen. England was on the rise: her courtiers and her merchant class—which were well inter-mingled—knew it. If Pocahontas mattered at all to them, it was as a symbol of their own achievement.[21]

When the curtain rose that January evening in 1617, the audience saw before them a simple street scene, a drawing in perspective meant to create a sense of depth, as if the avenue led back toward a large, fair building in the rear.[22] Unlike Pocahontas and Uttamatomakin, most people in the audience knew more or less what to expect next. A masque was neither a play nor a dance but rather a spectacular show lasting as long as three hours. Dancers and musicians paraded and performed, some with lines to say or sing, all relying on extraordinary settings and costumes to create a magical effect. In the midst of the extravaganza would come at least one antimasque, in which the per-formers would be gaudily, vulgarly, or humorously attired and do their best to make the audience laugh. Ultimately, a masque was about the resolution of discord: in the end, the personifications of virtue always regained their precedence, and the beautiful and ele-gant masquers would descend to join their noble audience in revels, dancing the night away.

Under King James, it had become court custom to have the play-wright Ben Jonson write the annual Twelfth Night masque and the Italian architect Inigo Jones design spectacular scenic effects. In the past few years the two artists' joint efforts had been somewhat more muted than in earlier days, but the events still cost the state at least three thousand pounds. Even a scholar who loves the genre has ad-mitted, "The masque did embody self-congratulation within con-spicuous consumption on a massive scale."[23]

The Vision of Delight, as the performance of 1617 was called, may well have mystified those unfamiliar with the tradition. After the character Delight addressed the audience, a large model of a monster was pulled onto the stage, and out of her belly came six *burratines*, dancers from Italian comedy, who made their ridiculous pirouettes in a long performance. Eventually the star-spangled chariot of Night rose up over the stage, hanging from wires, the moon following. Night sang, "Break, Fantasy, from thy cave of cloud, and spread thy purple wings; now all thy figures are allowed, and various shapes of things." The backdrop changed to clouds—probably by virtue of scene-changing shutters that could be flipped up or down, perhaps with some smoke added for effect. Fantasy, having been freed, now gave vent to a long and vulgar monologue that would have had those "in the know" laughing uproariously: "And then it were an odd piece to see the conclusion peep forth at a codpiece." A second antimasque of "phantasms" followed. Fantasy finished, "Behold the gold-haired Hour descending here, that keeps the gate of heaven and turns the year, already with her sight how she doth cheer, and makes another face of things appear."

The scene changed again, to the bower of Zephyrus, the beautiful and gentle god of the west wind. As the masquers danced in the role of the glories of the spring, Wonder recited a poem that was an ode to the beauty of the earth and asked whose hand had made it all. "Whose power is this? What god?" And she was answered: "The herds, the flocks, the grass, the trees, Do all confess him, but most these who call him lord of the four seas, King of the less and greater isles, and all those happy when he smiles." There he sat, King James, lord not only of this land but of the four seas. They danced before him, until Aurora spoke to bid them all good-bye, throwing flowers in the paths of the dancers. All was well. At the end of the chaotic night, dawn had come with the glories of the new year, allowing all to worship a king of divine right, whose power extended here and across the ocean.

Ben Jonson's *Vision of Delight* has been called "an anatomy of the conventions of masques." For his intended audience, it answered every expectation.[24] It reconfirmed him as a great man in their minds. He was a court favorite; his collected works had just been published the preceding year. And the Lady Rebecca made an impression on him. He was, of course, a part of the London literary world that found the New World fascinating, and she was a pretty, exotic, and well-spoken young woman whom everyone was talking about. Nine years later, when the flurry was past, he still had not forgotten her. Pocahontas would reappear in *The Staple of News* as "a princess, and a great one, come forth of a tavern." But it would be naïve to interpret this as a simple tribute. It is safe to assume that in 1617 Jonson's interaction with the woman herself was laced with the possibility of mockery. Later in *The Staple* he gave away his attitude toward the princess in the tavern: he had, after all, only been trying to get people to laugh. And he was only partly sorry for any injustice he might have done her. In fact, he mentioned how sorry he was— only in order to make people laugh again. Toward the end a narrator says he should censure the playwright "for the princess' sake—Pokahontas, surnamed the Blessed—whom he has abused indeed, and I do censure him, and will censure him: To say she came forth of a tavern was said like a paltry poet."

Others at the masque were polite to the "well-placed" Lady Rebecca and "her father's counselor," as they called Uttamatomakin. These same courteous people were, however, quite ready to belittle them behind their backs. John Chamberlain, a genteel town gossip who had several friends at court, heard all about the "Virginia woman's" presence at the masque. At first he noted it only tersely in a letter to a friend abroad, adding, "She is on her return (though sore against her will) yf the wind wold come about to send them away." He wanted to believe that the departure was "sore against her will"; indeed, many have wanted to believe that Pocahontas was desperate to remain in London, a savage reveling in the metropolis, though only a single item of secondhand party gossip substantiates the claim. A month later Chamberlain let some uglier feelings show. He had seen an engraving of the "princess." "Here is . . . no fayre Lady," he wrote, "and yet with her tricking up and high stile and titles you might thincke her and her worshipfull husband to be somebody, yf you do not know that the poore companie of Virginia out of theyre povertie are faine to allow her fowre pound a week for her maintenance."[25]

That she was "no fayre Lady" certainly had racial overtones; the words "tricking up" demeaned her sexually. Interestingly, though, the real dart was aimed not at Pocahontas herself but at John Rolfe, who was from the same class as the letter-writer, yet present at the masque, sitting near the king, claiming to be married to royalty. Pocahontas was only caught in the crossfire: she herself did not really matter to London society, except insofar as she had any impact on their internal concerns.

It would be delightful to be able to eavesdrop on the comments undoubtedly passed between Uttamatomakin and Pocahontas under their breath, in their own language. While they left nothing as transparent as Chamberlain's letters, they are not entirely silent. Of the two, Uttamatomakin can be heard making the clearest statements. We know little about him, except that he was there on Powhatan's behalf and was married to Pocahontas's half sister, Matachanna. He also mentioned a connection to Opechankeno, cousin to the king and chief of the Pamunkey. That the delegate should have been Pamunkey makes sense, for that tribe, the most populous in the paramountcy, was central to the king's authority; at that point it even seemed likely that Opechankeno might inherit the kingship, rather than Powhatan's next-younger brother.[26]

Uttamatomakin held a position of spiritual as well as political authority, a typical arrangement in the Algonkian world. He said he was a priest, and his name indicates as much. The English could not decide if he was really "Uttamatomakin" or something like "Tomacomo" or "Tomakkin," as they had heard both. The second name is in fact embedded in the first. The prefix *uttama-* in other contexts indicated "spiritual" or "priestly": indeed, the kingdom's principal temple, located in Pamunkey territory, was called Uttamussack.[27] It is probable that the English simply had not realized that the two appellations were actually the same, the one including the man's priestly title, the other not.

The man who was an honored priest and adviser to two chiefs back home was not enjoying himself here in London. He told the English that when he had first been chosen to travel to their country, he had gone to pray, to speak to his okee in the temple. He had outlined the trip's agenda and its probable duration. But, he said, his god had corrected him, warning him that it would probably turn out to be longer than he thought. The god had been right, of course. Ships had already left that Uttamatomakin had hoped to be on. He lived here with a sense of disappointed frustration, desiring to be gone.[28]

Uttamatomakin irritated Samuel Purchas by refusing to accept the Christian god, expounding on the glories and wisdom of his own gods, and correcting English understandings of the latter. (That Pocahontas was also busy clarifying English misapprehensions is implied by John Rolfe's saying to Samuel Purchas that Alexander Whitaker had been wrong in much of what he said about Powhatan religion in his book, *Good News from Virginia.*) Uttamatomakin also scored more secular points. He said scathingly to John Smith and others that their ruler was not a true king, as he had been too mean and stingy to offer Uttamatomakin a gift to bring home. He had expected something far grander than the white dog that had been sent to Powhatan years ago.[29]

Those who talked to Uttamatomakin also claimed that he had been instructed by Powhatan to count the people he saw and keep a record on a notched stick. The story was probably apocryphal.[30] The English were constructing a condescending anecdote out of something that had a grain of truth in it. The Powhatan Indians did keep records on notched sticks, but their previous experiences would have been enough to convince them that you couldn't count ants that way. Powhatan no doubt told Uttamatomakin to estimate the population; Uttamatomakin may well have remarked that even making an estimate was going to be impossible. The great population was certainly one of the most glaring realities that he encountered very early on. He also mentioned his surprise at the existence of extensive English agriculture: it had apparently been a working hypothesis on Powhatan's part that the Europeans were trying to take over his country because they suffered from an extreme shortage of food. The English chose to see him as naïve; in fact, from the vantage point of someone daily more aware of the threat to his king and country, he spoke cogently and perceptively.

Pocahontas is more difficult to hear. Given her position, she was probably more circumspect than Uttamatomakin. And she was a woman, and so less likely to be taken seriously by the men who were chronicling events. We have only two traces of her self-presentation— a portrait that she sat for, and one impassioned statement that was heard by several men and recorded by one. The picture conveys a stately pride, the words a sense of anguish.

Late in 1616, Simon Van de Passe, a well-known Dutch-German engraver working in London, was commissioned to sketch her portrait for an engraving that would be used to make a piece of memorabilia that could be distributed. He was considered eminently suitable: his father had also been a noted artist, and he would do portraits of famous men—including John Smith and King James himself—before he left England. Two years ago an image of an Indian in St. James's Park had been used to advertise a fund-raising lottery for the Virginia Company; but this picture was to be entirely different. Here would be no animal skins or bows and arrows. This Indian was to be a great lady of the Jacobean court.[31]

Van de Passe was still very young, only about twenty-one years old. Some unusual choices that he made in doing the portrait indicate that he respected Pocahontas's wishes as to her representation. A sympathy may have existed between the artist and his sitter, who was after all very close to him in age. Beneath the portrait the artist wrote in Latin that she was twenty-one. In fact, she was almost certainly no more than nineteen, but the Virginia Company officials would have wanted to hide that, as they needed to present a convert who was a consenting adult in order to make their point effectively.[32]

On one hand, the engraving is full of symbols that are relatively easy to read: the woman who looks out at us from the past is wearing the most beautiful and costly of materials, layers opening to reveal more layers, and a lace ruff of the finest workmanship. Long, delicate fingers hold a fan of ostrich feathers, a symbol of royalty. This is a princess indeed. Unobtrusively appears a sign that she is from the New World and specifically Virginia: she wears pearl earrings. Virginia had been seen as a rich source of pearls from the beginning of the colonization project. These, indeed, are one element of the portrait that would have felt like "home" to Pocahontas.

Not everything about the portrait, however, is so predictable. Certain elements reveal distinct decisions that were made by Pocahontas and others involved in arranging for the sitting: she would adopt some elements of royalty, but not its frivolousness. The hat, for example, is in certain ways remarkable. The high capotain, once worn only by men, had recently been adopted by some women. Queen Anne wore one, for example. But such women were subject to criticism for being unfeminine. (Later, in fact, after Anne died, James would direct that women be prohibited from wearing men's fashions.) Pocahontas, apparently, had no desire to appear either frail or behind the times but would wear the hat of a man. And the headcovering says more than this: noblewomen usually did not wear hats in their portraits, unless they were specifically represented as being outdoors, while middle-class women did. This hat is closer to the kind favored by the bourgeois Puritans than it had to be. Rather than being covered with embroidery or velvet, Pocahontas's hat is decorated only with a relatively simple band and feather. Here sat less a princess than the wife of John Rolfe, the evangelical Protestant. Likewise, many noblewomen chose to have much of the neck or arms or hair exposed, but Pocahontas did not choose that path. Well aware of what was said about naked savages, she shows nothing but her face.[33]

An engraving based on a sketch taken from life.
Published in John Smith's *General Historie*, 1624.
*(Simon Van de Passe, 1616, courtesy of the New York
Public Library)*

Remarkably, Van de Passe represented Pocahontas's features as indigenous. Rather than making her look as European as possible—as
painters of later generations would do—the engraver clearly shows
her high cheekbones, almond eyes, and black hair. In a most unusual
pose for a woman, her large, dark eyes look straight out, observing all
the world. Portraits of men in that era often show them doing just
that; women more often tilted their heads down or to the side, sub-
serviently, flirtatiously. Pocahontas showed her straight-backed pride.
John Rolfe and Sir Edwin Sandys are unlikely to have insisted on

this—as they might have on some of the other elements of the portrait. It would have been Pocahontas herself who wanted it this way.

Lady Rebecca had something to say about the byline as well. Around the portrait are words obviously written by the Latin scholars with whom she kept company: "MATOAKA, ALS REBECCA FILIA POTENTISS, PRINC. POWHATANI IMP. VIRGINIA." But underneath, in smaller print, the text reads: "Matoaka als Rebecka daughter to the mighty Prince Powhatan Emperour of *Attanoughskomouck* als virginia converted and baptized in the Christian faith, and wife to the worthy Mr. Joh. Rolff." Attanoughskomouck? It was always a struggle to capture an Indian word phonetically, but the word that the English represented elsewhere as "Tsenacomoc(o)"—that is, the Indians' name for their own country—clearly peeps out of the confusion.[34] It would not have been John Rolfe or Sir Edwin who gave the term to Van de Passe but Matoaka. The English men probably wouldn't have cared to include it, but if they did, they would have spelled it as the English always did. This rendition was obviously the result of Matoaka's sounding it out for a Dutchman, just as it was undoubtedly the woman herself who insisted on using the name Matoaka rather than her more famous and attention-grabbing nickname, which everyone else was using. She knew Pocahontas was a name for a child; they did not.

During that same autumn John Smith came to visit the Lady Rebecca in her lodgings in Brentford. He apparently expected her to be overjoyed to see him. He was disappointed: "After a modest salutation, without any word, she turned about, obscured her face, as not seeming well contented; and in that humour her husband, with divers others, we all left her two or three hours." Smith presumed she was embarrassed at having lost rather than gained in fluency in English. But after a couple of hours she reappeared and ended her silence. Smith remembered her saying, somewhat accusingly, "You did promise Powhatan what was yours should bee his, and he the like to you; you called him father being in his land a stranger, and by the same reason so must I doe you." Smith tried to interrupt her with a style of flattery befitting their London context, saying he dared not let her call him "father," as she was a king's daughter. Pocahontas responded with the seventeenth-century equivalent of "Get real." She spoke in a torrent of anger, her countenance set:

> [You] were . . . not afraid to come into my father's Countrie, and cause feare in him and all his people (but mee) and [yet] feare you here I should call you father. I tell you then I will, and you shall call mee childe, and so I will bee for ever and ever your Countrieman. They did tell us always you were dead, and I knew no other till I came to Plimoth; yet Powhatan did command Uttamatomakkin to seeke you, and know the truth, because your Countriemen will lie much.[35]

These words, of course, come through John Smith, who was perfectly capable of making things up—and yet this story has the ring of truth. The incident was witnessed by several others, to whom Smith admitted he had bragged ahead of time. He had claimed the "princess" would be adoring, but instead she had expressed anger and bitterness. He seems to have felt a need to explain an interaction to others that he had certainly not predicted. The human details—the initial silence, his attempt to interrupt her, the irritation visible in her face—all bespeak a conversation that actually took place; they are not at all in keeping with the balladlike adventure story that Smith was so adept at making up on his own. Her attitude as he described it certainly was not what everyone else claimed she was feeling—an overwhelming joy at being in London, a spoiled darling, the toast of the town. Thus it is likely to have been the attitude that Smith actually observed.

Some historians have taken this speech as evidence that Pocahontas was desperately in love with Smith. But even Smith did not claim that. She was clearly expressing profound sadness and anger, not unrequited love. She spoke rather of political matters. Her father had established a kin relationship with this man, implying reciprocity and honesty. Smith had defaulted on both counts. He had not prevented the depredations of the English or kept his promises. He had simply slipped away, leaving a lie to explain his absence and his failure to live up to his word. At the same time Pocahontas reminded him that she herself had honored the claims of reciprocity and honesty and intended to continue doing so. It is hard not to hear the note of judgment and superiority: she embodies her people's virtues, while she deprecates not just Smith but all the English. Years before, she or one of her companions had said to Smith, "*Kator nehiegh mattach neer uttapitchewayne.* Truly . . . I do not lie." Now the grown woman said scornfully, "Your Countriemen will lie much." She had learned a great deal in her years with the English.[36]

In March the Rolfe household was ready to depart. The wind was right, and if they made good speed, they would be home within a year of when they left. At the last moment Rolfe had a meeting with Edwin Sandys. Money had been collected during their visit to be used toward converting the natives. It was only fair that the couple should have a share of it. The company now gave the tidy sum of one hundred pounds to "Mr. Rolfe and his Ladye, partly in doing honor to that good example of her conversion, and to encourage other of her kindred and nation to do the like, And partly upon promise made by the said Mr. Rolfe on behalfe of him selfe and the said Ladye, that bothe by their godlye and vertuous example . . . as also by all other good means of perswasions and inducements, they would employe their best endevours to the winning of that People to the knowledge of God." It may have been profoundly distressing to Pocahontas that John had promised on behalf of both to participate in this project, which was to consist of removing Indian children from their homes and raising them in a soon-to-be-founded Christian school. But perhaps not: Rolfe seems to have been careful to promise nothing specific. He would act "as occasion hereafter shall require"; and in any case, the statement said clearly that the money was first and foremost a thank-you gift to them. They packed their trunks.[37]

Samuel Argall was to be their captain again, although they traveled on a different ship this time. In fact, Argall had been made deputy governor of the colony, as Lord De La Warr was in no hurry to return to the New World. The ordinary ship captain must have considered himself well repaid indeed for his kidnapping of an unarmed young woman in the spring of 1613. The party seemed eager to be home, for they decided to travel even though almost none of the Virginia Indians felt well, struggling against colds, flus, and apparently pneumonia. They made their way down the Thames, leaving the city behind, passing through a marshy, dreary land. Twenty miles downriver they could see a tall church and a three-story inn on rising ground in the town of Gravesend. John Rolfe told Argall they needed to stop: Pocahontas was too ill to continue.

They went to the inn at Gravesend, and Pocahontas was put to bed. They surely sent for a doctor, but a medical man in that era would have been able to do little that would actually help. If they bled her, it would have hastened her demise. Her infected lungs were filling with fluid. Most of the other Indians were sick, too; they could do little to comfort one another.[38]

Pocahontas died there in the inn. Only a few months before she and Uttamatomakin had told Samual Purchas that their people "helde it a disgrace to feare death, and therefore when they must dye, did it resolutely."[39] What her last words were to John we will never know. Myths have grown up around that moment, but John never recorded what she said. He kept his last exchange with her for himself. He did write of looking down at his son, also at death's door. He must have suffered a sickening sense of history repeating itself: mother and child were both to be taken from him once again. Then God gave him a miracle. Thomas struggled, and survived—"even as a brand snatched out of the fier," said his grateful father. It was proof, he said, that God had his good at heart after all.[40]

On March 21 they held a small funeral for Pocahontas at the church of St. George in Gravesend. The clerk got John's name confused and put down "Thomas" as her husband instead. The pastor said what he always said, reading from the Book of Common Prayer: "I am the resurrection and the life saith the Lord: he that believeth in me, yea, though he were dead, yet shall he live. And whosoever liveth and believeth in me, shall not die forever." At the grave, which no one ever managed to mark with a stone, they read a prayer that was, unbeknownst to the English standing there, a universal human cry, present in all surviving preconquest Native American poetry as well as in the Bible: "Man that is born of a woman hath but a short time to live, and is full of misery. He cometh up and is cut down like a flower; he flieth as it were a shadow, and never continueth in one stay." Uttamatomakin, a priest himself, undoubtedly prayed in his own way.[41]

Captain Argall said they had to go if they were not to miss the wind. Rolfe probably had little desire to stay. Argall told him to leave his child with someone, as it was impractical to take him. Rolfe said no. At least one of the other Indians in the party had died as well, and three were even now too sick to travel. Those who were able to do so boarded the ship, Uttamatomakin among them, and they made their way down the English Channel. Thomas was still weak and vulnerable, his lungs not yet fully cleared. He was two now, careening about as toddlers do. For the first time in his life, John was solely responsible for his care, "as they who looked to him had need of nurses themselves." He broke under the pressure. When they stopped for supplies in Plymouth, he spoke to Sir Louis Stukely, the vice admiral for Devonshire, and arranged for him to keep the child until John's brother, Henry, could come from London to collect him. The act did not come easily to him. "I know not how I may be censured for leaving my child behind me."[42]

In Thomas, Rolfe saw "the lyving ashes of his deceased mother." Now he was to leave all the ashes behind, the living and the dead. In the letter he left for Henry, he asked that the child be sent to him when he was older and stronger. They sailed. John never saw Thomas again.

NINE

1622, and Queen Cockacoeske

"All must die, but tis enough that her child livith."
—Anonymous Virginia Indian,
as quoted by John Rolfe (June 1617)

The return passage was uneventful, without hurricanes or hangings. They were en route only thirty-five days, and only one man died at sea. As the travelers drew near the mouth of the Chesapeake, then made their way up the river, John Rolfe must have dreaded the telling of it all. Alexander Whitaker, it turned out, was not there to greet his famous protégée or to learn of her death—he had drowned in one of the rivers while they were away. Jamestown in general was in a pitiful state. The houses were in disarray, and the one well in town had been spoiled. Conditions were such that some colonists continued to run away to the Indians: Harry Potter even managed to steal a calf to take with him. Captain—now Governor—Argall had his work cut out for him.[1]

Rolfe went to speak with some Virginia Indians; he did not record which ones, or where. He had to tell them of Pocahontas's death and explain where Thomas was. He also needed to start recruiting students for the proposed school. The Indians wanted all his news and were glad to talk to the father of young Thomas. They made friendly nonpromises on the other issue. "The Indyans [are] very loving," Rolfe wrote to Sir Edwin, "and willing to part with their children. My wive's death is much lamented; my childe much desired, when it is of better strength to endure so hard a passage."[2]

Politically, relations with the Indians were in fact much more strained than Rolfe let on. Argall sent another letter back to England on the same boat that carried Rolfe's, and he gave more specific information. Powhatan had retired to a village on the Potomac River, leaving the kingdom to his younger brother, with Opechankeno still chief military man. Opechankeno had come to Jamestown to meet with Argall on his return and had at least pretended to feel great joy when presented with an expensive gift from England. But Uttamatomakin was making his presence—and his information—felt. In his letter Argall wrote, "Tomakin rails against England, English people, and particularly his best friend Thomas Dale." The new governor claimed to feel no real concern, saying that Opechankeno was dismissive of Uttamatomakin: "All his reports are disproved before Opachankeno & his Great men [his advisors] whereupon (to the great satisfaction of ye Great men) Tomakin is disgraced."[3] It seems odd, however, that Argall should have been so aware of arguments among the political factions advising Opechankeno; more likely, he had been taken in by a scripted scene arranged by the chief to disarm the English. Given Opechankeno's subsequent behavior, it appears that he listened intently to all that Uttamatomakin had to say.

Later in the summer of 1617, the microbes that had come off the boat from England—probably the same ones that had killed Pocahontas—spread throughout the indigenous population, carrying death in their train. It was a hard winter. "The Indians [are] so poor they can't pay their debts and tribute," wrote Argall in March 1618. In a period of mounting tension, they were talking again about Pocahontas and especially Thomas. They seemed to envision the boy as a potential mediator: "Powhatan goes from place to place visiting his Country taking his pleasure in good friendship with us. [He] laments his daughters death but glad her child is living. So doth Opachankeno. Both want to see him." Company officials grew irate when Argall later reported that Opechankeno was refusing to part with any more land except to Pocahontas's son, Thomas: "Wee cannot imagine why you should give us warninge that Opachankano and the Natives have given their Country to Mr. Rolfe Child and that they will reserve it from all others till he comes of yeares except as some do here report it to be a Devise of your owne to some especiall purpose for yourselfe."[4]

That young Thomas was not really in line to inherit any chieftainship or territory within the Powhatan tradition should not confuse us: Opechankeno was clearly doing the best he could to preserve his people's land. He was looking for a reason to keep it out of English hands, which the English themselves might approve of. And if the land ever really did pass to Thomas in legalistic English fashion, the chief could at least comfort himself with the thought that young Rolfe was the one Englishman to whom he was related by ties of blood. Though the Londoners accused Argall of making up the story, he would never have done so: he had no reason to alienate his metropolitan backers by claiming that Opechankeno was refusing to part with land if he was not. Other governors would later be similarly berated by the company for treating Opechankeno as if he were a legally relevant player.[5] Safe across the Atlantic Ocean, the London businessmen could afford to operate in a theoretical universe of English law in which the Indians did not exist. The on-the-spot governors had no such luxury.

The following year, 1619, relations remained tense as settlers continued to establish new plantations without any formal agreement with the indigenous people. Powhatan had died in 1618, and his

younger brother had fully succeeded him, but Opechankeno continued as military chief. The settlement pattern was clear to him: within
a few more years all the territory bordering the James would be
claimed by the whites, excepting only that belonging to the Nansemonds. Colonists acted with less and less fear of the Indians. One
Captain John Martin and some of his servants attacked a canoe full
of people who had refused to trade with them. Opechankeno complained to the Assembly of Burgesses, then beginning to meet in
Jamestown. John Rolfe had apparently taken Opechankeno's part in
some way, as Martin wrote him a threatening, hate-filled letter,
which Rolfe presented to the Assembly, demanding redress. The
council members chastised Martin, but only a few years later he
would write a treatise entitled *The Manner How to Bring the Indians
into Subjection.* By that point, the authorities were disposed to listen.[6]

As the summer of 1619 wore on, other problems unfolded as well.
Disease spread again among the Indians, the second epidemic in two
years. By then Argall had been so roundly criticized on so many fronts
that he had been recalled to London. Lord De La Warr had died, and
another governor, the newly knighted Sir George Yeardley, now
served. Henry Spelman, back in the colony, older but still no wiser,
said very publicly to Opechankeno that he needn't listen to Yeardley
or treat his demands seriously, as he was nobody important, and a real
nobleman would shortly be sent. Another bilingual English boy heard
him and tattled. Chaos and mutual recriminations ensued; Spelman
was tried in Jamestown in August. It was considered extremely dangerous to give the Indians any reason to despise any colonial authority—especially now, when they seemed disposed to resist. Because of
his youth—and perhaps because of his bilingual value—Spelman was
not executed but rather sentenced to seven years' labor as interpreter
to the governor: "This sentence being read to Spelman, he, as one that
had in him more of the Savage then of the Christian, muttered certain words to himselfe neither shewing any remorse for his offenses,
nor yet any thankfulness to the Assembly."[7]

Because individual Englishmen continued to establish farms here and there, none of which had Opechankeno's blessing, Yeardley feared for the safety of the "straggling Plantations." Believing that the Spelman incident had weakened his authority, he decided to send Rolfe to speak to him. "Opachankano professeth much love to me, and giveth much credite to my worde," claimed Rolfe. It was worth a try. One evening when the wind was right, Rolfe, Henry Spelman, and a trusted man named Thomas Hobson sailed as far as they could up the York River; then, where the water divided into the much smaller Youghtanund and Mattaponi Rivers, they clambered into a small shallop and rowed quickly upstream toward the heart of Opechankeno's home territory. They stopped within five miles of his village, and then Spelman and Hobson continued on foot. Rolfe, who was a significant figure in the colony, probably thought—quite rightly—that he stood in greater danger of being made captive than did a messenger and his interpreter. They reached the village at almost the same moment as an Indian runner.

It was the first time in Opechankeno's experience that the English had traveled faster than news of their coming, and he did not like it. The two visitors were at first treated harshly, but the chief relented when he understood that they came representing Pocahontas's husband. He asked why Rolfe had not trusted him enough to come himself and decided to accept it when they answered that he was ill with a horrible cold and did not want to leave the boat: Rolfe, who knew something of Opechankeno's world from his years with Pocahontas, claimed he had prepared the messengers for the question and had supplied them with a culturally acceptable answer.[8]

Political relations were reestablished. Opechankeno still did not say anything favorable about the parceling out of land with which the Assembly was then occupied, but he offered a compromise concerning the indoctrination of young people. He would not "upon any terms" part with any children, but he would assign whole families to go and live with the colonists, if they would be given houses, land, and cattle.

Yeardley, in his attempt to convince the thrifty Sir Edwin Sandys that this was the best they could do, pointed out that they would still have "the opportunity to instruct their children" without having to grow food for them, which their families would do "by their own labors."[9]

When Rolfe wrote his report of these events to Sandys in January 1620, he tacitly presented himself as the widower of Pocahontas and a bridge to the Indians. He failed to mention that he was newly married to a young English woman named Joan Pierce, the daughter of a good friend and neighbor, William Pierce. Later that year a daughter named Elizabeth was born to the couple. Precariously prosperous, they owned three oxen and used them to grow both the profitable tobacco and the requisite corn. White indentured servants now provided much of the labor.[10]

Rolfe knew he needed to protect his assets in the fledgling polity. Indeed, his long letter to Sandys was part of his effort to remain a player in the unfolding colonial world by renewing his ties to a former patron in London. Under Argall, Rolfe had served as recorder for the company, and several edicts were issued under his hand and sent back to the capital. Under Yeardley, he served on the governing council that organized the convening of the annual Assembly of Burgesses. He was also friends with Abraham Piercey, who was cape merchant (in charge of the company's stores of goods), and he tried to use that friendship as well as his London connections to help his new ally, William Pierce. The colonists claimed that the company store owed Rolfe, and that Rolfe owed Pierce; London officials could therefore repay Rolfe by paying the Pierce family in London. Three debts would be instantly settled. The company turned Rolfe's proposal down twice—on this and on another occasion when his brother presented it.[11]

John's brother, Henry, Thomas's guardian, became his advocate in London. He became a shareholder in the company and dealt on several occasions with the company's officials. When, for example, Lady De La Warr claimed a portion of a 1621 shipment of Rolfe's tobacco, in exchange for the value of some goods her husband had left with him years ago, Henry deftly stepped in and swore that this latest shipment had all been grown on the land of his brother's neighbor, William Pierce, and thus was not Rolfe's property. He was sure, however, that his brother would be delighted to prepare a complete list of all the De La Warr goods in his possession, so the company could assess their value.[12]

Meanwhile, John Rolfe had joined with other colonists in petitioning the king for changes in the tobacco importation law, and in 1621 he was named to one of two colonial councils as a government reorganization took place. One council consisted of members carefully selected by the London officers of the company and was to conduct most of the colony's business; the other, meeting once a year only, contained two elected representatives from each plantation or town. Rolfe was sufficiently well connected and respected to be named to the elite body.[13]

It was no accident. By now Sir Edwin Sandys was treasurer of the company. One's power in the colony depended to a great extent on the standing of one's patron or patrons back in London. It was, after all, no different for those actually living in the metropolis. Ex-governor Argall, for example, made sure to retain powerful friends no matter what happened. When he was forced to resign from the governorship in 1619, he returned immediately to London and began to attend all the business meetings of the company. He defended himself and continued to develop his connections with men in high places. The powerful Duke (formerly Earl) of Buckingham—the same George Villiers who had done such remarkable dancing in front of Pocahontas in *The Vision of Delight*—became a strong advocate of Argall's and hired him to carry out overseas missions until Argall's death in 1626. John Smith, on the other hand, was not so good at ingratiating himself. He became actively involved with attempts to colonize New England (a place name he invented) but was never actually sent himself. He supported himself with some success by writing copiously until his death in 1631.[14]

The three Virginia Indians left behind in London in 1617 because they were too ill to travel—one man and two women—were absolutely and completely dependent on powerful patrons. Important figures were interested in them as potential converts but relatively uninterested in what they had to say. The young man lived with George Thorpe, who later—in 1620—traveled to Virginia to found a school for Indian children in hopes of removing them from their parents' influence. Thorpe called the young man Georgius, after himself, and put him to work copying out documents related to the future school. He pressed him to convert. Georgius accepted the faith in the autumn of 1619, as he lay dying from the lung condition that had haunted him for more than two years. Seventeen days later he expired. He would have been able to tell Thorpe and the company officials that removing Powhatan children from their parents was going to be problematic, but clearly no one was encouraging him to speak freely.[15]

Two young women also remained in London. They recovered somewhat from their illness and were baptized as Mary and Elizabeth. Mary lived as a servant to a textile merchant in Cheapside. Elizabeth lived with one Captain Maddison, and the company paid her room and board. She was related to Powhatan's successor—though it is unclear exactly how—and probably had traveled as a social companion to Pocahontas. When Mary became seriously ill again in the spring of 1620, she was moved to the home of Whitaker's cousin, the Reverend William Gough of Blackfriars. Gough said he took great pains to comfort her "both in soul and in body": whether his zealous style was actually comforting is doubtful, for he spoke openly of her upcoming death. The company agreed to pay for room and board and all necessary medicines—though they in fact were slow in doing so, and the medical expenses had to be covered by Sir William Throckmorton, who was George Thorpe's cousin and a close relative of Sir Thomas Dale's wife.[16]

In the fall of that year, the corporation's accountant suggested that both women be placed in apprenticeships at company expense, so that they might learn trades and eventually cease to be a financial burden. Nothing came of his idea, however. The following summer, in June 1621, the same man proposed something quicker and cheaper: why not send the two of them to Bermuda as brides for colonists? Implicitly, returning them to Virginia involved untold social and political complications. What might the women say? Should they be encouraged to marry white men? If they married Indians, would they be lost to the faith? In Bermuda, however, the wife-hungry colonists would be delighted to have them.

The chair of the meeting tabled the motion for unspecified reasons. Apparently he actually wanted to ask the women what they thought, for two days later it was decided to send them to Bermuda— "whither," someone said, "they are willing to go." Someone important saw them as people; to have sent them to Bermuda against their will was tantamount to selling them into slavery. Two impoverished boys were to accompany them as indentured servants. They would be the women's dowry, enabling them to marry someone a cut above the ordinary. The company would write a letter to the governor requesting "the carefull bestowing of them."[17]

In late July they boarded the *James* and set sail. Traveling with them were a number of impoverished white women who were to be given to colonists as wives in exchange for a hundred pounds of tobacco each. Mary and Elizabeth had reasonable hope of getting more gentlemanly husbands: thirty pounds, it turned out, had been enough to contract four young servant boys, not two, so they had an impressive dowry. They were given food and drink for the journey and a box of clothing, bedding, and soap. They were to share a new Bible and a psalter. If they had been shown even a rough map, they knew they were headed to a place only a few days' sail from Tsenacomoco—from home.[18]

Mary died at sea. In early October 1621, Elizabeth arrived in Bermuda alone. Governor Nathaniel Butler read the company's letter demanding that he find a good husband for her and grumbled that "it was a harder task in this place than they were aware of." He did nothing about the matter for more than four months. Then in March there came a ship from Virginia, bearing letters and gifts from the new governor there. Butler remarked that it was a good time to marry off the girl, while the crew was on his shores, as all of Virginia, white and Indian, would thereby hear that he had done what he should. Elizabeth had learned to write, and he made her sit down and craft a letter to her royal brother. He hosted a grand party, with more than a hundred guests, and sent the woman off to her plantation home with "as fit and agreeable a husband as the place would afford." There, after her wedding day, all trace of Elizabeth disappears from the record.[19]

There is better information about what happened to Pocahontas's second husband in that same month. In the winter of 1622, when he was approximately thirty-seven years old, John Rolfe became seriously ill. He took to his bed and on March 10 sent for witnesses to make his will. Reverend Richard Bucke came, the same man who had buried Rolfe's daughter, Bermuda, twelve years earlier. Sir George Yeardley's wife, Temperance, was also there, probably helping the still-young Joan cope with caring for an invalid and a toddler at the same time. In the old formula the scribe wrote, "I, John Rolfe of James City in Virginia, Esquire, being sicke in body, but of perfecte minde and memory (laude and prayse be given to Almightie god therefore) doe make and ordaine this my laste and finall will and testament."

Rolfe did not die easy in his mind: "Almightye god hath bestowed upon me two small children of very tender age." Even the older Thomas, after all, was still only about seven. Rolfe asked his good friend and father-in-law, William Pierce, to oversee the education and property of both children. He left the plantation he was living on, across the river from James Town, to Thomas. The boy was to be given full control when he turned twenty-one or married, whichever happened first, provided he married with William's consent. If he died without issue, the land was to pass to his half sister, Elizabeth, upon exactly the same conditions. Rolfe left a less valuable and more distant land claim, on a peninsula downriver called Mulberry Island, to his wife, Joan, for use during her lifetime, and then to Elizabeth and her heirs during all eternity. His goods and chattel were to be sold, and the profits divided equally among Joan, Thomas, and Elizabeth, except that his oxen and best sword, girdle, and armor were to be given to William, and twenty pounds were to be given to a favorite indentured servant named Robert Davies when his term was up in two years' time.

As he lay dying, John Rolfe ordered his world as he saw fit, imagining that he left a peaceable kingdom to his and Pocahontas's son, Thomas, whenever the lad should come to take up his estate. Richard Bucke, whose comforting voice Rolfe had known so long, led the little group in prayer.[20]

A month later, in April, the Reverend Patrick Copland preached a sermon before the Virginia Company officials and shareholders back in London, thanking God for the "Happie Successe" of their colonial venture.[21] Copland, too, entertained the fantasy of the peaceable kingdom. If it had existed, his words would have made a fit ending for Pocahontas's story, stretching Rolfe's desires across the Atlantic to touch little Thomas in his pew. But there was something the churchgoers did not know that Sunday in April, for in 1622 word spread slowly across the sea.

Pocahontas's people had had enough.

MARCH 10, when Rolfe dictated his will, had been a Sunday. On Friday, March 22, the Powhatan people launched a great assault against the colony, killing approximately one-quarter of the residents—somewhere between 350 and 400. The Indians used to their advantage their age-old techniques of warfare—intertribal cooperation, advance planning, and the preservation of secrecy, enabling simultaneous attacks in multiple places. They used creativity and trickery to surmount the problem of their lack of equivalent weaponry. The night before and early that morning, groups approached settlements up and down the James River in an apparently friendly fashion, in some cases even breakfasting with the colonists. At an appointed time they attacked with deadly suddenness. At Mulberry Island, for example, where a young relative of William Pierce was living on the land that the Pierces and the Rolfes claimed, all were killed: Thomas Pierce and his wife and child, two English serving men, and a young French boy they had with them. Jamestown and its immediate environs, including the Rolfe plantation, went unscathed: an Indian boy who was living with a colonist "as his son" leaked word of the coming assault. Some say more than one person told. At any rate, those within easy rowing and riding distance of the fort were warned, and a military defense was mounted that apparently caused the Indians to abandon any plan of entering the area near the town. It is even possible that the Indians never intended to attack this most densely populated section.[22]

For years, various theories have been floated to explain the Indians' decision to reverse their former policy so suddenly and so completely. Most acknowledge that the Indians were losing their land, but only a few have given that idea central importance. Specifically, some have blamed Argall's harshness and then the policies of the new councils. Others have argued that the Indians were more incensed about religious questions, including the new efforts to indoctrinate their children. Some have insisted that the Indians responded almost spontaneously because the English had shortly before murdered a famous warrior with almost mythic status—Nemattanew, or Jack-of-the-Feather. A few have found compelling the fact that the attack coincided with the religious celebration of the four-year anniversary of Powhatan's death. It is also true that as the Indians took up their positions on the eve of the attack, it was the five-year anniversary of Pocahontas's funeral. But the vast majority of them would not have known that and probably would not have cared much if they had.[23]

In hindsight, the Indians' motivations seem quite clear. They had information now, after all. Pocahontas had died, but Uttamatomakin had returned and spoken of what he had seen in London. If any doubted him at first, the last few years of continued importation of people and supplies from England, and the increasing number of set-tlements, would have provided compelling corroborating evidence. His lessons could not have been lost: England's technology was su-perior, its population vast. Rather than having seen England's most powerful weapons and greatest concentration of goods, the Powhatans in Virginia had glimpsed only the tip of the iceberg. The Europeans were not even desperate for food, as had once been believed. They wanted land, and to get it, they would destroy the Indians eventually. There was only one moment when the Indians were stronger, and that was in the earliest period of settlement, before the English had transferred their people and their power. That was now. If there was any hope for the Indians, it was to take action immediately, while they still could. With the element of surprise on their side, they might yet eliminate so high a percentage of the settlers as to convince the others to leave. Conservatives may have hoped merely to cause the English to confine themselves to Jamestown, while younger, angrier warriors probably believed they could yet kill them all, if the Indians worked together effectively enough. In any case, they would take their river and their kingdom back. Other factors may have been proximate causes, may even have determined the exact timing of the attack. The ultimate cause, however, seems clear enough.

But it was already too late. In 1607 the Indians might have done better, but they did not then have the information to make full-scale hostilities seem rational. And even if they had acted at once, their ef-forts would only have delayed matters, not changed the course of his-tory. The technological differential remained what it was. No one could change the fact that eleven thousand years ago farming had made sense in the Fertile Crescent and had made no sense in the Virginia Tidewater. Sedentary living and the ensuing inventions over the course of millennia had given the Old World inhabitants untold advantages over those of the New.

In March 1622, however, the long-term results of the chain of Indian raids were not at all clear. To a large extent, the Indians had been successful; it remained to be seen how the English would respond. March was a good time for the assault, the tail end of winter, when the Indians were still living inland, broken into small units and families, not yet having regathered at their major riverside villages, where they would be vulnerable to counterattack. If all went well, the surviving English would abandon the place, and by summer the Indians could plant their old lands again. As the Indian warriors moved inland into the denser trees, along winding deer paths and footpaths that they knew but the English did not, they brought away with them about twenty prisoners, most of them young women. These would have the option of becoming mirror images of Pocahontas— of becoming Indians if they chose. Some did. Anne Jackson, who stayed with the Pamunkey until 1626, then was ransomed, was unable to fully break her ties with those whom she had learned to love. The colonial authorities shipped her back forcibly to England. Even Jane Dickinson, who apparently had wanted to be ransomed in 1623, implied in 1624 that her life with the landowner who had bought her freedom in order that she might work for him was a worse kind of slavery than she had experienced with the so-called savages.[24]

Most of the colonists, however, did not share these feelings. Never having lived among the Indians, failing to see them as people, most of the settlers felt only hatred. They might have decided to leave if they had believed the danger would stretch on interminably. But there was to be no standoff between matched adversaries. Instead, they meant to kill the Indians. When Londoners blamed the disaster on them, for having grown too cozy with the natives, they wrote back in rage: "You pass soe heavie a Censure upon us as yf we alone were guiltie. You may be pleased to Consider what instructions you have formerly given us, to wynn the Indyans to us by A kinde entertaiyninge them in our howses, and yf it were possible to Co-habitt with us, and how ympossible it is for any watch and warde to secure against secret Enemies." Well, they said, now they were at last free from any and all instructions to win the Indians by kind enter-taining. "We have slaine divers, burnt theire Townes, destroyed theire [fishing] Wears & Corn. Sir George Yardley in his last expeditione brought into the Colonie above a Thowsande bushel of corne . . . By Computatione and Confessione of the Indyans themselves we have slayne more of them this yeere, then hath been slayne before since the begininge of ye Colonie."[25]

Indeed, the initial report written in the colony about the "bar-barous massacre" made the claim that in the long run, the event was a net positive: at last the colonists were free to remove the Indians and take the country for themselves without complications: "This Massacre must rather be beneficiall to the Plantation then impaire it . . . Now by vanquishing of the Indians, [it] is like to offer a more ample and faire choice of fruitfull habitations, then hitherto our gen-tlenesse and faire comportment to the Savages could attaine unto."[26] In words reminiscent of a modern-day killer who claims he would never have hurt his victim so badly if she had not been foolish enough to struggle, the colonial chronicler continued to insist it had never been his choice to fight, even as he loaded his gun and drew on his armor. The policy of extermination had been born.

William Pierce joined actively in the expeditions sent against the Indians. Perhaps he wore the armor, girdle, and sword that the dying John Rolfe had left him. If so, the sword that Pocahontas had once handled was now turned against her own friends and family. When the area had been "pacified"—that is, all Indian resistance had been broken—Pierce established a plantation at Mulberry Island, where he owned lands adjoining those that he held in trust for Rolfe's daughter, Elizabeth. He was named captain of the guard and com-mander of Jamestown, so he also maintained a small household in the town, where he had three servants, including an enslaved African woman, one of twenty who had come off a Dutch ship in 1619—the first African slaves to arrive in the future United States. His daughter Joan, Rolfe's widow, married a wealthy man named Captain Roger Smith. Thomas's half sister, Elizabeth, grew up in her new stepfather's household.[27]

When Thomas was approaching twenty, Pierce paid for his passage to Virginia and thereby gained more land in the headright system.[28] What the boy's youth had been like is unknown. What is certain is that when he attained adulthood, he wanted to cross the sea. In 1641, at least six years after his arrival, he asked the colonial officials for permission to visit Opechankeno "to whom he was allied." He did not hesitate to refer openly to his blood relationship to the enemy chief, who had eluded capture after the events of 1622 and had therefore remained in power, as it seemed beyond the ability of the English to oust him. Thomas also asked to visit "Cleopatra, his mother's sister." Behind the English nickname there existed a real woman whom Thomas wanted to see. Was this "Cleopatra" a sister who had gone to London with Pocahontas, survived, and returned with Uttamatomakin? It seems quite plausible. There is no record of what transpired between them.[29]

A few years later, in 1644, the unrelenting Opechankeno, now at least an octogenarian, led another great rebellion. It was less successful than the last, for the English were by now much stronger. This time, the chief was captured, caged, and executed. Now Thomas was forced to choose sides. He participated in the war against his mother's people. He must have done so with apparent alacrity, for by 1646 he held the title of lieutenant and was rewarded with the assignment to keep Fort James in the Chickahominy territory. By a new law, this meant that the four hundred adjoining acres would become his property in perpetuity, provided that he and at least six working men lived on it at their own expense for three years and put the fort in good repair. Thomas was eager to establish himself in this area. The lands he had inherited from his father, where he had been born, had been worked by others after Rolfe's death, and little by little Thomas had sold most of them to those who were actually living there. He focused his efforts on the Chickahominy territory instead, and in 1656 and 1658 purchased 350 additional acres. Thomas would die a rich man.[30]

At about the same time he went to the "fort lands," he married the daughter of a colonist. They apparently had a daughter named Jane. Like her grandmother Pocahontas, Jane grew up to bear one son, then died when he was very young. He lived to have children, and the children to have children. They were among the colony's elite.[31] Thomas and his wife may also have had sons: in the 1660s a Thomas and William Rolfe or Relfe, whose connections make them sound suspiciously like such sons, moved from Virginia to North Carolina. Perhaps they did not want to wait to inherit land when there was so much available immediately in the Carolinas; and perhaps they were not at all loath to leave behind an area where their father was openly referred to as Powhatan's grandson.[32]

While Thomas was establishing his fortune and founding his dynasty in the 1640s, the world of Pocahontas's other family members— that of her siblings, cousins, nieces, and nephews—fell apart. In October 1646, in the wake of the rebellion of 1644, Opechankeno's successor, Necotowance, dubbed "King of the Indians" by the British, was forced to sign a peace treaty in which the Indians ceded most of their lands, acknowledged that their right to remain on certain territories was due to the generosity of the English king, and promised to pay an annual tribute to the colonial governor. Necotowance told his people, "The English will kill you if you go into their bounds."[33]

When Necotowance died, all semblance of a paramount chieftainship disappeared; each tribe struggled to survive on its own, following its own tactics. Elizabeth, a daughter of the chief of the Nansemond, married an English minister named John Bass who was a member of the House of Burgesses. They were able to preserve their lands and their family history for generations.[34] By 1649 the Pamunkey were governed by Totopotomoy and his wife Cockacoeske, both of whom claimed a relationship with Opechankeno and may well have been cousins. When Totopotomoy was killed fighting alongside the English against mutual Siouan enemies, Cockacoeske continued to rule. She did so for the next thirty years. Disease and relentless English expansion into lands the Indians relied on for food caused her people's population to drop, but she did her best by those who lived.[35]

In 1676 erratic Indian raids on the part of outlying Iroquoian groups such as the Susquehannocks helped to spark a rebellion on the part of poorer white settlers. They were led by Nathaniel Bacon, and their uprising became known as Bacon's Rebellion. Before events had progressed far, Cockacoeske was summoned to Jamestown so that the colonial authorities might ask her people to fight with the English against the Iroquoians. It was a memorable event: "She entered the chamber with a comportment gracefull to admiration, bringing on her right hand an Englishman interpreter, and on her left, her son, a stripling twenty years of age." She wore a crown of braided strips of black and white shell beads, and a deerskin cloak that reached from shoulders to feet, the edges worked into long, twisted fringe. Moving with "grave courtlike gestures and a majestick air in her face," she walked over to the head of the council table and sat down, announcing in Algonkian that she would speak only in her own language and communicate only through her interpreter—though the English had good reason to believe from past encounters that she understood their language perfectly well. The committee of the Governor's Council delegated to meet with her asked her how many men she would provide to help the English in their campaign.

As Powhatan and Pocahontas had also done, Cockacoeske remained silent, with all eyes turned to her. They asked her their question again. This time she spoke volubly: "With an earnest passionate countenance as if tears were ready to gush out and with a fervent sort of expression [she] made a harangue about a quarter of an hour." She used an argument that she apparently thought would be more effec-

tive than any complaints about longstanding injustice: out of virtu-
ous, wifely affection, she reminded the English repeatedly that it was
in just such circumstances that her dear husband had been killed,
along with one hundred other men. She was not going to make the
same mistake now. At length, she agreed to provide twelve men, no
more, though the English believed she had 150 at her command.[36]

In their rage at Indians in general, Nathaniel Bacon's followers
chose to attack those nearest at hand rather than pursue those actually responsible for the continuing raids. Though Cockacoeske had
just signed an agreement and had provided the twelve men to serve
as guides to the English military, her village was sacked and some
women killed; she herself was forced to flee to the woods. Afterward
the colonial government was unsympathetic; they focused their efforts on the rebellious Nathaniel Bacon and his followers and ignored their allies. Fortunately, in 1677 commissioners of the king
arrived from England to investigate the situation in the colony and
make recommendations. They advocated a meaningful peace agreement with the Virginia Indians. On May 29, 1677, at least four tribes
gathered to sign the Treaty of Middle Plantation. It would govern
colonial relations with the Indians for the next hundred years, until
the American Revolution.

Endorsing the treaty were the queen of the Weyanok, the king of
the Nottoway, and the king of the Nansemond, as well as Cockacoeske, the queen of the Pamunkey, and her son, John West. The Appomattock were there, and in favor of the accord but forbidden to
sign because some of their members were on trial for murder. Several
other tribes were said to be subsumed under Cockacoeske's chieftainship, as in the Powhatan days of old, among them the Mattaponi,
the Chickahominy, and the Rappahannock. The latter two groups,
however, had traditionally been both populous and powerful, and
their young men were quick to reject Cockacoeske's rulership after
the treaty was signed, though they accepted the document itself. Two
of the land reservations established in that moment still exist today,

albeit in much reduced form. The groups represented then form, to-gether with the Monacans, the core of the state-recognized tribes of Virginia at the start of the twenty-first century—the Chickahominy, Mattaponi, Nansemond, Pamunkey, and Rappahannock. They strug-gle today to keep their traditions alive.[37]

It is fashionable in some circles to lament Pocahontas's death, not for herself or her family or her people, but for the sake of history: it is said that had she lived, advocating for her people in the tumul-tuous decades that followed and encouraging more intermarriage, events might have turned out differently. Indian-white relations might have been more harmonious. It is naïve to think so.

The destruction of Virginia's Indian tribes was not a question of miscommunication and missed opportunities. White settlers wanted the Indians' land and had the strength to take it; the Indians could not live without their land. It is unfair to imply that somehow Poca-hontas, or Queen Cockacoeske, or others like them could have done more, could have played their cards differently, and so have saved their people. The gambling game they were forced to play was a dan-gerous one, and they had one hand, even two, tied behind their backs at all times. It is important to do them the honor of believing that they did their best. They all made decisions as well as they could, managing in what were often nearly unbearable situations. There is nothing they could have done that would have dramatically changed the outcome: a new nation was going to be built on their people's de-struction—a destruction that would be either partial or complete. They did not fail. On the contrary, theirs is a story of heroism as it exists in the real world, not in epic tales. Their dwindling people did survive, against all odds. There is a loop in the Pamunkey River that has surrounded Indian land time out of mind. It is called the Pa-munkey Reservation now, and the people there say it shelters Pow-hatan's bones. In the summer, wildflowers grow at the edge of the water, and Pocahontas's people can still catch a faint smell of the sea, just as they could in 1606.

Notes

LIST OF ABBREVIATIONS USED IN CITATIONS

CWCJS Philip Barbour, ed., *The Complete Works of Captain John Smith*, 3 vols. (Williamsburg, Va.: Institute for Early American Culture, 1986).

VMHB *Virginia Magazine of History and Biography*

WMQ *William and Mary Quarterly*

ONE
Amonute's People

1. Most of what we know about the lives of the Virginia Algonkians comes from the written works of English people who lived among them, however briefly, such as John Smith and Henry Spelman, or who interviewed Indians and questioned them about their lives, such as William Strachey (in Jamestown) and Samuel Purchas (in London). Through these sources we learn about such things as their dugout canoes, their use of rivers and creeks for rapid communication, and the structure of village life. The best scholarly synthesis and analysis of what we know of the Powhatan Indians from such sources is to be found in the work of anthropologist Helen Rountree, especially *The Powhatan Indians of Virginia: Their Traditional Culture* (Norman: University of Oklahoma Press, 1989). For an overview of the ways in which our knowledge is enriched by archaeological studies, see Rountree's work with E. Randolph Turner III, *Before and After Jamestown: Virginia's Powhatans and Their Predecessors* (Gainesville: University Press of Florida, 2002). Karen Ordahl Kupperman, *Indians and English: Facing Off in Early America* (Ithaca, N.Y.: Cornell University Press, 2000), offers an excellent treatment of very early contacts before official colonization began, and of the knowledge that the Indians had gathered before Europeans planted their flags. At

Plymouth, for example, the Pilgrims were met by an Indian who said "Welcome," having learned proper English greetings from fishermen in Canada (34–35).

2. Archaeologists have recently uncovered the remains of Werowocomoco at today's Purtan Bay (a traditional name conceivably based on "Powetan Bay") on the York River. The nature of the artifacts, the position given the village by three seventeenth-century mapmakers, John Smith's description of the site, and the distance he reported it to be from Jamestown together prove beyond doubt that investigators have indeed found Powhatan's seat. The Werowocomoco Research Group includes Deanna Beacham (Virginia Council on Indians), Martin Gallivan (Department of Anthropology of the College of William and Mary), Danielle Moretti-Langholtz (American Indian Resource Center of the College of William and Mary), E. Randolph Turner III (Virginia Department of Historical Resources), and archaeologists David A. Brown and Thane Harpole. Property owners Bob and Lynn Ripley have been generous and cooperative, envisioning themselves as stewards of the land. The Research Group's 2003 press release is available from the College of William and Mary. For a discussion of the importance of the collaboration occurring among the property owners, the archaeologists, and the Virginia Indian community, see Michelle Tirado, "Artifacts: Werowocomoco Discovered," *American Indian Report* 19:7 (July 2003): 24–26. For a sense of what the village probably looked like, scholars turn to a 1580s painting of the Indian "Town of Secotan" by Roanoke colonist John White. In 1590, Theodor de Bry made an engraving based on this painting (see frontispiece) and published it with Thomas Harriot's text, *A Briefe and True Report of the New Found Land of Virginia*. De Bry aligned the houses in a slightly more orderly fashion than did White, in keeping with European expectations, but his work still captures much of what was real in the villages of the relatively unified cultural region of today's Virginia and North Carolina.

3. Exactly where residents of Werowocomoco stored most of their canoes has not been proven. It would have been in one of the two creeks wrapping around the village, however, and the one on the left is far smaller and muddier than the one on the right. Furthermore, at the opening to the cove on the right there is some evidence of a landing. Interested readers should remain on the lookout for reports to be published by the Werowocomoco Research Group (see note 2). The site may have had important political associations even before the time of Powhatan. For a consideration of the ways in which political hierarchies rose and fell, see Jeffrey L. Hantman and Debra L. Gold, "The Woodland in the Middle Atlantic: Ranking and Dynamic Political Stability," in *The Woodland Southeast*, ed. David G. Anderson and Robert C. Mainfort, Jr. (Tuscaloosa: University of Alabama Press, 2002). For a brief and accessible discussion of more typical Indian villages' usual location and relationship to the land, see Helen Rountree, "Beyond the Village: A Colonial Parkway Guide to the Local Indians' Use of Natural Resources," available from the Jamestown-Yorktown Foundation.

4. Pocahontas may not have been exactly nine when the English arrived in 1607, but John Smith, who spoke with her often, believed her to be ten years old in 1608, and Strachey and the other colonists believed her to be eleven or twelve in 1609. They said she was prepubescent at that time. She married in about 1610, when she would have been expected to be twelve or thirteen. Only later was Pocahontas's age raised in European accounts so as to render her a young woman at the time of these events. For further discussion of the issue of her age, see chapter 8.

5. The Powhatans referred to the whites as coat-wearers on several occasions. Daniel Richter in *Facing East from Indian Country: A Native History of Early America* (Cambridge, Mass.: Harvard University Press, 2001), 13–15, discusses all the names Algonkians had for them, including "woodworkers," "cloth-makers," "metal-workers," and "axe-makers."

6. David Quinn, *England and the Discovery of America, 1481–1620* (New York: Alfred A. Knopf, 1974), 419–29.

7. Paul Hoffman, *A New Andalucia and a Way to the Orient: The American Southeast During the Sixteenth Century* (Baton Rouge: Louisiana State University Press, 1990), Chapters 8 and 10. Hoffman uses Spanish archival documents. Extant documents on the Jesuit venture are collected in Clifford M. Lewis and Albert J. Loomie, eds., *The Spanish Jesuit Mission in Virginia, 1570–1572* (Chapel Hill: University of North Carolina Press, 1953). Additional research has been done by Charlotte Gradie. See her "Spanish Jesuits in Virginia: The Mission that Failed," *VMHB* 96 (1988): 131–56, and "The Powhatans in the Context of the Spanish Empire," in Helen Rountree, ed., *Powhatan Foreign Relations, 1500–1722* (Charlottesville: University Press of Virginia, 1993). Gradie was the first to point out that Don Luis may well have been lying when he said he could not find his homeland with soldiers aboard. He may have been picked up south of his family's territories, but only one Spaniard, who was wrong about other issues, mentioned that. Nor do we know for certain which tribe Luis came from. The Spanish recorded that he was from "Ajacán": either it was a small village that never became known to the English, or they misunderstood the name. Spanish records make it clear that the Jesuits landed in what would have been Paspahegh territory, and that Don Luis considered himself related to the people there, though they were not his immediate family. When they crossed the neck of land to settle on the next river up, the York, they would have been in Chiskiak territory, and that was where Don Luis's brother lived, so he was probably Chiskiak himself. Further evidence for this interpretation is the fact that the Chickahominy considered Don Luis to have been, symbolically or politically speaking, Powhatan's father, and the Chiskiak were often added to the list of tribes that formed Powhatan's initial power base. Scholarly debate on Luis's exact relationship to Powhatan—which we will in fact never know—has been ably summarized by Helen Rountree in *Pocahontas's People: The Powhatan Indians of Virginia Through Four Centuries* (Norman: University of Oklahoma Press, 1990), 15–20. Readers should be aware that there is no basis at all for the story, which has been accepted by some scholars, that Don Luis was in fact Opechankeno, who appears later in these pages. I have benefited in my detective work on these issues from the insights of archaeologist Randolph Turner, made in personal communications, July 2003. Continuing research is being conducted by Daniel K. Richter, director of the McNeil Center for Early American Studies at the University of Pennsylvania.

8. Fathers Luis de Quirós and Juan Baptista de Segura to Juan de Hinistrosa, September 12, 1570, in Lewis and Loomie, *Spanish Jesuit Mission*, 91–92.

9. Ralph Hamor, *A True Discourse of the Present State of Virginia* (1615; Richmond: Virginia State Library, 1957), 13. They said they hated the Spanish for having brought Powhatan's father—indicating any elder kinsman—to their shores. They lived next door to the Paspaheghs, and the Spanish could easily have thought they were landing in the same territory as the first expedition had. It is logical that they themselves did not foresee being mistaken for the Paspaheghs, with whom they had tense relations.

10. For the full story, see Alden Vaughan, "Sir Walter Ralegh's Indian Interpreters," *WMQ* 59 (2002): 341–76. For the word *boy* in Pocahontas's language, see John Smith, *A Map of Virginia with a Description of the Country* (London: Joseph Barnes, 1612), in *CWCJS* 1:136. There were of course other ways of saying *boy* in other related languages. See Frank T. Siebert, "Resurrecting Virginia Algonquian from the Dead: The Reconstituted and Historical Phonology of Powhatan," in *Studies in Southeastern Indian Languages,* ed. James M. Crawford (Athens: University of Georgia Press, 1975). The literature on "the lost colony" in general is substantial. A classic work is Quinn, *England and the Discovery of America.* Newer work includes Giles Milton, *Big Chief Elizabeth: The Adventures and Fate of the First English Colonists in America* (New York: Farrar, Straus & Giroux, 2000), and Lee Miller, *Roanoke: Solving the Mystery of the Lost Colony* (New York: Arcade Publishing, 2000).

11. The debate on what became of the Roanoke colonists is extensive. Rountree has summarized it in light of Powhatan's political context in *Pocahontas's People,* 21–27, and Miller in *Roanoke* provides strong evidence that they were sold as slaves.

12. An excellent summary of Powhatan's rise to power is Rountree, *Pocahontas's People,* chap. 1. Frederick Gleach also treats it in *Powhatan's World and Colonial Virginia: A Conflict of Cultures* (Lincoln: University of Nebraska Press, 1997), as does Margaret Holmes Williamson, *Powhatan Lords of Life and Death: Command and Consent in Seventeenth-Century Virginia* (Lincoln: University of Nebraska Press, 2003). Importantly, archaeologist Randolph Turner assesses evidence left not by British writers but by the indigenous themselves in their trade goods and settlements, in "Native American Protohistoric Interactions in the Powhatan Core Area," in Rountree, *Powhatan Foreign Relations.* A sophisticated treatment of traditionally coexisting forms of political power and influence with Powhatan society, which did not always privilege the chieftainships, is Martin D. Gallivan, *James River Chiefdoms: The Rise of Social Inequality in the Chesapeake* (Lincoln: University of Nebraska Press, 2003).

13. Daniel Richter discusses the extent to which such changes constantly took place in the Native American world, even before the arrival of the Europeans, in *Facing East from Indian Country,* 36–39. In the case of the Powhatans, we should remember that they were dealing not only with Iroquoian enemies but also with threats from the Piedmont Siouans (the Monocans), Maryland's Algonkian paramount chieftainship (the Piscataway), and, internally, the populous Chickahominy. See Rountree, *Powhatan Foreign Relations.*

14. William Strachey, *The Historie of Travell into Virginia Britania,* ed. Louis B. Wright and Virginia Freund (1612; London: Hakluyt Society, 1953), 68.

15. Sources generally agree on what her names were, though their meanings are debatable, or lost. Pocahontas's private name may have been Matoaka. (See the discussion in chapter 7.) We have no hard evidence that the Powhatans really gave their children private names, only an ambiguous comment by Samuel Purchas, but the practice was widespread among Native Americans in general. Henry Spelman describes an infant's naming ceremony in his "Relation of Virginia" in *Travels and Works of Captain John Smith,* ed. Edward Arber and A. G. Bradley (Edinburgh: John Grant, 1910), cix.

16. Ibid., cxi.

17. It is important to note that the word *princess* is therefore inapplicable to Pocahontas or any other Algonkian woman.

18. Strachey, *Historie of Travell*, 63–69. Numerous scholars mention that Powhatan made political use of intermarriage and, separately, that he often set his own sons to rule over subject tribes. They have not tended to point out the way in which he was using matrilineality and polygyny at the same time, but the pattern is immediately obvious to scholars familiar with Native American state-building practices in Mesoamerica and the Andes.

19. Spelman, "Relation of Virginia," cviii.

20. See Pedro Carrasco, "Royal Marriages in Ancient Mexico," in *Explorations in Ethnohistory: Indians of Central Mexico in the Sixteenth Century*, ed. H. R. Harvey and H. Premm (Albuquerque: University of New Mexico Press, 1984).

21. Strachey, *Historie of Travell*, 61–62. Hamor also talks about this favored daughter in *True Discourse*, 40–43.

22. For a remarkable treatment of women's work, see Helen Rountree, "Powhatan Indian Women: The People Captain John Smith Barely Saw," *Ethnohistory* 45 (1998): 1–29. She has gone beyond the texts left by English men, actually performing some of the work herself and studying the available plants in the region.

23. Rountree, "Powhatan Indian Women," 3.

24. Strachey, *Historie of Travell*, 65. Rountree, in "Powhatan Indian Women," 18–19, has proven that collecting the special blue feathers needed for one cloak would have taken several years.

25. Strachey, in *Historie of Travell*, 101, told the story secondhand, having gotten it from Captain Argall, who visited the Potomacs while Henry Spelman, the young interpreter, resided there.

26. A number of scholars do accept the notion of the dichotomy between a benevolent and a terrible deity. However, Mexicanists for years likewise accepted the Spaniards' belief that the Aztecs had worshipped a benevolent Quetzalcoatl and a bloodthirsty Huitzilopochtli; only recently has greater attention to sources written in their own language disproved the notion. One of Powhatan's priests, interviewed by Samuel Purchas, categorically denied the dichotomy. See *Purchas, His Pilgrimage*, 3rd ed. (London: William Stansby, 1617), 955. Frederick Gleach notes the embedded morpheme *manito* in *mamanitowik* in *Powhatan's World*, 33. The concept of the *okee* has proven particularly difficult for scholars, but the idea of a physical manifestation of a local god who is at the same time part of the larger divinity of the universe, and who is both a benefactor and a terror to his people, is quite common in other Native American cultures. Students might compare the notion of the Andean *huaca*, for example. Smith and Strachey captured the concept; only in later sources did it become confused. See Williamson, *Powhatan Lords of Life and Death*, 176–80. Some Virginia Indians today practice their own version of their ancestors' religion.

27. Strachey, *Historie of Travell*, 102. This god was the great Hare, a significant presence in Algonkian religion in general. See Williamson, *Powhatan Lords of Life and Death*, 174–75. On priests tending to the temples, and on ordinary people not understanding their formulaic prayers, see the interview with the priest Uttamatomakin in *Purchas, His Pilgrimage*, 3rd ed., 954–55.

28. Strachey, in *Historie of Travell*, 40, records the three-hundred-year tradition. Rountree, in *Pocahontas's People*, dismisses it, given the archaeological evidence of con-

tinuous cultural development; but in *Powhatan Indians of Virginia* (49–50) she gathers together every mention of pictoglyphic counting or mapping records. Dan Richter, in *Facing East from Indian Country*, 3–5, summarizes the agricultural revolution on the East Coast.

29. This is the purport of the Pulitzer Prize–winning book by Jared Diamond, *Guns, Germs and Steel: The Fates of Human Societies* (New York: Norton, 1997). There is, of course, more to the argument, and the text deserves a close reading by all serious historians. Traditionally people exaggerated the technological power of the English in the seventeenth century, and in response scholars have recently tended to dismiss it to an unrealistic extent, in some cases even asserting that the Europeans did not really have a technological advantage since they were dependent on the Indians for food for the first few years. In an era of increasing political sensibilities, it has seemed impolitic on the part of professors to say anything that might be construed by some as tantamount to a statement that Europeans were "more advanced" or in any way "superior." Diamond allows us to proceed without self-consciousness, as the technological differential resulting from the presence or absence of suitable plant species thousands of years ago obviously has nothing to do with intelligence.

30. It is even conceivable that Don Luis was still alive, but it is highly unlikely, as Powhatan himself was already an old man and Luis would have been older still. Powhatan also would have evinced even greater understanding of the Europeans if a man who had lived in Mexico City and Madrid had been sitting at his side.

TWO
What the English Knew

1. Peter Martyr, *The Decades of the Newe Worlde or West India* (London, 1555), trans. Richard Eden from Pietro Martire d'Anghiera, *De rebus oceanicis et orbe novo decades tres* (Basel, 1533), 35 verso. Smith's writings give indication of his having read widely, but here he is shown reading only those books he explicitly declared he had read.

2. Ibid., 36.

3. Sir Walter Ralegh, *The Discoverie of the Large, Riche and Bewtiful Empyre of Guiana*, ed. Neil Whitehead (Norman: University of Oklahoma Press, 1997), 196.

4. Martyr, *Decades*, 208. On the sixteenth-century use of the image of the naked Indian woman, see the classic article by Rayna Green, "The Pocahontas Perplex: The Image of Indian Women in American Culture," *Massachusetts Review* 16 (1975): 698–714. Rebecca Faery treats the theme in depth in *Cartographies of Desire: Captivity, Race, and Sex in the Shaping of an American Nation* (Norman: University of Oklahoma Press, 1999), esp. 88–91. Concerning the older tradition of broadside images representing people from overseas in general as naked, particularly sexual, and often in naturalized family units, and the contempt for this tradition on the part of Richard Eden and other scholars who deemed themselves serious about colonization, I have been informed by Thomas Hahn, "*Of the Newe Landes*: Text and Image in the First English Book on the New World," Colgate University Humanities Colloquium, April 8, 2003.

5. Richard Hakluyt, *Principal Navigations, Voyages, Traffiques & Discoveries of the English Nation*, ed. Irwin R. Blacker (New York: Viking, 1965), 39–40. Other captive Indians are mentioned throughout.

6. Ibid., 293–94.

7. Hakluyt, "Epistle Dedicatorie," in first edition of *Principal Navigations*.

8. John Smith, *A Description of New England* (London, 1616), in *CWCJS* 1:349.

9. For an overview of the recent literature debating China's reasons for not exploring in this period, see Gale Stokes, "The Fates of Human Societies: A Review of Recent Macrohistories," *American Historical Review* 106 (2001): 508–25.

10. Francisco López de Gómara, *Historia de la conquista de México* (Saragossa, 1554); translated by Thomas Nicholson as *The Pleasant Historie of the Conquest of the West India, now called New Spain, atchieved by the worthy prince Hernando Cortes, most delectable to reade* (London: Henry Bynneman, 1578). Malinche is introduced as a "true Interpreter" on pp. 55–56. Juan de Acosta's Spanish work was likewise translated into English and widely read. That English proponents of colonization knew Malinche to have been crucial is evidenced by the fact that Samuel Purchas included her in the synthetic account he completed in 1612, *Purchas His Pilgrimage* (London: William Stansby, 1613), 654.

11. The literature on the Spanish conquests and on the defeat of the Spanish Armada is vast. Classic works that would make good starting places include Hugh Thomas, *Conquest: Montezuma, Cortés, and the Fall of Old Mexico* (New York: Simon & Schuster, 1993), John Hemming, *The Conquest of the Incas* (New York: Harcourt Brace, 1970), and Geoffrey Parker and Colin Martin, *The Spanish Armada* (New York: Norton, 1988).

12. The best treatment of the Irish precedent remains Nicholas Canny, "The Ideology of English Colonization: From Ireland to America," *WMQ* 30 (1973): 575–98. The most complete study of the era as a whole is David Quinn, *England and the Discovery of America, 1481–1620* (New York: Alfred A. Knopf, 1974).

13. The best treatment of this topic is Edmund Morgan, *American Slavery, American Freedom: The Ordeal of Colonial Virginia* (New York: Norton, 1975), chap. 1.

14. On the events of 1606, see Philip Barbour, introduction to *The Jamestown Voyages Under the First Charter, 1606–1609* (Cambridge, Eng.: Hakluyt Society, 1969).

15. Robert Gray, "Epistle Dedicatorie," in *A Good Speed to Virginia* (London, 1609).

16. Ibid., C3 verso. For a discussion of the ambivalence of the colonizers, see Karen Ordahl Kupperman, *Indians and English: Facing Off in Early America* (Ithaca, N.Y.: Cornell University Press, 2000), 16–18, and especially Andrew Fitzmaurice, *Humanism and America: An Intellectual History of English Colonisation, 1500–1625* (New York: Cambridge University Press, 2003).

17. Ibid., 214.

18. English rhetoric about colonization has been extensively treated by historians and literary critics. Noteworthy books that are particularly relevant include Morgan, *American Slavery, American Freedom*; Francis Jennings, *The Invasion of America: Indians, Colonialism, and the Cant of Conquest* (New York: Norton, 1975); and Peter Hulme, "John Smith and Pocahontas," in *Colonial Encounters: Europe and the Native Caribbean, 1492–1797* (London: Methuen, 1986).

19. Sir Thomas More, *Utopia*, ed. David Harris Sacks (1516; Boston: Bedford Books, 1999), 142.

20. George Peckham, *A True Report of the Late Discoveries by Sir Humphrey Gilbert* (1583), in *Envisioning America: English Plans for the Colonization of North America*, ed. Peter C. Mancall (Boston: Bedford Books, 1995), 64–65.

21. Thomas Harriot, *A Briefe and True Report of the New Found Land of Virginia*, in Mancall, *Envisioning America*, 77.

22. Joyce Chaplin, *Subject Matter: Technology, the Body, and Science on the Anglo-American Frontier, 1500–1676* (Cambridge, Mass.: Harvard University Press, 2001), 36–37. The powder horn is difficult to make out and has often been taken to be a doll in Elizabethan dress. I am grateful to Buck Woodard for pointing out to me that it was almost certainly a horn.

23. King James, "Instructions for Government," November 20, 1606, in Barbour, *Jamestown Voyages*, 1:43.

24. London Council, "Instructions Given by Way of Advice," written between November 20 and December 19, 1606, in Barbour, *Jamestown Voyages*, 1:52.

25. Ralph Hamor, *A True Discourse of the Present State of Virginia* (1615; Richmond: Virginia State Library, 1957), 44. De Bry included engravings of ancient Picts with Harriot's *Briefe and True Report*; they are reproduced in Mancall, *Envisioning America*, 103–6. For scholarly discussion of the matter, see Kupperman, *Indians and English*, 58–59, and Chaplin, *Subject Matter*, chap. 3, as entrées into an extensive literature.

26. Smith, *Description*, in *CWCJS* 1:360. "All the Romanes were not Scipios; nor all the Geneweses, Columbuses; nor all the Spanyards, Corteses." Scholars who have noted Smith's fascination with Cortés include Morgan, *American Slavery, American Freedom*, 77, and John Hart, *Representing the New World: The English and French Uses of the Example of Spain* (New York: Palgrave, 2001), 214–18.

27. George Percy, "Observations Gathered Out of a Discourse of the Plantation of the Southerne Colonie in Virginia," in Barbour, *Jamestown Voyages*, 1:129.

28. Pedro de Zúñiga to Philip III, September 22, 1607, in Barbour, *Jamestown Voyages*, 1:115–16.

29. William Strachey, *Historie of Travell into Virginia Britania*, ed. Louis B. Wright and Virginia Freund (1612; London: Hakluyt Society, 1953), 92.

30. Ibid., 93. For a general discussion of mixed English feelings regarding Spain, see Hart, *Representing the New World*, chap. 5.

31. Strachey, *Historie of Travell*, 93–94. Strachey was familiar with the story of Malinche Gómara's account of the conquest of Mexico, as he elsewhere cited Nicholson's 1578 translation titled *A Pleasant Historie*. He had almost certainly read other Spanish accounts of the conquest as well.

THREE
First Contact

1. This "gentleman of ye colony" was almost certainly Gabriel Archer. Indeed, the "Relation" is generally cited as his. See "A relation of the Discovery of our River written and observed by a gentleman of ye Colony," in *The Jamestown Voyages Under the First Charter, 1606–1609*, ed. Philip Barbour (Cambridge, Eng.: Hakluyt Society, 1969), 1:80–98.

2. Opechankeno was often called Powhatan's "brother," but that relationship almost certainly existed on a symbolic level. Biologically, they were probably cousins.

3. John Smith, *A True Relation of Such Occurrences and accidents of noate as hath happned in Virginia* (London: John Tappe, 1608), in *CWCJS* 1:45–47. Smith's account is borne out as much as it can be by the testimony of others who were on a barge that went partway up the river with him and by the fact that the two other men he took with him as he continued on the smaller canoe were indeed killed. I have omitted from the story his assertion that he was surrounded by two hundred warriors, all aiming at him: this is obviously a wild exaggeration, which he included in order to excuse himself for having fallen into their custody. The commentary on what he did not know, and on what Opechankeno probably intended to convey, is my own.

4. Ibid., 1:47.

5. Ibid., 1:49–53. Scholars have found several references to some sort of list or even dictonary prepared by Thomas Harriot, but it is no longer extant. Lists of words that have been found in works published by Harriot have been collected in *A Vocabulary of Roanoke* (Southampton, Pa.: Evolution Publishing, 1999). See Archer, "Relation of the Discovery," in Barbour, *Jamestown Voyages*, 1:82, 88, for an example of a settler using specific Algonkian words at first contact, and recording his use in a report written in June 1607.

6. Stories of the Spanish finding sacrifice victims being fattened in cages appear, for example, in Francisco López de Gómara, *Historia de la conquista de México* (Saragossa, 1554), which was translated by Thomas Nicholson in 1578 (see chapter 2, note 10).

7. Smith, *True Relation*, in *CWCJS* 1:47.

8. A good biography of Smith is Alden T. Vaughan, *American Genesis: Captain John Smith and the Founding of Virginia* (Boston: Little Brown, 1975). Readers should understand that our information on Smith's early years comes only from his own later writings, in which he tends to exaggerate. I have culled a bare outline of what I believe can be considered facts, being more conservative than Vaughan in my willingness to believe Smith.

9. Neither Smith nor anyone else on board knew with certainty who had been named as council members. Instead, Captain Christopher Newport was given a locked box containing the list of names, with instructions to open it only after they had landed at an appropriate site. It was thought best not to divide authority on the voyage over. Still, Smith undoubtedly had an inkling.

10. The most detailed English account of these earliest of interactions is George Percy, "Observations gathered out of a Discourse of the Plantation of the Southerne Colonie in Virginia," in Barbour, *Jamestown Voyages*, 1:129–46. After the earliest weeks, the most detailed account of relations with the Indians is John Smith's *True Relation*, in *CWCJS* 1. Other helpful accounts are by Gabriel Archer, Francis Magnel, Francis Perkins, and Edward Maria Wingfield, all in Barbour, *Jamestown Voyages*. The remainder of this chapter is built from all these sources, without citation wherever they agree. Whenever I have relied on a specific statement made by only one individual, however, I have noted it.

11. Helen Rountree, *Pocahontas's People: The Powhatan Indians of Virginia Through Four Centuries* (Norman: University of Oklahoma Press, 1990), 30–31.

12. Archaeological excavations at Jamestown have revealed hundreds of shattered projectile points. The English said they "burst" against their armor. See Helen Rountree and E. Randolph Turner III, *Before and After Jamestown: Virginia's Powhatan Indians and Their Predecessors* (Gainesville: University Press of Florida, 2002), 127.

13. The best summary of these events from the indigenous point of view is Philip Barbour, *Pocahontas and Her World* (Boston: Houghton Mifflin, 1970), 11–13.

14. Archer, "Relation of the Discovery," in Barbour, *Jamestown Voyages*, 1:98.

15. Percy, "Observations," in Barbour, *Jamestown Voyages*, 1:143–45.

16. Smith, *True Relation*, in *CWCJS* 1:33.

17. Until recently scholars tended to accept Smith's version that he and a hunting party had accidentally collided. Undoubtedly that is how it felt to him. But it is impossible to believe that the Pamunkey men in their hunting season, noting and analyzing every movement in the woods, would have been unaware of the travels of a barge full of Englishmen. For the new interpretation, see Helen Rountree, "Pocahontas: The Hostage Who Became Famous," in *Sifters: Native American Women's Lives*, ed. Theda Perdue (New York: Oxford, 2001), 17.

18. All settlers who met Powhatan described this type of reception. Smith, *True Relation*, in *CWCJS* 1:53. Smith used the word "wenches" in later accounts; they were "many young women" here. A more accurate phonetic transcription of the Powhatan word for "raccoon" is probably *a-reh-kan*. Certain tribes had a completely different nomenclature. See Frank Siebert, "Resurrecting Virginia Algonquian from the Dead: The Reconstituted and Historical Phonology of Powhatan," in *Studies in Southeastern Indian Languages*, ed. James M. Crawford (Athens: University of Georgia Press, 1975), 371.

19. The story appeared in John Smith, *The General Historie of Virginia, New England and the Summer Isles* (London: Michael Sparkes, 1624), in *CWCJS* 2. A few have been so eager to believe some version of the story as to claim that Smith's 1624 account is likely to have been more, not less, accurate than the 1608 report, in that the colony was by then successfully launched and it was therefore no longer necessary to hide the sufferings of the colonists. Certainly the Virginia Company investors had much to hide in 1608. The assertion, however, that Smith was thus more honest in 1624 ignores the myriad obvious exaggerations in other parts of the narrative, as well as the fact that to have claimed Pocahontas and her father had taken a shine to him in 1608 would have been helpful to the colonial venture, not detrimental to it.

20. John Smith, *The True Travels, Adventures and Observations of Captain John Smith* (London: Thomas Slater, 1630), in *CWCJS* 3:187. Editor Barbour notes that the word *banyo* is bath in Turkish, and that there is a description of these baths in Hakluyt. Literary critics have made apt analyses of Smith's texts. An excellent place to begin is Mary C. Fuller, "Mastering Words: The Jamestown Colonists and John Smith," in *Voyages in Print: English Travel to America, 1576–1624* (Cambridge: Cambridge University Press, 1995).

21. Quoted in Smith, *True Travels*, in *CWCJS* 3:145.

22. J. A. Leo Lemay, *Did Pocahontas Save Captain John Smith?* (Athens: University of Georgia Press, 1992). For those who are interested in the nineteenth-century debate, Lemay provides an excellent entrée.

23. Rountree, "Pocahontas," 17–18. For her analysis Rountree draws on narrations of captivity among other Algonkian groups up and down the East Coast over the ensuing century. For Henry Spelman's description of "their manner of execution," see his "Relation of Virginia," in *Travels and Works of Captain John Smith*, ed. Edward Arber and A. G. Bradley (Edinburgh: John Grant, 1910), cxi.

24. Scholars who have supported this theory include historians Kathleen Brown, in "In Search of Pocahontas," in *The Human Tradition in Colonial Latin America*, ed. Ian Steele and Nancy Rhoden (Wilmington, Del.: Scholarly Resources, 1999); Karen Ordahl Kupperman, in *Indians and English: Facing Off in Early America* (Ithaca, N.Y.: Cornell University Press, 2000); Daniel Richter, in *Facing East from Indian Country: A Native History of Early America* (Cambridge, Mass.: Harvard University Press, 2001); as well as anthropologists Frederic Gleach, in *Powhatan's World and Colonial Virginia: A Conflict of Cultures* (Lincoln: University of Nebraska Press, 1997); and Margaret Holmes Williamson, in "Pocahontas and Captain John Smith," *History and Anthropology* 5 (1992): 365–402. Rountree in her previously cited works acknowledges that such an adoption might have occurred, but she is not absolutely convinced and certainly does not believe a young girl would have been present at such a ceremony rather than doing evening chores.

25. Smith, *True Relation*, in *CWCJS* 1:53–57. In his next book, written when he had had more effective communication with the Indians, Smith claimed Powhatan said that whoever told him there was a great salt sea across the mountains was lying. John Smith et al., *The Proceedings of the English Colonie in Virginia* (London: Joseph Barnes, 1612), in *CWCJS* 1:236. Rountree has pointed out that the Indians frequently traveled long distances and were familiar with a wide terrain. They may well have wanted to hide all that they knew from the English, or the English may have failed to understand them. "The Powhatans and Other Woodland Indians as Travelers," in Rountree, *Powhatan Foreign Relations, 1500–1722* (Charlottesville: University of Virginia Press, 1993).

26. Smith et al., *Proceedings of the English Colonie*, in *CWCJS* 1:213.

27. Smith, *General Historie*, in *CWCJS* 2:151.

28. Williamson demonstrates that it might have meant "my son" in "Pocahontas and Captain John Smith," 378.

29. Smith et al., *Proceedings of the English Colonie*, in *CWCJS* 1:248.

30. Alan Gallay makes the apt comparison to the confederacies in the Deep South, which survived longer, in *The Indian Slave Trade: The Rise of the English Empire in the American South, 1670–1717* (New Haven, Conn.: Yale University Press, 2002).

31. For an assessment of the importance of trade goods in this context, see Stephen R. Potter, "Early English Effects on Virginia Algonquian Exchange and Tribute in the Tidewater Potomac," in *Powhatan's Mantle: Indians in the Colonial Southeast*, ed. Peter H. Wood, Gregory A. Waselkov, and M. Thomas Hartley (Lincoln: University of Nebraska Press, 1989); and Martin Quitt, "Trade and Acculturation at Jamestown, 1607–1609: The Limits of Understanding," in *WMQ* 52:2 (1995): 227–58. The Chesapeake may well have been destroyed before Powhatan met Smith, but probably after the English first appeared.

32. Williamson, "Pocahontas and Captain John Smith," 369 (quotation). Gleach in *Powhatan's World* makes assumptions like Williamson's. Anthropologists and liter-

ary critics often privilege Native Americans' cultural framework in assessing their actions. They do this with the best of intentions, in response to the more traditional "Western" narrative, which often judged indigenous actions in the light of Western assumptions and thus made Indian choices look foolish or naïve. They have, however, often taken this view to an extreme, implicitly (and occasionally even explicitly) denying Indians the ability to change their worldviews and their methods when faced with entirely new conditions. A famous example in another arena has been scholars' insistence until recently that Moctezuma, the astute and successful twenty-year emperor of the Aztecs, assumed that Hernando Cortés was a god when his priests told him so and proceeded to make political and military decisions based on this conviction. Historians have now taken that notion apart. See Camilla Townsend, "Burying the White Gods: New Perspectives on the Conquest of Mexico," *American Historical Review* 108 (2003): 659–87. Powhatan was undoubtedly influenced by his religion and his priests, but probably no more so than were the English.

33. To determine what Algonkian Indians really wanted to buy, historians consult merchants' records. For a list of the best-selling goods, see Richter, *Facing East from Indian Country*, 43. On Spelman's statement that since the arrival of the English the people wanted to do their farming with iron tools, see his "Relation of Virginia," in Arber and Bradley, *Travels and Works*, cxi.

34. Smith, *General Historie*, in *CWCJS* 2:106, and *Proceedings of the English Colonie* in *CWCJS* 1:213, 232. For comments on earlier English fantasies in this regard, see William Hamlin, "Imagined Apotheoses: Drake, Harriot, and Ralegh in the Americas," in *Journal of the History of Ideas* (1996): 405–28.

35. Smith, *General Historie*, in *CWCJS* 2:149. The Indians' attitude toward European writing is debatable. Scholars have not reached consensus, and some would argue that it was indeed mystifying to the Indians.

36. For a transcription and rough translation of one mocking song about the English, see William Strachey, *The Historie of Travell into Virginia Britania*, ed. Louis B. Wright and Virginia Freund (1612; London: Hakluyt Society, 1953), 85–86. An interesting article on Algonkians' condescending attitudes toward the French is Cornelius Jaenen, "Amerindian Views of French Culture in the Seventeenth Century," in *American Encounters: Natives and Newcomers from European Contact to Indian Removal, 1500–1850*, ed. Peter C. Mancall and James H. Merrell (New York: Routledge, 2000).

37. Thomas Harriot, *A Briefe and True Report of the New Found Land of Virginia*, in *Envisioning America: English Plans for the Colonization of North America*, ed. Peter C. Mancall (Boston: Bedford Books, 1995), 79.

38. Pepiscuminah, werowance of the Quioccohannock, cited in Strachey, *Historie of Travell*, 101. It should be noted that Kupperman in *Indians and English* discusses another possibility at some length—namely, that the Algonkians believed the newcomers were their own ancestors, returned from the dead, strengthened by their experiences in the other world. But I have found no evidence for this theory among the Powhatan specifically.

39. Joyce Chaplin writes incisively: "Indian interpretations of nature and responses to colonization were innovative, profound, witty and ironic." See her *Subject Matter: Technology, the Body, and Science on the Anglo-American Frontier, 1500–1676* (Cambridge, Mass.: Harvard University Press, 2001), 34. For the religious views of Pocahontas's brother-in-law, see Samuel Purchas, *Purchas, His Pilgrimage*, 3rd ed. (London:

William Stansby, 1617), 954–55. Pepiscuminah, cited in note 38 above, who said he thought the Christian gods were stronger, also absolutely refused to convert.

FOUR
Jamestown

1. John Smith, *A True Relation of Such Occurrences and accidents of noate as hath hapned in Virginia* (London: John Tappe, 1608), in *CWCJS* 1:63.

2. Ibid., 1:65.

3. Ibid., 1:79. On Namontack being presented in England as a son of Powhatan, see Pedro de Zúñiga to His Majesty the King of Spain, June 26, 1608, in *The Jamestown Voyages under the First Charter, 1606–1609*, ed. Philip Barbour (Cambridge, Eng.: Hakluyt Society, 1969), 1:163.

4. Smith, *True Relation*, in *CWCJS* 1:79.

5. John Smith, *A Map of Virginia with a Description of the Country* (London: Joseph Barnes, 1612), in *CWCJS* 1:137. The word is defined here as "friend," but it had to have been "my friend." See Frank T. Siebert, "Resurrecting Virginia Algonquian from the Dead: The Reconstituted and Historical Phonology of Powhatan," in *Studies in Southeastern Indian Languages*, ed. James M. Crawford (Athens: University of Georgia Press, 1975).

6. Archaeological excavations at Jamestown have proved a marvelous complement to the documentary record. The fort was considerably smaller than the colonists had boasted. The unexpected outbuilding is considered to have been a very early trading post because of the high percentage of copper bits found among the artifacts, the presence of a 1607–1609 James I halfpenny, and the nature and date of the artifacts later used to fill in the cellar around 1610. William Kelso, J. Eric Deetz, Seth Mallios, and Beverly Straube, *Jamestown Rediscovery* (Richmond: Association for the Preservation of Virginia Antiquities, 2001), 7:1–8, 15–34.

7. Smith, *True Relation*, in *CWCJS* 1:93. Captain Nelson, who had sailed with Newport but become separated from him, arrived in Jamestown after Newport's departure for England. He left again, carrying Smith's report, on June 2.

8. Ibid., 1:95. On Opechankeno's daughter coming to represent her father, see 1:75.

9. William Strachey, *The Historie of Travell into Virginia Britania*, ed. Louis B. Wright and Virginia Freund (1612; London: Hakluyt Society, 1953), 72. Strachey leaves it somewhat unclear whether he himself ever saw Pocahontas, but his arrival in May 1610 renders it virtually impossible. Furthermore, if he had seen her himself, he probably would have said so, as he did about other people he met there.

10. Kathleen Brown, "In Search of Pocahontas," in *The Human Tradition in Colonial Latin America*, ed. Ian K. Steele and Nancy L. Rhoden (Wilmington, Del.: Scholarly Resources, 1999), 77.

11. Karen Robertson, "Pocahontas at the Masque," *Signs: Journal of Women in Culture and Society* 21:3 (1996): 552.

12. Frank T. Siebert, "Resurrecting Virginia Algonquian," is the best treatment of the subject. The piece has been rendered accessible to the general public in the work of Helen Rountree, "Powhatan Indian Words," distributed by the United Indians of

Virginia through their Web site (www.unitedindiansva.org). Smith and other first-hand observers wrote about the mutual intelligibility existing in the region among the Powhatans, and explicitly excluded those whom we now know to have been of Iroquoian or Siouan stock. Some Virginia Indians are currently attempting to use linguists' techniques to reconstruct the probable language of the predecessors of the Powhatans (Proto-Algonkian): this can be done to some extent by comparing living Algonkian languages and what is known of Powhatan in order to derive most likely roots. For a leading example of the ways in which texts in Indian languages, wherever they exist, can be made to yield insights into a culture, see James Lockhart, *The Nahuas After the Conquest* (Stanford, Calif.: Stanford University Press, 1992).

13. Smith, *Map of Virginia*, in *CWCJS* 1:137–39.

14. Ibid., 1:137. See editor Barbour's commentary regarding the appearance of *uttasantosough* in North Carolina in 1701. Siebert, in "Resurrecting Virginia Algonquian," has separate entries for *boat* and *canoe*, 318 and 322.

15. See chapter 1, note 4, on Pocahontas's age.

16. The notion of girls in "primitive" societies reaching menarche early is purely a racist fabrication. In fact, with their more physically demanding lifestyle, contact-period Indian girls would have arrived at puberty later on average than urban and suburban girls in our modern world.

17. Smith et al., *The Proceedings of the English Colonie in Virginia* (London: Joseph Barnes, 1612), in *CWCJS* 1:274–75. Rebecca Faery has analyzed the sexual innuendo concerning Pocahontas in Smith's texts in *Cartographies of Desire: Captivity, Race and Sex in the Shaping of an American Nation* (Norman: University of Oklahoma Press, 1999), 103–7. The reference to the council's investigation of Smith's conduct is very interesting. Most of the records of the Virginia Company are missing from this period, so we have no transcript of the proceedings, but the investigation undoubtedly took place if Smith and his advocates mentioned it. We know that several gentlemen who had been in the colony, including Edward Maria Wingfield and George Percy, made very negative reports about Smith's behavior—indeed they had to, having been mutinous under his presidency—and that Smith struggled to regain the favor of his London allies: it makes perfect sense that such an investigation occurred in this period.

18. "The Nansemonds still remember this incident," writes Deanna Beacham in a personal communication. In 1988, a remembering ceremony was conducted by then—Assistant Chief Oliver Perry and the Nansemond people, in which representatives from Jamestown formally returned some corn.

19. Philip Barbour, *Pocahontas and Her World* (Boston: Houghton Mifflin, 1970), 39.

20. Smith et al., *Proceedings of the English Colonie*, in *CWCJS* 1:237.

21. Ibid., 1:239.

22. Ibid., 1:256. Richard Wiffin, William Phettiplace, and Anas Todkill signed this piece.

23. Ibid., 1:242–48.

24. Ibid. These words all come to us through Smith, of course, and may not represent what Powhatan actually said. However, they are hardly true to the typical English fantasy of such conversations, and what Powhatan purportedly outlines here is in fact what he went on to do.

25. Helen Rountree makes this point in "Pocahontas: The Hostage Who Became Famous," in *Sifters: Native American Women's Lives*, ed. Theda Perdue (New York: Oxford, 2001), 20. Compare Smith's brief and vague reference in *Proceedings of the English Colonie* (*CWCJS* 1:275) to the melodramatic description of tears streaming down Pocahontas's face in *General Historie* (*CWCJS* 2:198–99).

26. Smith et al., *Proceedings of the English Colonie*, in *CWCJS* 1:261–62.

27. Ibid., 1:257. The rest of the section is equally interesting. An excellent brief scholarly overview of the differences between sedentary and nonsedentary cultures in the Americas is John E. Kicza, *Resilient Cultures: America's Native Peoples Confront European Colonization, 1500–1800* (Upper Saddle River, N.J.: Prentice Hall, 2003).

28. George Percy, the only English nobleman present, became president after Smith left. He later wrote a report to his brother, Lord Percy, about this horrible period. "A Trewe Relacyon of the Precedinges and Ocurrentes of Momente wch have happned in Virginia . . . ano 1609 untill my departure outt of the Country wch was in ano Dni 1612" was reprinted in *Tyler's Quarterly Historical and Genealogical Magazine* 3:4 (1922): 259–82. Percy, from whom we learn that Powhatan's children were aboard the pinnace, said explicitly that he wrote in order to counteract "falseties and malicious detractions" that others had printed. One of the objectionable texts was probably Henry Spelman's, who in 1613 published the first version of the Ratcliffe debacle—claiming that he had been sent to Jamestown by Powhatan, with whom he had been living, specifically to invite Ratcliffe and the others to come and trade and, having no idea of Powhatan's perfidiousness, had done so. This account is usually accepted, but that Powhatan asked the settlers to come is undoubtedly false. Percy did not say there was any invitation to come and trade; he said he sent the pinnace only because his calculations showed they would shortly run out of food. It would have made no sense for him to have denied the invitation if there was one: that would have provided him a perfect excuse for the disaster that followed. Spelman, on the other hand, whom everyone apparently knew to have accompanied the expedition, and who had undoubtedly bragged of his ability to communicate with the "savages," had every reason to fabricate. He disappeared immediately after they anchored, before the slaughter, and was not seen again for many months, so when he eventually managed to return to London, some fast talking was in order. The problems in Jamestown caused everyone involved to feel defensive and to accuse one another of lying. Given everything we know about the policies of Powhatan and the characters of George Percy and Henry Spelman (one apparently acting in good faith, the other a self-avowed miscreant), it seems unthinkable that the paramount chief attempted to lure English people upriver in order to kill them, knowing full well they were only a fraction of the total. On the contrary, he clearly wanted them to stay away. He was showing the colonists what he would do to them if they did not.

29. The best study of Jamestown's rising and falling population is in the appendix of Frederick Fausz, "An 'Abundance of Blood Shed on Both Sides': England's First Indian War, 1609–1614," *VMHB* 98 (1990), 55–56.

FIVE

Kidnapped

1. William Strachey, *Historie of Travell into Virginia Britania*, ed. Louis B. Wright and Virginia Freund (1612; London: Hakluyt Society, 1953), 62, mentions the marriage.

Helen Rountree points out the significance of Kocoom's not having been a chief in "Pocahontas, the Hostage Who Became Famous," in *Sifters: Native American Women's Lives*, ed. Theda Perdue (New York: Oxford, 2001), 20–21. See Ralph Hamor, *A True Discourse of the Present State of Virginia* (1615; Richmond: Virginia State Library, 1957), 42, on the marriage of Pocahontas's eleven-year-old sister.

2. Strachey, *Historie of Travell*, 59, 62.

3. Henry Spelman, "Relation of Virginia," in *Travels and Works of Captain John Smith*, ed. Edward Arber and A. G. Bradley (Edinburgh: John Grant, 1910), cvii, provides our best description of the marriage ceremony. Rountree analyzes what we know of courtship and marriage in "Pocahontas," 20–23. Margaret Holmes Williamson discusses the symbolism of white beads in *Powhatan Lords of Life and Death: Command and Consent in Seventeenth-Century Virginia* (Lincoln: University of Nebraska, 2003), 253.

4. William Strachey (see note 1) wrote about the marriage in 1612. His book was never published at the time and thus might conceivably be discounted as evidence of what the English knew, but it is significant that Strachey noted the event even though he himself had not met Pocahontas. That is, he was getting his information about her from fellow colonists in Jamestown and from Indian visitors to the fort. It seems clear that her doings were a subject of gossip and were generally known.

5. Rountree, "Pocahontas," 23.

6. John Smith made this claim after speaking to her and her English husband in his *General Historie of Virginia, New England and the Summer Isles* (London: Michael Sparkes, 1624), in *CWCJS* 2:232–32. (All three of them had special reason to dislike Spelman and note his doings.) Spelman himself says nothing of the kind, it must be admitted, but he hated John Smith and all those associated with him, and the story he offered instead about how he got to the Patowomeck makes no sense at all. He was the third son of a knight, but having behaved badly in early adolescence, according to his own testimony, he got himself shipped off to America, whereupon Smith deposited him with one of Powhatan's sons to learn the language, incorporating him in part of a trade deal. Spelman never forgave him: "Unknown to me he sold me to him." After Ratcliffe and his men had been killed, the boy began to feel less welcome. He recalled: "It happned that the Kinge of Patomeck cam to visit the great Powetan, wher beinge a while with him, he shewed such kindness to [Thomas] Savage, Samuell [a Dutchman], and myself as we determined to goe away with him." Spelman said that Thomas Savage had a change of heart as they left, ran back to Powhatan, and told him what was up. Angry at the possibility of losing his translators, Powhatan sent warriors after them. The Dutchman ended up being killed. With perfect bravado Spelman explained, "I shifted for myself and gott to the Patomeckes cuntry." Since he was a complete stranger to the region, it certainly seems that he left something out of the story here. The piece that Smith offers—that Pocahontas had a connection with the Patowomeck and used it to help him—seems to offer the solution. Spelman, who was encouraged by patrons to blame John Smith for virtually all of the colony's ills, had every reason to avoid acknowledging the young woman whose name was often paired with Smith's by the time he published his account. See his "Relation of Virginia," in Arber and Bradley, *Travels and Works*, ci–cxv.

7. I have not seen the tombstone myself. I am using Philip Barbour's translation from the Latin, provided in *Pocahontas and Her World* (Boston: Houghton Mifflin, 1970), 113. Barbour does a fine job of collecting all the evidence that we have about the

Rolfes of Heacham, while still acknowledging that there is no definite proof that the John Rolfe in Virginia was the same as the one born in Heacham. There is a strong folk tradition that John Rolfe was descended from the Heacham line.

8. David A. Price has used his expertise as a financial journalist to calculate the approximate modern equivalence. See *Love and Hate in Jamestown: John Smith, Pocahontas, and the Heart of a New Nation* (New York: Alfred A. Knopf, 2003), 239–41. Of course, we must understand that this is only an approximate value: it is impossible to do a final mathematical calculation based on a rate of inflation, for what an average person consumed in the year 1600 bears almost no resemblance to what an average American consumes today.

9. Pedro de Zúñiga to Philip III, March 15 and April 12, 1609. Reproduced in *The Jamestown Voyages Under the First Charter, 1606–1609*, ed. Philip Barbour (Cambridge, Eng.: Hakluyt Society, 1969), 2:256, 259. Extracts of the 1609 tradesmen's guild records are printed in Alexander Brown, *The Genesis of the United States* (1890; New York: Russell & Russell, 1964), 1:276–78.

10. William Symonds, *Virginia: A Sermon Preached at White-Chapel, in the Presence of many, Honourable and Worshipfull, the Adventurers and Planters for Virginia, 25 April, 1609* (New York: Da Capo Press, 1968), 10, 15, 25.

11. Ibid., 30, 35.

12. Ibid., 54; preceding quotation, 52.

13. "Instructions, orders and constitucions by way of advise . . . to Sir Thomas Gates knight" (1609), reproduced in Barbour, *Jamestown Voyages*, 2:266.

14. "Instructions, orders and constitucions to Sir Thomas West knight" (1610), reproduced in Susan Myra Kingsbury, *The Records of the Virginia Company* (Washington, D.C.: U.S. Government Printing Office, 1933), 3:27.

15. William Strachey, *A True Reportory of the Wreck and Redemption of Sir Thomas Gates, Knight, upon and from the Islands of the Bermudas* (London, 1610), in *A Voyage to Virginia in 1609: Two Narratives*, ed. Louis B. Wright (Charlottesville: University of Virginia Press, 1964), 3–8.

16. Strachey, *True Reportory*, 10–15. Silvester Jourdain, "A Discovery of the Bermudas, Otherwise Called the Isle of Devils," in Wright, *A Voyage*, 105–7.

17. Strachey, *True Reportory*, 17–53.

18. Ibid., 54. Strachey was clearly touched by the birth and death of Bermuda.

19. Ibid., 63–64.

20. William Strachey, "For the Colony in Virginea Britannia, Lawes Divine, Morall and Martiall" (London, 1612), in *Laws Divine, Morall and Martiall*, ed. David Flaherty (Charlottesville: University of Virginia Press, 1969). Edmund Morgan (among others) has analyzed the militaristic tone of this moment in *American Slavery, American Freedom: The Ordeal of Colonial Virginia* (New York: Norton, 1975), 79–80. Frederick Fausz argues forcefully that hostilities were such that the period should be referred to as the First Anglo-Powhatan War. He shows that the Indians could more than hold their own in the earliest period, before many English arrived. "An 'Abundance of Blood Shed on Both Sides': England's First Indian War, 1609-1614," *VMHB* 98 (1990): 3–54.

21. Strachey, *True Reportory*, 92; previous quotation, 90.

22. George Percy, "A Trewe Relacyon of the Predecinges and Ocurrentes of Mo-mente wch have happned in Virginia . . . ano 1609 untill my departure outt of the Country wch was in ano Dni 1612," *Tyler's Quarterly Historical and Genealogical Magazine* 3:4 (1922), 271–72. Helen Rountree, in *Pocahontas's People: The Powhatan Indians of Virginia Through Four Centuries* (Norman: University of Oklahoma Press, 1990), 55, discusses the fate of the Paspaheghs. "It rankles that De la Warr, who murdered women and children, has a state named after him, and Powhatan only a county, which wasn't even really a part of his territory," writes Deanna Beacham, Virginia Council on Indians, in a personal communication. In 1993, in the course of creating the Governor's Land housing complex and golf course in Williamsburg, eighteen Paspahegh skeletons were discovered. Nicholas Luccketti of the James River Institute of Archaeology conducted immediate excavations, the results of which have been studied by scholars. The bones were respectfully reburied later that year under the leadership of Oliver L. Perry, chief emeritus of the Nansemond. The procedures used in the Paspahegh case have become a model: Indian remains from numerous sites in Virginia have since been repatriated, rather than being allowed to remain in museum drawers. In this country, in the past, only Indian skeletons have become the property of scholars; other uncovered human remains have regularly been reburied. In the year 2000, the Governor's Land Foundation installed a stone marking the new gravesite of the eighteen slaughtered Paspaheghs. See Bill Tolbert, "Paspahegh Indians Honored," *Virginia Gazette*, December 20, 2000.

23. Strachey first wrote about this incident in *True Reportory*, 94, which he sent back to England for publication not long after reaching Virginia in 1610. When he wrote the manuscript, the English still had the king's son in custody and still planned to send him to England. Later, after the story had fully unfolded, he wrote about it again in *Historie of Travell*, 65–66. Juxtaposing the two accounts provides a glimpse of the way in which the English often misunderstood Indian statements and then perpetuated inaccurate accounts if time did not offer them a corrective. Strachey called the king's son Kainta, for example, in the first account, and only later said that his name was Tangoit. Since the name of the werowance was Tackone-kinta-co, it seems likely that a morpheme sounding like *kinta* or *kainta* denoted royalty but was not an actual name, as he had first thought.

24. Percy, "Trewe Relacyon," 273. Other accounts mention the attack as well.

25. "The Relation of the Lord De La Warr, 1611," in *Narratives of Early Virginia, 1606–1625*, ed. Lyon Gardiner Tyler (New York: Charles Scribner's Sons, 1907), 212, 213. Philip Barbour has done the best job of piecing together all known references to Argall in order to offer an overview of his preceding life, in *Pocahontas and Her World*, 67–85. Barbour sees Argall as a relatively sympathetic character.

26. Barbour, *Pocahontas*, 97–103. Barbour draws largely from Argall's own writing. (See note 27.)

27. Argall wrote to his friend Nicholas Hawes in England in June 1613. Hawes let the letter pass into the hands of Samuel Purchas, who was compiling all the missives he could from the New World. It was later published in *Purchas, His Pilgrimes* (1625; Glasgow: James MacLehose, 1906), 19:90–95. In the letter Argall displays remarkable awareness of Algonkian political perspectives.

28. Argall to Hawes. The spelling of *Yapassus* and *Pasptanzie* deserve comment. The werowance's name is represented by different Englishmen as *Iapassus* or *Japazuz*,

leading me to believe that the name began with what we would today call a soft (or palatal) *y* sound, as I have represented it here. The village was called Pastancie by Argall, but Pasptanzie by Henry Spelman, who actually lived there and spoke the language.

29. Ralph Hamor, *A True Discourse of the Present State of Virginia* (1615; Richmond: Virginia State Library, 1957), 5. Hamor's account of these events (3–6) is the one on which we must rely, as Argall himself passed lightly over the way in which Yapassus tricked Pocahontas into boarding the ship, giving no details at all. Another account appears in Smith's *General Historie*, but it is only a garbled version of Hamor's; indeed, Smith says at the beginning of the section that he got it from Hamor's book. In interpreting Hamor, who was in Jamestown and would have spoken to Argall and Ensign Swift, we must proceed with caution: he was writing a book to appeal to a London audience. The kidnapping of a fair damsel had to be made to appear a good and even noble deed, not a dastardly one. So Hamor left out information that Argall supplied about his own general conduct and that of the Indians: Hamor said instead that Yapassus would have sold anyone, even his own father, for the miserable copper kettle that Argall paid him, and that his wife was as evil and conniving as all women tend to be and cried copious crocodile tears—implying, in short, that Pocahontas was well out of their clutches. Ignoring such obviously gratuitous and even falsified details, however, we can see in the account the essentials of what took place. For an analysis of Hamor's construction of events, see Karen Robertson, "Pocahontas at the Masque," *Signs: Journal of Women in Culture and Society* 21:3 (1996): 566–67.

30. Hamor, *True Discourse*, 6. Robertson has commented on Pocahontas's significant silences in "Pocahontas at the Masque." For a future werowansqua's use of silence before making an impassioned speech, see Martha McCartney, "Cockacoeske, Queen of Pamunkey: Diplomat and Suzeraine," in *Powhatan's Mantle: Indians in the Colonial Southeast*, ed. Peter H. Wood, Gregory A. Waselkov, and M. Thomas Hartley (Lincoln: University of Nebraska Press, 1989), 177.

31. Argall to Hawes, in *Purchas, His Pilgrimes*, 19:93. Messengers generally used the waterways, but when a communication had to travel between two villages far upriver, it sometimes made more sense to send runners over the narrow necks of land. See Helen Rountree, "The Powhatans and Other Woodland Indians as Travelers," in *Powhatan Foreign Relations, 1500–1722* (Charlottesville: University Press of Virginia, 1993), 33.

32. Because of the problems resulting to the colony as a whole from individual acts of violence, the new laws promulgated under the second charter explicitly forbade rape: "No man shall ravish or force any woman, maid or Indian, or other, upon paine of death." Strachey, *Lawes Divine, Morall and Martiall*, 12. The rigid law does not seem to have been enforced, in this as in other matters. Frances Mossiker raises the issue of the disappearance of Pocahontas's former acquaintances in *Pocahontas: The Life and the Legend* (New York: Alfred A. Knopf, 1976), 161.

33. Situating the kidnapping of Pocahontas within her own understanding of what abductions were is a complex matter and open to debate. It is possible that she saw the kidnapping as a perfectly natural and even expected political event. Danielle Moretti-Langholtz, director of the American Indian Resources Center at the College of William and Mary, is currently engaged in research on this issue.

34. Strachey, *True Reportory*, 81–82.

35. John Rolfe was apparently living in Henrico, another settlement farther up-river. By July, a Londoner had the news. See *The Letters of John Chamberlain*, ed. Norman Egbert McClure (Philadelphia: American Philosophical Society, 1939), 470. Ralph Hamor, by his own admission in his introduction, had been casting about for a Virginia-related book topic that had not already been treated by "diverse others." When these events unfolded, he quickly began work and put "Powhatan's daughter" in the subtitle to *A True Discourse*.

SIX

Imprisonment

1. Diego de Molina to Diego Sarmiento de Acuña, 1614, in Alexander Brown, *Genesis of the United States* (1890; New York: Russell & Russell, 1964), 743.

2. The Reverend Whitaker was studying religion at Cambridge during the time when the King James Bible was being prepared, 1604–11. It was published at about the time he sailed, and as a religious enthusiast of the new order, he may well have had a copy of the huge, gothic-lettered folio edition with him in his trunks. But the book we know he had with him, which he had been using since boyhood, was the Geneva Bible, first printed in 1560 by Puritan exiles and used ever since by Protestant enthusiasts at Cambridge, like his father and his colleagues. Whitaker's language gives evidence of his close knowledge of that text. That Bible was smaller (a quarto rather than a folio) and used the more modern Roman typescript. It contained numerous illustrations, including a representation of well-armed Egyptians chasing Israelites to the Red Sea. Whitaker would have purchased just the pages, then taken them to a binder to be put in a cover designed according to his specifications. Given his station in life, the binding would have been fine and expensive. See Olga Opfell, *The King James Bible Translators* (London: McFarland, 1982), and Alister McGrath, *In the Beginning: The Story of the King James Bible* (New York: Doubleday, 2001). Ralph Hamor provides information on Powhatan's first offer of ransom in *A True Discourse of the Present State of Virginia* (1615; Richmond: Virginia State Library, 1957), 6.

3. Don Diego de Molina, unaddressed letter to "His Lordship," 1613, in *Narratives of Early Virginia, 1606–1625*, ed. Lyon Gardiner Tyler (New York: Charles Scribner's Sons, 1907), 218–24.

4. Archaeology tells us what the colonists failed to mention in their reports: Indian women lived in the fort. The prevalence of their pots and cooking utensils proves this, the implements being present in greater numbers than gifts and purchases alone could explain. See William Kelso, J. Eric Deetz, Seth Mallios, and Beverly Straube, *Jamestown Rediscovery* (Richmond: Association for the Preservation of Virginia Antiquities, 2001), 7:41–47.

5. Hamor, *True Discourse*, 29–31. It is a common misconception that the better houses had glass windows, because Jamestown was known for having had a glassworks. The latter industry, however, lasted only a few months before it was abandoned due to constant skirmishing with the Indians; it was not reestablished until the 1620s.

6. Reverend William Crashawe asserted that Whitaker was unmarried in his "Epistle Dedicatorie" to Alexander Whitaker, in *Good News from Virginia* (London: Felix Kyngston, 1613), C1. Karen Robertson, in "Pocahontas at the Masque," *Signs: Journal of Women in Culture and Society* 21:3 (1996): 551–83, and Kathleen Brown, in "In

Search of Pocahontas," in *The Human Tradition in Colonial America*, ed. Ian K. Steele and Nancy L. Rhoden (Wilmington, Del.: Scholarly Resources, 1999), both comment on the traumas that would have been associated with the changing of her clothing.

7. Whitaker himself tells us what he ate out of his garden in *Good News from Virginia*, 43.

8. On Whitaker's background, see Harry Culverwell Porter, "Alexander Whitaker: Cambridge Apostle to Virginia," *WMQ* 14 (1957): 317–43. William Crashawe gives a contemporary's view of him in his "Epistle Dedicatorie." Opfell, *King James Bible Translators*, 43–47, offers a picture of life at Cambridge University.

9. Whitaker, *Good News*, 5.

10. Whitaker to William Crashawe, August 1611, in Brown, *Genesis*, 497.

11. Whitaker, *Good News*, 8, 21, 23–24, respectively.

12. Ibid., 28, is an example of Whitaker's references to "whoring." Marquis de Flores (Zúñiga) to Philip III of Spain, August 1612, in Brown, *Genesis*, 572–73, tells of the complaints against him. Zúñiga's information undoubtedly came originally from Molina, who was in Jamestown and regularly passing on information through various conduits. The letter does not mention Whitaker by name but says, "A zealous minister of their sect was seriously wounded in many places because he reprehended them."

13. Whitaker, *Good News*, 24–25.

14. Ibid., 11.

15. John Rolfe to Sir Thomas Dale, 1614. A handwritten manuscript, which may have been the original or a copy made of it, is housed in Oxford's Bodleian Library. Philip Barbour published an exact transcription in *Pocahontas and Her World* (Boston: Houghton Mifflin, 1970), 247–52, and I have worked with his text; quotation on p. 248. Whitaker describes his schedule in a 1614 letter to his cousin William Gough, reprinted in Hamor, *True Discourse*, 59–61. It should be noted that the schedule did not appear in the first printing of Hamor's book, but only in the second, where it replaced an impolitic statement on Whitaker's part that Virginia was a good place for zealous Protestants to escape from High Church dress codes and ceremonies. That Hamor obviously replaced the lines himself does not mean that the outline of the schedule was inaccurate: he had been there, and so had a number of his readers.

16. Because the letter later appeared in print as an appendix to the book by his friend Ralph Hamor, which was written to advertise the first conversion of a Virginia Indian, one must ask if the letter could not have been written by someone else after the event, with publication frankly in mind. We have proof, however, that it was not. The writer of the original missive, which is housed in Oxford's Bodleian Library, declares he does not fear to marry an infidel, since their children will still be Christians, but the text made public by Hamor in 1615, though faithful to the handwritten document in all else, omits that section entirely. By 1615 Pocahontas had converted and was being advertised as a Christian; to have announced that Rolfe had wanted to marry her willy-nilly and live with a "barbarian" would have been counterproductive to the Virginia Company's publicity campaign. That something significant needed to be cut proves that Hamor did not simply create (or elicit) a document to suit his purposes. Philip Barbour has examined Rolfe's signature everywhere it is known to exist and asserts that the signature on the letter at Oxford appears to be that of Rolfe himself: *Po-*

cahontas and Her World, 279. The sentences on the religion of the children appear in the transciption in Barbour, *Pocahontas*, 250–51. Readers who examine Hamor, *True Discourse*, will see that the text there omits them, 66–67.

17. Rolfe in Barbour, *Pocahontas*, 249.

18. Nehemiah 13:24.

19. Rolfe in Barbour, *Pocahontas*, 250.

20. Ibid., 250–51.

21. Clara Sue Kidwell, "Indian Women as Cultural Mediators," *Ethnohistory* 39 (1992): 104–5, makes this point very effectively.

22. Readers who are interested in theories about objectification will note that the traditional vision of Pocahontas is in essence a pornographic narrative. Most modern men agree that what they find so enticing about pornography is that the women in that world generally adore and desire them unquestioningly. Such women have no needs or demands of their own, resent no injustices, never think of lodging a complaint or criticism. They are, indeed, much easier to have around than are real, human partners; they inspire fewer self-doubts. It is this same psychological dynamic that is at work in the imaginations of many Americans, male and female, who enjoy stories about "good Indians" who were happy to see their people conquered.

23. Daniel Richter, *Facing East from Indian Country: A Native History of Early America* (Cambridge, Mass.: Harvard University Press, 2001), 77–78. Other historians have made similar statements about the motivations of Indian women elsewhere. Susan Sleeper-Smith, for example, writing about the marriages Algonkian women made with French fur traders, asserts: "While encounter changed indigenous communities, it also encouraged the evolution of strategic behaviors that ensured cultural continuity." *Indian Women and French Men: Rethinking Cultural Encounter in the Western Great Lakes* (Amherst: University of Massachusetts Press, 2001), 2.

24. Sir Thomas Dale to D.M., in Hamor, *True Discourse*, 53–54. Deanna Beacham first pointed out to me the inconsistency of assuming that Pocahontas made her decisions entirely for cultural and political reasons. No one ever really does that, and Pocahontas certainly had good personal reasons for doing what she did.

25. Robertson, "Pocahontas at the Masque," 580.

26. Richter, *Facing East from Indian Country*, 73, mentions the possible need to escape from Whitaker's "oppressive tutelage."

27. There is significant documentary evidence concerning this event. A good treatment is Barbour's in *Pocahontas and Her World*, 119–24.

28. Hamor, *True Discourse*, 7.

29. Rolfe in Barbour, *Pocahontas*, 251. The events themselves are described in Hamor, *True Discourse*, 8–11, and again in a letter from Sir Thomas Dale to D.M., which Hamor appended to his book, 51–55. The two accounts contain interesting discrepancies. Dale clearly wanted it to appear that his own military prowess, and not the arrangements made by Pocahontas, had been decisive in bringing the peace. He even writes, "Now may you judge Sir, if the God of battailes have not a helping hand in this." As a result, he obfuscates in his narrative. Rolfe and Sparkes are never mentioned by name and appear only in the initial encounter, when the English were still

below Matchcot; it is left entirely unclear who actually spoke to whom in the talks that ended the standoff. He does not mention Pocahontas's marriage until the close of his account. Hamor obviously felt some pressure, not only to include this account but even to amend his. For in his account, after events have unfolded as they did specifically because of Pocahontas's willingness to marry Rolfe, Hamor suddenly says that Powhatan later heard of the "pretended marriage," as though it hadn't been on the table before, when it clearly was.

SEVEN
Pocahontas and John

1. Ralph Hamor says they came back downriver at the very end of March; Pocahontas was converted, then was married on April 5. *A True Discourse of the Present State of Virginia* (1615; Richmond: Virginia State Library, 1957), 10–11. It might be thought that Whitaker and Pocahontas had simply been waiting for the Easter season to perform the baptism, but Easter that year fell on April 24. They were thus in the middle of Lent when Pocahontas made her statement; it was not a time that they would have selected for religious reasons.

2. Whitaker's and Dale's statements are included in Hamor, *True Discourse*, 55, 60. See *The Book of Common Prayer*, ed. John E. Booty (1559; Washington, D.C.: Folger Shakespeare Library, 1976), 273. Pastors with radical tendencies, like Whitaker, sometimes departed from the Book of Common Prayer, especially in the wilds of Virginia, as he himself said. In this case, however, his own statement, and the obvious need to ensure that the baptism was never questioned, tell us that he followed the rules.

3. There is a rich literature on the complexities of Native American religious conversion. Due to the nature of the sources, the most detailed studies concern Mexican and New Mexican Indians. See, for example, Louise Burkhart, *The Slippery Earth: Nahua-Christian Moral Dialogue in Sixteenth-Century Mexico* (Tucson: University of Arizona Press, 1989); Ramón Gutiérrez, *When Jesus Came, the Corn Mothers Went Away: Marriage, Sexuality and Power in New Mexico, 1500–1846* (Stanford, Calif.: Stanford University Press, 1991); and James Lockhart, *The Nahuas After the Conquest: A Social and Cultural History of the Indians of Central Mexico, Sixteenth Through Eighteenth Centuries* (Stanford, Calif.: Stanford University Press, 1992). For Indians closer to the Powhatans, see, for example, James P. Ronda, "Generations of Faith: The Christian Indians of Martha's Vineyard," in *American Encounters: Natives and Newcomers from European Contact to Indian Removal, 1500–1850*, ed. Peter C. Mancall and James H. Merrell (New York: Routledge, 2000). The most compelling indigenous myth concerning a mortal girl being impregnated by a god that survives today is probably the Andean story of Caui Llaca in *The Huarochirí Manuscript: A Testament of Ancient and Colonial Andean Religion*, ed. Frank Salomon and George Urioste (Austin: University of Texas Press, 1991).

4. Genesis 24:18 (King James Version).

5. Genesis 25:22–23.

6. Genesis 24:63–64.

7. William Strachey, *The Historie of Travell into Virginia Britania*, ed. Louis B. Wright and Virginia Freund (1612; London: Hakluyt Society, 1953), 113–14.

8. Some English wrote "Matoka" or "Matoke," but enough wrote "Matoaka" to suggest that they were hearing *Matowka* rather than *Matoka*. On the root *matow-*, meaning "kindle," see Frank Siebert, "Resurrecting Virginia Algonquian from the Dead: The Reconstituted and Historical Phonology of Powhatan," in *Studies in Southeastern Indian Languages*, ed. James M. Crawford (Athens: University of Georgia Press, 1975), 352. On the likelihood that the suffix *-k* (which would be *k* + vowel in some situations) indicated "that which has a certain quality," see Siebert, 420. The idea that the name meant "Little Feather" was an invention of later generations.

9. Samuel Purchas, *Purchas, His Pilgrimage*, 3rd ed. (London: William Stansby, 1617), 941.

10. Alexander Whitaker was actually the first to mention the name Matoaka, in a letter to England dated June 18, 1614, reprinted in Hamor, *True Discourse*, 59, and he would have been delighted to learn that it had been hidden out of superstition on Pocahontas's part, which was now vanquished, but he asserts no such thing. Deanna Beacham first pointed out to me the unlikelihood of Pocahontas's choosing to use the name on a Virginia Company advertisement if it were indeed a secret identity in the traditional indigenous style.

11. Hamor, *True Discourse*, 11.

12. We know where Rolfe held lands, thanks to his will and to surviving Virginia Company records. There is a local tradition in Virginia that the couple lived on a plantation near Henrico called Varina and that the land had been given them by Powhatan. But there is absolutely no evidence for this. Frances Mossiker was the first to research this issue in *Pocahontas: The Life and the Legend* (New York: Alfred A. Knopf, 1976), 193.

13. Strachey in *Historie of Travell* and Hamor in *True Discourse* mention an unpleasant smoke associated with the Virginia variety. Mossiker gives excellent coverage of Rolfe's role in the early cultivation of tobacco in Virginia in *Pocahontas*, 173, 199–201. For general treatment of the emerging importance of tobacco in British culture, see Jeffrey Knapp, "Divine Tobacco," in *An Empire Nowhere: England, America and Literature from Utopia to The Tempest* (Berkeley and Los Angeles: University of California Press, 1992).

14. John Rolfe, *A True Relation of the State of Virginia*, ed. Henry C. Taylor (1616; Charlottesville: University of Virginia Press, 1951), 5; and Mossiker, *Pocahontas*, 199–201.

15. Mossiker, *Pocahontas*, 199. See also Paula Gunn Allen, *Pocahontas: Medicine Woman, Spy, Entrepreneur, Diplomat* (San Francisco: HarperCollins, 2003).

16. The salary in 1619 was twenty pounds per annum. *The Records of the Virginia Company of London*, ed. Susan Myra Kingsbury (Washington, D.C.: Government Printing Office, 1906), 1:74.

17. "The Will of John Rolfe," ed. Jane Carson, *VMHB* 58 (1950): 64.

18. Hamor, *True Discourse*, 37–47.

19. Helen Rountree has collected mentions of several instances of Indians learning to shoot in this period: *Pocahontas's People: The Powhatan Indians of Virginia Through Four Centuries* (Norman: University of Oklahoma Press, 1990), 61. Both Hamor and Dale include accounts of the negotiations with the Chickahominy in their

narratives in Hamor's *True Discourse*. Hamor says explicitly that the peace with them was due to Pocahontas's marriage.

20. Rolfe, *True Relation*, 5. It is important to acknowledge that in some regards Rolfe's statement was written as an advertising tract (see chapter 8), but he uses such personal and joyful language that it seems beyond doubt that he meant most of what he said. We can certainly use it very safely to prove that Rolfe had disputes with the Indians with whom he lived (see following notes), as on a conscious level he would have been tempted only to hide such matters, not advertise them.

21. Ibid., 1.

22. Ibid., 12; and Purchas, *Pilgrimage*, 3rd ed., 952.

23. Rolfe, *True Relation*, 6, 14.

24. Ibid., 12–13.

25. Dale's comment is in Hamor, *True Discourse*, 56. The subject of Indian-white intercultural relations is almost impossible to reduce to a single footnote: I will provide an interested student with only a starting point. A classic article is Rosalie Wax and Robert Thomas, "American Indians and White People," *Phylon* 22 (1961): 305–17. Cornelius Jaenen attempts to come to terms with another Algonkian group's views of Europeans in Pocahontas's era in "Amerindian Views of French Culture in the Seventeenth Century," in Mancall and Merrell, *American Encounters*.

26. Purchas, *Pilgrimage*, 3rd ed., 944.

EIGHT
In London Town

1. Several contemporary accounts of the London visit refer to the size of the entourage. The roles of the individuals involved are only uncovered little by little in context. For information on the Lembri affair, see the letters among Spanish officials demonstrating that he really was a spy, published in Alexander Brown, *The Genesis of the United States* (1890; New York: Russell & Russell, 1964), 509–24; and John Smith, *General Historie of Virginia, New England and the Summer Isles* (London: Michael Sparkes, 1624), in *CWCJS* 2:254–55. Smith said the dead man had been the pilot who guided the Spaniards to England in 1588, but that seems highly unlikely.

2. Samuel Purchas, *Purchas, His Pilgrimage*, 3rd ed. (London: William Stansby, 1617), 957. In keeping track of the distance, he counted each day's travel as two days, as he was unused to making progress at night.

3. Francis Mossiker, *Pocahontas: The Life and the Legend* (New York: Alfred A. Knopf, 1976), 210–15, discusses life aboard ship in this era very effectively.

4. Ralph Hamor, *A True Discourse of the Present State of Virginia* (1615; Richmond: Virginia State Library, 1957), 38. On Namontack's death, see Smith, *General Historie*, in *CWCJS* 2:350. The latter account is somewhat cryptic, but it is clear that Namontack was on a local trip with the English; perhaps he had even gone with George Somers to Bermuda to look for wild hogs.

5. Both Purchas in *Pilgrimage* and Smith in *General Historie* assert that Uttamatomakin came to gather information for his king.

6. Sir Thomas Dale to Sir Ralph Winwood, June 3, 1616, in Brown, *Genesis*, 783.

7. For an overview of the city at this time, see *Material London, ca. 1600*, ed. Lena Cowen Orlin (Philadelphia: University of Pennsylvania Press, 2000).

8. Philip Barbour did meticulous research on the name of the inn; see *Pocahontas and Her World* (Boston: Houghton Mifflin, 1970), 159, 270. An eighteenth-century wit renamed the inn, which had remained famous for housing Pocahontas, the Belle Sauvage.

9. John Rolfe's later correspondence with the Virginia Company was addressed to Sir Edwin Sandys and implied a warm relationship based on patronage. Sandys figures prominently in all traditional histories of the company. Those who immediately mentioned the arrival of Pocahontas included the indefatigable letter-writer John Chamberlain as well as Sir George Carew, vice chamberlain to Queen Anne, whose letter appears in Brown, *Genesis*, 789.

10. Surviving documents from the continuing lawsuits have been published in *The Records of the Virginia Company of London*, ed. Susan Myra Kingsbury (Washington, D.C.: U.S. Government Printing Office, 1933), 3:34–57.

11. John Rolfe, *A True Relation of the State of Virginia* (1616; Charlottesville: University Press of Virginia, 1951), 2–3, 11.

12. Samuel Purchas, *Purchas, His Pilgrimage*, 1st ed. (London: William Stansby, 1613), 631.

13. Samuel Purchas, *Purchas, His Pilgrimes* (1625; Glasgow, 1906), 19:118.

14. Eric Gethyn-Jones argues that the actions taken by George Thorpe indicate that this period altered his life course. *George Thorpe and the Berkeley Company: A Gloucestershire Enterprise in Virginia* (Gloucester, Eng.: Alan Sutton, 1982), 60.

15. Barbour discusses the move in *Pocahontas and Her World*, 162–63. Jane Schneider discusses woad and Queen Elizabeth's edict in "Fantastical Colors in Foggy London: The New Fashion Potential of the Late Sixteenth Century," in Orlin, *Material London*, 112. We know the move took place in the fall because John Smith said he visited her in Brentford as he was making preparations for a trip to the West Country that occurred in the autumn.

16. Much has been made of *The Tempest*'s negative portrayal of the character Caliban, answering to the audience's fear of demon-natives, but the author, on a conscious level at least, was not at all sure he favored the current mania for exhibiting Indians. Says the character Trinculo: "When they will not give a doit [a coin] to a lame beggar, they will lay out ten to see a dead Indian."

17. Purchas, *Pilgrimage*, 3rd ed., 954–55, discusses the men's hairstyle. The wedding masque was performed at White Hall. "Virginian Princes, ye must now recounce / Your superstitious worship of the Sun, / Subject to cloudy darknings and descents; / And of your sweet devotions turne the events / To this our Britain Phoebus, whose bright skie / Enlighted with a Christian piety / Is never subject to black error's night." The piece was extremely popular. For excerpts of the script and contemporary commentary on it, see Brown, *Genesis*, 605–6. Karen Kupperman offers insight into London's fascination with the New World in *Indians and English: Facing Off in Early America* (Ithaca, N.Y.: Cornell University Press, 2000), 73–74.

18. Smith included a summary of what he had purportedly written earlier in his *General Historie*, in *CWCJS* 2:258–60.

19. John Chamberlain, extremely sensitive to social hierarchy, commented on their placement at the masque. Letter to Sir Dudley Carleton, January 18, 1617, in *The Letters of John Chamberlain*, ed. Norman Egbert McClure (Philadelphia: American Philosophical Society, 1939), 2:50. A later statement of Lady De La Warr's also indicates that her husband reposed great confidence in John Rolfe at that time. Kingsbury, *Records of the Virginia Company*, 1:507.

20. Karen Robertson contrasts Pocahontas's situation with that of the visiting Danish prince in "Pocahontas at the Masque," *Signs: Journal of Women in Culture and Society* 21:3 (1996): 555. Barbour comments on Villiers's position in *Pocahontas and Her World*, 176. A remarkable painting of Villiers is reproduced in Christopher Breward, *The Culture of Fashion: A New History of Fashionable Dress* (Manchester, Eng.: Manchester University Press, 1995), 79.

21. For treatment of this theme, see Schneider, "Fantastical Colors," in Orlin, *Material London*. Mossiker provides a description of lavish celebrations of Christmas at court in this era in *Pocahontas*, 248–49.

22. No record of the music or choreography for *The Vision of Delight* survives. Jonson's complete script, however, which includes some instructions for staging, is reproduced in *Ben Jonson: The Complete Masques*, ed. Stephen Orgel (New Haven, Conn.: Yale University Press, 1969), 245–55.

23. Ibid., 2–3.

24. Orgel calls it "an anatomy of the conventions," ibid., 34–35. Robertson does a more psychoanalytical analysis of the way in which the masque answered its audience's needs in "Pocahontas at the Masque," 574–75.

25. John Chamberlain to Sir Dudley Carleton, January 17 and February 22, 1617, in McClure, *Letters of John Chamberlain*, 50, 57. Chamberlain was equally scathing when other people of his class set themselves as something more. He mocked George Yeardley mercilessly when he was later made a knight and sent to assume the governorship of the colony.

26. The best contemporary summary of Uttamatomakin's position is found in Purchas, *Pilgrimage*, 3rd ed., 954–55.

27. William Strachey, *The Historie of Travell into Virginia Britania*, ed. Louis B. Wright and Virginia Freund (1612; London: Hakluyt Society, 1953), 95; John Smith, *A Map of Virginia with a Description of the Country* (Oxford: Joseph Barnes, 1612) in *CWCJS* 1:169–70.

28. Purchas, *Pilgrimage*, 3rd ed., 954–55.

29. Ibid., 954–56; Smith, *General Historie*, in *CWCJS* 2:261. Smith seems to have been too obtuse to understand Uttamatomakin and claimed the man literally did not believe he had seen the true king. An Algonkian king gave gifts in proportion to his status.

30. Samuel Purchas, an assiduous scholar, remarked that "it was said" he had done so, while in all else he asserted that he gained his information directly from Uttamatomakin himself, via their translator.

31. On Van de Passe and his work, see William Rasmussen and Robert Tilton, *Pocahontas, Her Life and Legend* (Richmond: Virginia Historical Society, 1994). For materials concerning the 1615 lottery, see Brown, *Genesis*, 761–65.

32. On Pocahontas's age, see chapter 1, note 4. The age given in this portrait has been assumed to be accurate by previous scholars, but it could not have been.

33. Robertson analyzes the print this way in "Pocahontas at the Masque," 572–73.

34. What to do, for example, with the single consonant that was something like *ts* but might have a vowel sound inserted just before on some grammatical occasions? What to do with a long *o*-like sound? Should it be written *ough* or simply *o* or even perhaps *ou*? Europeans weren't consistent even in the spelling of their own words; they certainly couldn't do justice to Algonkian. Nor could they understand that final vowels could appear and disappear depending on how a word was used in a sentence.

35. Smith, *General Historie*, in *CWCJS* 2:261.

36. Daniel Richter analyzes her speech this way in *Facing East from Indian Country: A Native History of Early America* (Cambridge, Mass.: Harvard University Press, 2001), 76–77.

37. Sir Edwin Sandys to Sir Thomas Smith (treasurer of the Virginia Company), March 10, 1617, in David Ransome, "Pocahontas and the Mission to the Indians," *VMHB* 99 (1991), 94. Kupperman in *Indians and English* raises the possibility that Pocahontas may have felt profoundly torn by this new development.

38. All sources agree that they stopped at the inn at Gravesend, but nothing else is sure. It is even theoretically possible that Pocahontas died of some other ailment, unrelated to the respiratory infections from which all the Indians were suffering, but given her youth and previous good health, that is unlikely.

39. Purchas, *Pilgrimage*, 3rd ed., 955.

40. John Rolfe to Sir Edwin Sandys, June 1617, in Kingsbury, *Records of the Virginia Company*, 3:70–73.

41. The parish records for the church of St. George in Gravesend read, "March 21: Rebecca Wrothe, wyffe of Thomas Wroth, gent. A Virginia Lady borne, was buried in the chancel." See Barbour, *Pocahontas*, 183. See *The Book of Common Prayer*, ed. John E. Booty (1559; Washington, D.C.: Folger Shakespeare Library, 1976), 309. The most accessible volume of preserved Mayan and Aztec poetry is *In the Language of Kings: An Anthology of Mesoamerican Literature, Pre-Columbian to the Present*, ed. Miguel León-Portilla and Earl Shorris (New York: Norton, 2001). The most faithful translation is John Bierhorst, *Cantares Mexicanos: Songs of the Aztecs* (Stanford, Calif.: Stanford University Press, 1985). The fleeting nature of life on earth, its likeness to flowers that fade, is a hallmark of Aztec poetry.

42. Rolfe to Sandys, June 1617, in Kingsbury, *Records*, 3:70–73.

NINE
1622, and Queen Cockacoeske

1. Reports from Governor Argall to the company, June 9 and October 20, 1617, in *Records of the Virginia Company of London*, ed. Susan Myra Kingsbury (Washington, D.C.: U.S. Government Printing Office, 1906, 1933), 3:73–74. John Rolfe to Sir Edwin Sandys, June 8, 1617, in ibid., 3:70–71.

2. Rolfe to Sandys, June 1617, ibid., 3:70–71.

3. Argall to the Company, June 1617, ibid., 3:73.

4. General Court of the Virginia Company, June 1622, reading a company letter dated August 1618 and written in response to one of Argall's dated March 1618, ibid., 2:52–53. Quotation from Argall in his report to the company, March 10, 1618, ibid., 3:92.

5. Sir George Yeardley was criticized for having granted land subject to confirmation from Opechankeno. See General Court, July 17, 1622, ibid., 2:94–95.

6. On settlement patterns in this period, see Helen Rountree, *Pocahontas's People: The Powhatan Indians of Virginia Through Four Centuries* (Norman: University of Oklahoma Press, 1990), 66–67. The incidents involving John Martin were dealt with in the General Assembly in Jamestown, in Kingsbury, *Records*, 3:157, 170. See John Martin, "The Manner How to Bringe the Indians into Subjection," December 1622, in Kingsbury, *Records*, 3:704–7.

7. General Assembly at Jamestown, ibid., 3:174–75. Various other reports and letters mention the incident.

8. Rolfe to Sandys, January 1620, ibid., 3:241–48.

9. Sir George Yeardley to Sir Edwin Sandys, 1619–20, ibid., 3:128. See also comments of the Council in Virginia, November 11, 1619, on 228.

10. John Rolfe's will was drawn March 10, 1622, and probated in London on May 21, 1630. The probate copy (PCC 1630) may still be consulted in London; a photocopy is held by the University of Virginia Library. A transcription was printed in "The Will of John Rolfe," ed. Jane Carson *VMHB* 58 (1950): 58–65. Elizabeth and Joan also appear in the Muster of 1625, available online at "Virtual Jamestown," www.iath. virginia.edu/vcdh/jamestown. Secondary sources commonly refer to Rolfe's wife as Jane, but this is an error.

11. This was a typical "bill of exchange," a transatlantic financial maneuver designed to deal with the insurmountable barrier of the ocean in a preelectronic era, at the same time resolving the shortage of specie in some areas. If one colonist owed another a debt that he did not have the ready cash to pay, he could write to a man who owed him money in London and instruct him to pay instead a particular person there in the capital who was owed money by the other colonist. In this case, the Mr. Pierce in London was almost certainly related to William Pierce in Virginia and had probably advanced his settler relation—and perhaps Rolfe as well—some money that the cash-poor colonist was now seeking a way to repay. Records of the General Court of the Virginia Company, 1619–22, in Kingsbury, *Records* 1:332, 400, 629–30.

12. Records of the General Court, April 1621, ibid., 1:459. See Henry's name on the list of the investors in the Virginia Company, c. 1618, ibid., 3:87.

13. Sir George Yeardley and the Council in Virginia to the company, January 1621; and Ordinance and Constitution for Council and Assembly in Virginia, July 1621, in ibid., 3:424, 483. See also Jon Kukla, *Political Institutions in Virginia, 1619–1660* (New York: Garland, 1989), 43–50.

14. The best summary of the close of these men's lives is Philip Barbour, *Pocahontas and Her World* (Boston: Houghton Mifflin, 1970), 215–26.

15. Eric Gethyn-Jones, *George Thorpe and the Berkeley Company: A Gloucestershire Enterprise in Virginia* (Gloucester, Eng.: Alan Sutton, 1982), 57–58. Gethyn-Jones does not present the conversion of Georgius in the same light that I do, but his research into Thorpe's papers and the local church register seems flawless.

16. These two women have until recently been known only through a few cryptic references in the Virginia Company records. Further discoveries were recently made in the Ferrar Collection in Magdalene College, Cambridge; the account by the governor of Bermuda is also far more detailed than most scholars realize. See notes 17, 18, 19.

17. General Court of the Virginia Company, 1619–1622, in Kingsbury, *Records*, 1:338, 427–28, 485, 496.

18. David Ransome, "Pocahontas and the Mission to the Indians," *VMHB* 99 (1991): 88–89. Ransome's careful research in the Ferrar Collection at Magdalene College has unearthed these details, as well as the fact that the two women were baptized and under what names.

19. A 1620s manuscript was published in London in 1882 for the first time and mistakenly ascribed to John Smith. The text itself, however, demonstrates that it was written by Nathaniel Butler, who was governor of Bermuda at the time, as scholars now agree. *The Historye of the bermudaes or Summer Islands* (1882; New York: Burt Franklin, 1964), 268–85. John Smith also referred to the Bermuda marriage of one of the Virginia Indians in his *General Historie of Virginia, New England and the Summer Isles* (London: Michael Sparkes, 1624), but he would have heard of it only secondhand through one of the guests.

20. Rolfe's will, in Carson, "John Rolfe's Will." That Rolfe liked Richard Bucke is evidenced by his comments about him in *A True Relation of the State of Virginia* (1616; Charlottesville: University Press of Virginia, 1961), 9–10, where he refers to him in much warmer terms than he does Whitaker. We do not know the date on which Rolfe died. He was close to death in early March, and presumably died shortly thereafter. He may have lingered on for a few weeks, and may even have been alive at the time of the great Indian assault on March 22. However, the raids did not come near the area in which he lived. If he had not yet closed his eyes for the last time, one wonders if his wife told him what had happened. In any case, news of his death was sent back to England at the same time as news of the assault. That fact probably explains certain historians' misreading of the Virginia Company records, and the assertion made by some that he was actually killed in the raids.

21. Cited in Karen Ordhal Kupperman, *Indians and English: Facing Off in Early America* (Ithaca, N.Y.: Cornell University Press, 2000), 223.

22. Edward Waterhouse, "A Declaration of the State of the Colony and . . . a Relation of the Barbarous Massacre," 1622, in Kingsbury, *Records*, 3:541–71. Frederic Gleach has pointed out that we have no actual proof that the Indians would have attacked Jamestown had the boy or boys not given the secret away; see *Powhatan's World and Colonial Virginia: A Conflict of Cultures* (Lincoln: University of Nebraska Press, 1997), 148–54.

23. Helen Rountree has suggested the word *assault* rather than the baggage-laden *massacre* or the inaccurate *uprising*—which presupposes that English authority was already established. Rountree has also provided the most down-to-earth and—in my view—coherent explanation for the assault in *Pocahontas's People*, 67–73. Gleach has argued extensively that religious and cultural factors were at least as important as material ones, in *Powhatan's World*. Spiritual explanations have also been profitably discussed by Frederick Fausz, "Opechancanough, Indian Resistance Leader," in *Struggle and Survival in Colonial America*, ed. David G. Sweet and Gary B. Nash (Berkeley: University of California Press, 1981), and Kupperman, *Indians and English*, 176, 189, 196.

24. Jane Dickenson's petition to the governor, March 30, 1624, in Kingsbury, *Records*, 4:473; Kupperman, *Indians and English*, 193–94.

25. Council in Virginia to the Virginia Company of London, January 20, 1623, in Kingsbury, *Records*, 4:9–10.

26. Waterhouse, "Declaration of the State," 564.

27. Muster of 1625, list of titles in colony in 1625, in Kingsbury, *Records*, 4:555–56.

28. Patent book entry for William Peirce [sic], 1635, in *Cavaliers and Pioneers: Abstracts of Virginia Land Patents, 1623–1800*, ed. Nell Marion Nugent (Richmond: Dietz, 1934), 1:29. Colonists at that time were allowed to claim land in proportion to the number of people whom they had paid to transport.

29. The Virginia Council's records for this period were destroyed in the Civil War. But Conway Robertson had copied some material from the 1630s and 1640s before the disaster occurred; his notes were published in *VMHB* 13 (1905–06): 389–401.

30. Act Two of the Grand Assembly of Virginia, October 5, 1646, in *Virginia Statutes at Large*, ed. William Waller Hening (1819; Charlottesville: University Press of Virginia, 1969), 1:327; Elizabeth Vann Moore and Richard Slatten, "The Descendants of Pocahontas: An Unclosed Case," *Magazine of Virginia Genealogy* 23 (1985): 5. The work of Moore and Slatten is based on references to Rolfe's holdings in Nugent, *Virginia Land Patents*.

31. The question of Pocahontas's descendants is a vexed one. Many wealthy Virginians have claimed descent from the "princess," producing dubious documentation. One of them, Wyndham Robertson, published a complete genealogy in 1887 (*Pocahontas, alias Matoaka, and Her Descendants*). By that time, however, the national myth surrounding Pocahontas was so popular that members of Virginia's leading families were well motivated to claim descent and "spin" family lore. There is in fact no marriage record for Thomas Rolfe, and the Bollings, who kept the tradition alive, were themselves not certain what the wife's name was. Though one Colonel Robert Bolling married a Jane Rolfe in 1675, who died in 1676, presumably in childbirth, there is no definite proof that she was Thomas's daughter, nor even absolute certainty that Colonel Bolling's oldest surviving child was in fact hers rather than the progeny of his second wife. Still, in 1705 Robert Beverly in *The History and Present State of Virginia* declared with certainty that Thomas's posterity was then "in good repute" in the area; and we know the story of being descended of Pocahontas existed in some branches of the Bolling family before any of the post-Revolutionary literary outpouring began, indicating that it was probably true. A French visitor was offered a number of details in 1782: Marquis de Chastellux, *Travels in North America in the Years 1780, 1781 and 1782*, ed. Howard Rice (Williamsburg, Va.: Institute of Early American History and Culture, 1963), 422–24. Chastellux clearly followed up by reading John Smith's account. For treatment of the explosion of mythology that originated after 1800, see Robert Tilton, *Pocahontas: The Evolution of an American Narrative* (Cambridge: Cambridge University Press, 1994).

32. Moore and Slatten, in "The Descendants of Pocahontas" make a compelling case that these Rolfes or Relfes were probably Thomas's sons. It is certain that Thomas was known in the neighborhood as Powhatan's grandson. In the 1650s through 1670s, apparently because he did not have a copy of his father's patent, he claimed that the lands he was still gradually selling off on the south shore of the James came to his family "by gift of the Indian king" when his parents were married. No one would have

quarreled with him that the lands were his (creeks and roads there were still named Rolph's), but he had to present something to the land patent office. (See Surry County patent books, cited in Moore and Slatten, "Descendants of Pocahontas," 5, 11.)

33. Cited in Martha McCartney, "Cockacoeske, Queen of Pamunkey: Diplomat and Suzeraine," in *Powhatan's Mantle: Indians in the Colonial Southeast*, ed. Peter H. Wood, Gregory A. Waselkov, and M. Thomas Hartley (Lincoln: University of Nebraska Press, 1989), 175.

34. The documents proving this are in private hands, but the most important one has been photographed and published in Helen Rountree and E. Randolph Turner III, *Before and After Jamestown: Virginia's Powhatans and Their Predecessors* (Gainesville: University Press of Florida, 2002), 152.

35. For excellent treatment of Cockacoeske's career, based on material in the British Public Record Office, Colonial Office, see McCartney, "Cockacoeske." Totopotomy died in today's Richmond at "Bloody Run." Knowledge of this still existed in the city in the nineteenth century. Personal communication from Buck Woodard.

36. McCartney, "Cockacoeske," 176–77.

37. The history of these tribes from the seventeenth century to the present day is recounted in Rountree, *Pocahontas's People*. Those seeking current information on the eight state-recognized tribes of Virginia should consult Sandra F. Waugaman and Danielle Moretti-Langholtz, *We're Still Here: Contemporary Virginia Indians Tell Their Stories* (Richmond: Palari, 2000), and the film *In Our Own Words: Voices of Virginia Indians*, produced by Danielle Moretti-Langholtz and narrated by Lenora and Troy Adkins, Chickahominy. There are approximately twenty-five hundred tribal members, living on two reservations (Pamunkey and Mattaponi) and throughout the state of Virginia.

Bibliographical Essay

People interested in Pocahontas and her era must come to terms with an apparent paradox: as sources, we have available to us everything and nothing. On the one hand, the colonial projects of Europeans were nearly all interconnected, and people taking part in any of the events wrote reams; people since then have preserved and pored over many of those papers. On the other hand, the number of documents giving us direct, reliable information about Pocahontas and her father is extremely small. The woman herself left us nothing. We must therefore make judicious use of what we have, neither extrapolating too much from too little, nor giving up entirely on the project of hearing the Native American voice.

As far as I know, I have read all relevant extant seventeenth-century documents. Many are printed texts of the era, others archival, but even the archival materials are almost all available in print today. In the citations, I have, wherever possible, referred to published editions, so that interested readers can access the primary sources themselves without traveling to the archives. The information as to where an original document is now housed is nearly always given in the published version I cite; if not, I mention the location myself. I would recommend that interested students read widely in the literature and documents pertaining to the Spanish New World and to early English colonies in general. That will provide a context for interpreting those few men who actually met and commented on Pocahontas or members of her family, either in Virginia or in London. These include not only John Smith and John Rolfe but also George Percy, William Strachey, Henry Spelman, Thomas Dale, Alexander Whitaker, Samuel Argall, Ralph Hamor, Samuel Purchas, and various officials of the Virginia Company. A recent collection conveniently draws together many of the relevant primary sources: Edward Wright Haile's *Jamestown Narratives: Eyewitness Accounts of the Virginia Colony, the First Decade* (1998). That book and an excellent set of maps of Virginia (or Tsenacomoco) as it was in 1607 are available from Roundhouse Press in Champlain, Virginia. John Smith was certainly the most prolific writer on the subject in question. A superb edition of all his publications is Philip Barbour's *Complete Works of Captain John Smith* (1986).

Only an extremely close reading of all the extant sources has made the present study possible. So many myths have grown up around Pocahontas that some have even made their way into the work of recent scholars. I have therefore accepted no purportedly factual statements about her life from anyone unless I can see exactly which evidence the author used in order to draw his or her conclusions. Existing documents often belie typical understandings. Some of the most common errors concerning the order of events are simply due to the shift from the Old Style to the New Style calendar: in the early seventeenth century, the New Year was marked at the end of March. A letter dated "January 1616," for example, was written in what we would understand to be January 1617. The only "liberty" I have taken concerns the edition of the Bible from which I assume Pocahontas read. It is possible that Alexander Whitaker had with him the brand-new King James Bible, but he may have sailed before it was available for sale. In any case, the Bible whose pages he had known for years was certainly the Geneva Bible. Yet I quote extensively from the King James Bible, on the grounds that it is truer to the spirit of the age and better represents the language with which Pocahontas was surrounded. She certainly would have been exposed to it on her trip to London.

Many scholars have written excellent works about the Jamestown experience, and about interactions between Algonkians and English more generally. Their perspectives are cited throughout the book. Interested readers might begin with important works such as James Axtell's *Natives and Newcomers: The Cultural Origins of North America* (2001), Francis Jennings's *The Invasion of America: Indians, Colonialism and the Cant of Conquest* (1975), Karen Ordahl Kupperman's *Indians and English: Facing Off in Early America* (2000), and Daniel K. Richter's *Facing East from Indian Country: A Native History of Early America* (2001), to name but a few. The foremost authority on Powhatan history and culture specifically is anthropologist Helen Rountree. Her works are cited throughout, and a fascinating triple biography promises to appear shortly: *Powhatan, Pocahontas and Opechancanough*, forthcoming 2005 from the University Press of Virginia. Her recent work with archaeologist E. Randolph Turner, *Before and After Jamestown: Virginia's Powhatans and Their Predecessors* (2002), helps readers to see how the archaeological record may be combined with documentary sources to give us clues about what happened. One of the most promising current archaeological sites is at Werowocomoco on the York River. The Werowocomoco Research Group is in the process of preparing materials for publication, as well as a Web site. A meeting of specialists on nearly every aspect of the Virginia experience occurred in March 2004, sponsored by the Omohundro Institute of Early American History and Culture in Williamsburg, Virginia. The papers presented at the conference, titled "The Atlantic World: Virginia, 1550–1624," will eventually be published and available to interested readers.

There are also numerous studies of John Smith and Pocahontas specifically, but they are mostly not by scholars and often accept uncritically the mythologizing narratives. A recent book by David Price, *Love and Hate in Jamestown: John Smith, Pocahontas, and the Heart of a New Nation* (2003), presents a dramatic and highly readable story—but it is essentially the narrative that John Smith himself provided, with little acknowledgment that he was motivated to tell the story a certain way. Three adult biographies of Pocahontas appeared years ago, contemporary with the American Indian Movement: Grace Woodward's *Pocahontas* (1969), Philip Barbour's *Pocahontas and Her*

World (1970), and Frances Mossiker's *Pocahontas: The Life and the Legend* (1976). Woodward and Mossiker were less concerned with accuracy, however, than with demonstrating that Pocahontas had been a "good" Indian, which was in effect consistent with the old myth about her. Barbour's work avoided a dichotomy between unfortunate savages and good Indians, but even he found the idea that the girl had been wildly in love with John Smith too charming to relinquish. Perhaps in response to books like these, Paula Gunn Allen recently published *Pocahontas: Medicine Woman, Spy, Entrepreneur, Diplomat* (2003). She tells a fascinating story, embedding Pocahontas within legends of various Native American tribes and rendering her powerful. Allen is, as she herself says, concerned not at all with accuracy but with providing an alternative telling. My book represents the first effort to piece together every shred of what we know with surety, listening carefully for hints of what the Powhatans and Pocahontas seemed to be saying about themselves, proceeding cautiously, taking nothing that tends to be repeated for granted.

I would suggest that readers expand their interest beyond Pocahontas and the Powhatans if they want to make serious efforts to understand Indians' views of themselves and others in the early colonial years, for we have significantly better sources in other areas. Among the Iroquoians, for example, Jesuit missionaries left us an extraordinarily rich record in their "Relations." Further afield, the Nahuas, whom we often call the Aztecs and who were at the center of the long-distance trade routes that brought corn to Pocahontas's people, wrote thousands of documents in their own language, many of which have been translated and studied. Students should begin with James Lockhart, *The Nahuas After the Conquest: A Social and Cultural History of the Indians of Central Mexico, Sixteenth Through Eighteenth Centuries* (1992). For interesting parallels with and contrasts to contact-era Powhatan women, see *Indian Women of Early Mexico* (1997), edited by Susan Schroeder, Stephanie Wood, and Robert Haskett. Another productive path for further reading would be the question of the technological imbalance between Old World and New—both its importance in explaining the conquest and the reasons for it. The best study of that subject that lays before readers the recent contributions of scientists concerning studies of ancient plants is Jared Diamond's *Guns, Germs and Steel: The Fates of Human Societies* (1997).

A subject only touched on in this book is the mythologizing of Pocahontas's life, which has been treated extensively by literary critics and art historians. Interested readers might begin with Robert Tilton's *Pocahontas: The Evolution of an American Narrative* (1994), and with a short work Tilton wrote in cooperation with William M. S. Rasmussen, *Pocahontas, Her Life and Legend*, cataloging a 1994 exhibit at the Virginia Historical Society in Richmond, which included images ranging from the original Van de Passe engraving to Disney's 1996 film.

Last but not least, interested readers might want to educate themselves about the many Indians who live today in the United States, including on the eastern seaboard, where they are largely forgotten and overlooked by others. For Powhatan descendant communities, see Sandra F. Waugaman and Danielle Moretti-Langholtz, *We're Still Here: Contemporary Virginia Indians Tell Their Stories* (2000), and the award-winning film *In Our Own Words: Voices of Virginia Indians* (2002), produced by Danielle Moretti-Langholtz and narrated by Lenora and Troy Adkins, Chickahominy. Public informaton on all the tribes is available from the Virginia Council on Indians in Richmond (804-225-2084). The Pamunkey welcome visitors at the museum on their reservation in King William County, Virginia, which is not far from Williamsburg.

Acknowledgments

In writing this book I accrued many debts, which the work itself is my only way of repaying. I offer it humbly, and with my thanks. Certain institutions deserve their share of the credit. Ten years ago the McNeil Center for Early American Studies in Philadelphia funded me in another study of the Chesapeake. This project had not been thought of then, but I remain grateful for their having accepted a scholar of Spanish America into their midst as an equal, and I am convinced that many of the ideas people there planted in my mind later bore fruit in this book. More recently and more concretely, the Research Council of Colgate University made it financially possible for me to visit major collections and to wander the byways of Tsenacomoco.

Librarians, as usual, made it possible for me to do the work. In New York City the staffs of the Hispanic Society and the New York Public Library Rare Book Room were extremely helpful. At the Colgate University Library, I am eternally indebted to Ann Ackerson, Ellie Bolland, Emily Hutton, and Ricki Mueller. I literally couldn't have done it without them.

Many people kindly offered to read the manuscript, in whole or in part. I am grateful to Danielle Moretti-Langholtz, Director of the American Indian Resource Center at the College of William and Mary, and to the American Portraits series editors Thomas P. Slaughter and Louis P. Masur. Members of the Virginia Indian community who interested themselves in the project include Chief Stephen R. Adkins (Chickahominy), Chief Emeritus Oliver L. Perry (Nansemond), Shirley "Little Dove" Custalow McGowan (Mattaponi), Debora Moore (Pamunkey), Reeva Tilley (Rappahannock), and Buck Woodard (Muskogee Creek, and a member of the Virginia Council on Indians). Deanna Beacham, program specialist for the Virginia Council on Indians and a member of the Werowocomoco Research Group, helped me distribute a draft of the manuscript among representatives of the Virginia Indian tribes, and was more generous with her time than I could have believed possible, making insightful comments that allowed me to see certain biases in my interpretation of the primary sources, nearly all of which she herself had read. From my experience, I would put in a plea that all scholars, no matter how extensive their experience, consult descendant communities as they analyze Native American history; many people in those communities have spent their lives thinking about the relevant issues, and new perceptions are sure to follow. Last but not least, I want to express my gratitude to Thomas LeBien at Hill and Wang, who often knew before I did what I wanted to say, and to his enterprising assistant, Kristina McGowan.

Other people took time out of their busy days to talk to me about what I was doing, offering key information and suggestions. I am most grateful to Joyce Krigsvold, who made me welcome at the Pamunkey Indian Museum; Helen Rountree, Professor Emerita of Anthropology at Old Dominion University; Randolph Turner, of the Virginia Department of Historical Resources; and Robert F. and C. Lynn Ripley, property owners of the Werowocomoco site, who consider themselves stewards of a national treasure, and without whose generosity there would be no archaeological study. The staffs of the Jamestown Settlement Living History Museum and the Jamestown Island National Historic Site patiently answered all my questions on some remarkably hot summer days. Last, I have been inspired in this project by conversations with my delightful colleagues at Colgate University, both in the History Department and in the Native American Studies Program.

The book's cover portrait is the work of Virginia artist Mary Ellen Howe, who worked for six years to produce the most accurate painting of Pocahontas possible. She based her work on a direct tracing of the Van de Passe engraving, taken from life, and consulted art and costume historians and producers of historical textiles. Studying nineteenth-century photographs from the Pamunkey and Mattaponi reservations and taking her own photos of living Rappahannock women, she noticed the same overbite, dimpled chin, and high cheekbones among the Powhatan people that Van de Passe once saw in Pocahontas. I am grateful to Ms. Howe for refusing to be satisfied with the mythologizing portraits of Pocahontas that have long dominated our cultural imagination and for insisting on trying to see the woman as she saw herself.

My chosen family makes the work I do worthwhile. My beloved partner John holds out his hand to me when I need him most, reminding me what I am trying to achieve when I study the words of those long gone. Our son, Loren, never ceases to ask questions, often about Pocahontas, refusing to accept it when I say some questions are unanswerable. And my foster daughter, Carmen, now all grown up, looks at me with her Taíno eyes and laughs at me when I need to be laughed at. But it is to my birth family that I offer special thanks—to my sister, Cindi, who believed in me from the time she was born, and to my parents, John Kenneth Townsend and Carolynn Erickson Townsend, who taught me what I know about human dignity and human worth.

Index

Acosta, Juan de, 185*n10*
African slaves, 32, 173–74
agriculture, *see* farming practices
Algonkians, 9, 55–56, 67, 70, 77, 119, 149, 190*n38*, 205*n29*; enemies of, 57, 103, 182*n13*; English technological superiority to, 64, 65; languages of, 13, 45, 73, 143, 176, 192*n12*, 206*n34*; marriage practices of, 86, 120, 200*n23*; matrilineal chieftainships of, 15; politics of, 102, 196*n27*; respect for privacy among, 134; spirit beings of, 21
Alonso (Spanish boy held hostage), 9, 10
Anne of Denmark, queen consort of James I, 144, 152, 204*n9*
Appomattock Indians, 12, 49, 177
Archer, Gabriel, 186*n1*
Argall, Captain Samuel, 99, 107, 123, 156–57, 196*n27*; French colony destroyed by, 121; as governor of Jamestown, 157, 159–62, 164, 165, 170; Pocahontas captured by, 101–5, 197*n29*; and Pocahontas's death, 157, 158; Pocahontas sails to England with, 136, 137; Warrascoyaks attacked by, 99–101

Arrohattock Indians, 12, 49
Aztecs, 16, 25, 36, 138, 183*n26*, 190*n30*; difference between North American Indians and, 81; human sacrifice practiced by, 37, 45–46; language of, 72; Spanish conquest of, 8, 30, 82

Bacon, Nathaniel, 176, 177
Barbour, Philip, 194*n7*, 199*n16*
Bass, John, 175
Beacham, Deanna, 196*n22*, 200*n24*, 202*n10*
Bermuda, 84, 99, 167–68
Beverly, Robert, 209*n31*
Bible, 29, 90, 91, 107–8, 111, 126, 158, 198*n2*; Nehemiah, 115
Bolling, Colonel Robert, 209*n31*
Book of Common Prayer, 125, 158, 201*n2*
Brathwait, Richard, 54
Brazil, 27
Brief and True Report of the New Found Land of Virginia, A (Harriot), 37
Britons, ancient, 40, 113
Browne, Edward, 50, 133
Bucke, Richard, 168, 169, 208*n20*

AMERICAN PORTRAITS
Edited by Louis P. Masur and
Thomas P. Slaughter